SPYING FOR THE RAJ

SPYING FOR THE RAJ

The Pundits and
the Mapping of the Himalaya

JULES STEWART

SUTTON PUBLISHING

First published in 2006 by
Sutton Publishing Limited · Phoenix Mill
Thrupp · Stroud · Gloucestershire · GL5 2BU

British Library Cataloguing in Publication Data
A catalogue record for this book is available from the British Library.

ISBN 0 7509 4200 2

Typeset in 12/15 Photina.
Typesetting and origination by
Sutton Publishing Limited.
Printed and bound in England by
J.H. Haynes & Co. Ltd, Sparkford.

To Spike

We shall not cease from exploration
And the end of all our exploring
Will be to arrive where we started
And know the place for the first time.

T.S. Eliot, 'Little Gidding'

Contents

List of Illustrations ix

Foreword xi

Acknowledgements xiii

Note on the Maps xiii

1 *To Tibet with a Cross* 1

2 *Mad Amirs and Englishmen* 23

3 *Enter the Pundit* 50

4 *All in the Family* 72

5 *Spies of the Wild Frontier* 84

6 *A Learned Man of Chittagong* 110

7 *The Holy Spy* 138

8 *Whither Flows the Tsangpo* 169

Notes 189

Bibliography 195

Index 199

List of Illustrations

1. General James Walker, Surveyor-General of India
2. Captain Thomas George Montgomerie, the man responsible for raising and training the corps of Pundits
3. The impenetrable Tsangpo Gorge
4. Map illustrating the journey of the Pundit Nain Singh through Great Tibet
5. Pundit Nain Singh, the first pundit
6. Pundit Kishen Singh
7. Map showing route followed by the Pundit Kishen Singh
8. Map showing routes of Sarat Chandra Das
9. Pundit Sarat Chandra Das astride a yak
10. Pundit Sarat Chandra Das
11. The Pundit Kintup
12. The Potala Palace in Lhasa, residence of the Dalai Lama
13. Major Frederick M. Bailey, adventurer, with the Maharajah of Bhutan
14. Frank Kingdon-Ward, botanist and explorer
15. Bust of Sir George Everest
16. Charanjit Kaur Mamik Senior Librarian, Survey of India, Dehra Dun
17. Surveying instruments at the Survey of India Museum, Dehra Dun

Foreword

The task of intelligence gathering is facing its most serious challenge since the Second World War. The terrorist attacks of 11 September, and subsequent atrocities in Bali, Madrid, London and elsewhere, have revealed an alarming lack of preparedness for what is today a real threat to Western society.

Jules Stewart's *Spying for the Raj* tells the tale of that incredibly courageous and resourceful corps of Indian secret agents who worked for the British in the nineteenth century. The book carries a relevant message to a world living in the shadow of terrorist violence. Satellite surveillance may be able to read a car number plate from miles above the Earth. But how useful is that to a security service that needs to know when and where Al Qaeda is planning to dispatch its next suicide bomber? Espionage tactics may need to shift 'back to basics' – that is, straight undercover work by skilled operatives – if we are to penetrate to the heart of the cells in which these plans are being hatched.

The Pundits provided the Government of British India with a wealth of Intelligence on the movement of Russian troops beyond the Himalaya and the devious machinations of Central Asian politics, as well as route surveys of totally unexplored territories. These men fixed the altitudes of peaks, traced rivers to their sources, kept secret logbooks of trade routes and mapped the exact location of territories and even cities that were previously blanks on the map. They were able to do so because they were prepared to spend months and sometimes years on the ground, travelling in disguise and suffering unspeakable hardships.

Like Kipling's hero in *Kim*, a novel that is in fact filled with characters drawn from the Pundits, these men were able to step into a new identity, with their mastery of the local language and customs, and risk their lives as secret agents in the employ of the Great Trigonometrical Survey of India.

In this book we meet a panoply of colourful and bigger-than-life characters, from the Sikkimese monk Ugyen Gyatso who took secret readings in Lhasa sitting under the protection of an umbrella, to the illiterate tailor's assistant Kintup, whose mission to solve the riddle of the link between the Tsangpo and Brahmaputra rivers turned into a four-year epic of pathos and personal tragedy.

The Pundits were key protagonists in the Great Game, that chess match of high intrigue played out on the roof of the world between Russia and Britain. They were explorers without parallel, fearless and determined to see the job through against all odds. They were the classic unsung heroes of the British Raj, living in a world of constant danger, with no hope of being rescued were their true identity to be detected by some bloodthirsty Central Asian potentate. *Spying for the Raj* is an entertaining and authoritative book that does justice to a band of men who risked all for the unfashionable ideals of duty and service.

Sir Ranulph Fiennes
January 2006

Acknowledgements

I am indebted to the entire staff at the Royal Geographical Society for their help and advice in researching manuscripts and maps, and to Dr Andrew Cook at the British Library for sharing his mapping skills with me. Thanks are due to Charanjit Kaur Mamik in Dehra Dun for making available the extraordinary archives of the Survey of India, and to R.S. Tolia, an outstanding authority on the Pundit Nain Singh. I am grateful to my agent, Duncan McAra, for his support and suggestions, and to Sutton Publishing for their skill in seeing the work to fruition. Many thanks to R.S. Rawat for his valuable information on the Singh clan, and to Nick Creagh-Osborne for his logistical help. Special thanks to Mark Baillie for his enlightened comments on the manuscript, and to Helen Crisp, whose help with every aspect of the book proved invaluable.

Note on the Maps

This book tells the story of a group of explorer-spies whose Intelligence gathering enabled the Great Trigonometrical Survey of India to produce maps of hitherto uncharted regions. These documents are held in the Map Room of the Royal Geographical Society, a treasure trove of some one million maps and related documents dating back more than five centuries, and the largest private collection of its kind in the world. Special thanks are due to the Society for permission to redraw or reproduce in full the maps in this book.

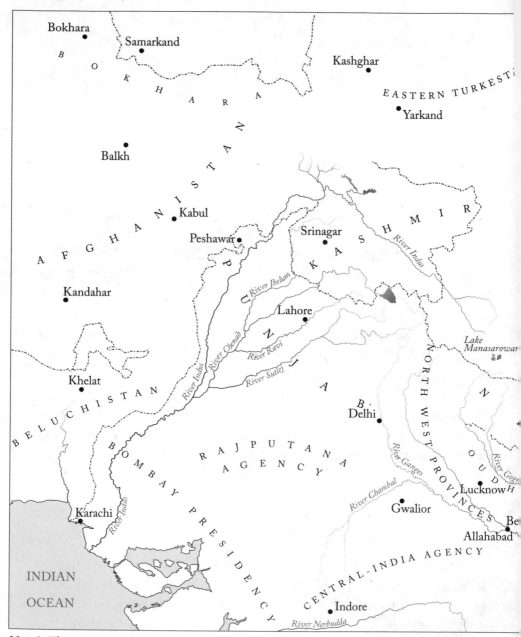

Map 1. The trans-Himalaya area of exploration

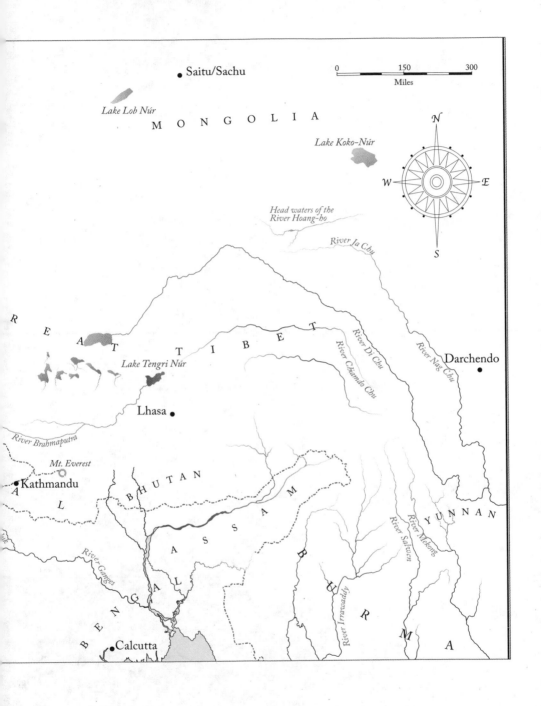

Map 2. Greater Tibet, showing routes taken by the major pundits

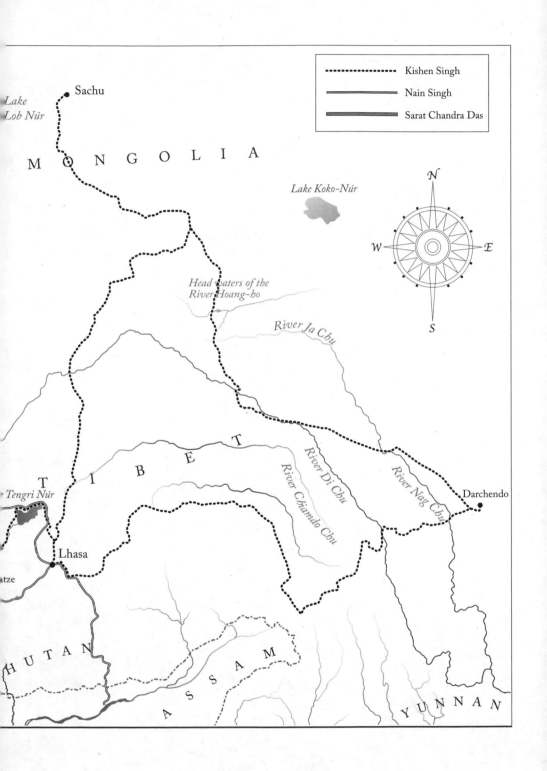

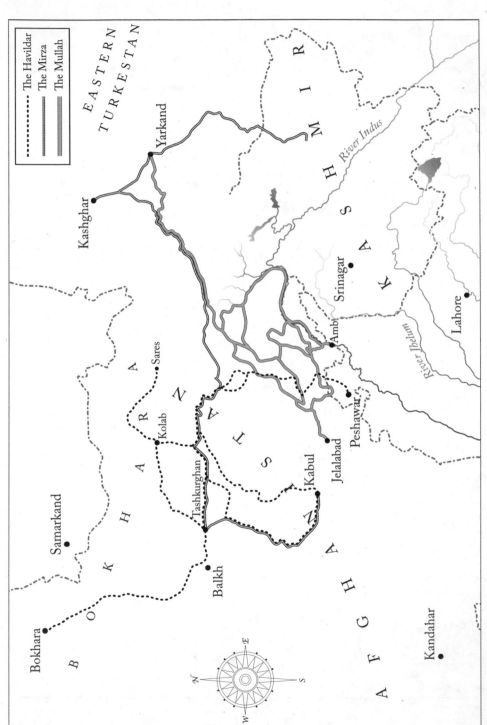

Map 3. The North-West Frontier, showing routes taken by the Muslim pundits

CHAPTER 1

To Tibet with a Cross

A passing yak herder might have dismissed the odd-looking individual as one of those eccentric, perhaps slightly mad Buddhist pilgrims who were often to be found performing their mysterious tantric rites by the banks of Tibet's sacred Tsangpo river. The shabby figure, clad in tattered sheepskin tunic and worn felt boots, crouched with his gaze fixed on the swiftly flowing water that rises on the Tibetan tableland to the west, to come crashing wildly across the bleak plateau, through the world's deepest gorge, whence it emerges as the Brahmaputra, sluggishly wending its way down to the Bay of Bengal.

Every day, he would release fifty small logs into the river, each cut exactly a foot long. A keen-eyed observer might have been puzzled by the small tin tubes that were bound to each of the logs with strips of bamboo. Had he been a Tibetan official, this discovery would almost certainly have cost the enigmatic 'pilgrim' his life. For the man perched by the river bank was Kintup, an illiterate peasant from Sikkim and one of the British Government's master spies, engaged on an espionage mission deep in Tibetan territory nearly 150 years ago.

The Tsangpo, which has yet to be navigated from its glacial source near Mount Kailash in western Tibet for the full length of its 1,800-mile course to its outlet in Bangladesh, was in the late nineteenth century an irritating conundrum to the geographers of the Great Trigonometrical Survey of India. Was this river, which zigzagged its way through the hidden canyons of southern Tibet, in fact linked to the Brahmaputra, thus ranking it among the world's greatest waterways? To find the answer, the British recruited specially trained undercover agents, known as Pundits, men who risked life and limb to infiltrate the forbidden land of Tibet, to gather intelligence about this disturbing blank spot on the Survey's map of Central Asia.

The Indian Pundits could by no means lay claim to being the first interlopers to penetrate *terra incognita* in High Asia. More than two centuries before the first Indian explorers set out to cross the Himalaya, a band of determined Catholic missionaries was suffering hunger, frostbite and highwaymen to salvage heathen souls in Tibet and China.

Tibet has exercised a magical power over travellers and religious pilgrims throughout history, from Marco Polo to Alexandra David-Neel, the early twentieth-century French opera singer-turned-Asian explorer. The pulse quickens at the mere mention of this mysterious land, the highest region on Earth, a vast, land-locked 14,000-foot-high plateau concealed behind frozen Himalayan ridges and barren, forbidding deserts. There is a compelling fascination about a people who carry their dead to mountaintops, their corpses to be dismembered and then devoured by hovering vultures, messengers who can run for days on end in a trance-like state of mind, their feet barely touching the ground, and holy men who are able to dip sheets into icy streams and dry them on their naked bodies while sitting cross-legged in the snow. The tantric practices of Tibet are chronicled in David-Neel's highly readable travelogues of Tibet, christened by Westerners the Roof of the World, the Abode of Snow or the Third Pole, and more prosaically known to its inhabitants as Bohd, literally 'followers of Bön', the ancient animistic religion that pre-dates the introduction of Buddhism into Tibet around the eighth century AD. The name Tibet is itself generally believed to derive from a composite of terms used by early Arabic, Mongol and Chinese traders and conquerors.

Tibet has always represented an irresistible enigma to those wishing to penetrate its mysterious ways. Nearly four centuries were to pass after Columbus had placed the New World on the map before Europeans were to acquire an accurate knowledge of this country's geography. As late as the mid-nineteenth century, the precise location of Lhasa was a subject of animated debate at meetings of the Royal Geographical Society.

As Britain expanded its rule over the Indian subcontinent, the Empire marching inexorably northward toward the Himalaya, with Russia methodically gobbling up the wild khanates of Central Asia on its southern borders, the matter of gaining a foothold in Tibet became a matter of urgency for the converging great European powers. But well before the celebrated Anglo-Russian rivalry, romantically dubbed the Great Game, began closing in on Tibet's borders, Europeans had begun to gatecrash this hidden Buddhist sanctuary, and appropriately enough they were arriving on a wave of religious zeal. Some four centuries ago, a band of intrepid clerics emerged from Portugal, of all places, to carry the evangelising fervour of the Society of Jesus to unbelievers on the other side of the world. The overland journeys of these dauntless globe-trotters would today be no less fraught with hardship and peril than when the Jesuits set out to reach Tibet in the early seventeenth century.

The Jesuit missionaries spent more than a century trekking across Central Asia. It was not a quest for knowledge of uncharted territories, there was no desire to fill in white spots on the map or unearth forgotten cities. This was to come more than 300 years later through the laborious fieldwork of geographers and archaeologists such as Sir Aurel Stein, Sven Hedin and the early

British explorers. The Portuguese clerics were first and foremost out to spread the Gospel.

Bento de Goes was 40 years old, a man well into middle age in 1602, when he stood before the ochre sandstone walls of Lahore, the Punjab capital of the great Moghul emperor Akbar, who had summoned the priest to his Court to learn about his curious form of worship. Brother Goes had marched more than 800 miles northward through the Indian desert from Goa, the Portuguese enclave where he had taken his Jesuit vows. At last he had arrived, fatigued and jubilant as he contemplated the splendour of the Moghul palaces, the hectic bustle of the bazaar, as well as the certainty that far more trying times lay ahead. For the priest's objective was to carry on to Xathai (Cathay, or China) and in that far-away kingdom to find a lost community of Christians, whose existence was based on the flimsiest of evidence. A Muslim merchant had returned to the Punjab after months of wheeling and dealing in the Orient, bearing tales of a considerable population of Isauitae (followers of Jesus) living in the remotest reaches of Asia. This trader's accounts, wholly unsubstantiated to be sure, were based on little more than a description of dress and custom that he had observed in his travels. They nevertheless aroused the Moghul emperor's curiosity. Thus Akbar granted Goes permission to go on his quest. The Islamic merchant may have been led to believe he had stumbled across a congregation of Nestorians, the ancient Christians of Iraq, Iran and Malabar, in India. The name relates to Nestorius, an abbot of Antioch, whom the Emperor Theodosius II appointed as patriarch of Constantinople in 428. The Nestorian missions in Asia were persecuted nearly to extinction by the Chinese, Hindus and Muslims, leaving fewer than 100,000 Nestorians practising today. Nestorius outraged the Catholic world by opposing the use of the title Mother of God for the Virgin Mary, on the grounds that, while the Father begot Jesus as God, Mary bore him as a man. This heresy served as a fertile expedient for wholesale massacres of Nestorian communities by Kurds and Turks as late as the nineteenth and early twentieth centuries.

The great period of expansion of the Nestorian Church was from the seventh to the tenth centuries, when missions were established in India and China, but since that time little had been heard of this mysterious sect. It was known that a famous monument had been erected by Chinese Nestorians in Sian (the ancient Su-cheu) in 781, and it was thither, through the trackless wilds of the Pamirs and Tien Shan mountains, that Goes set his sights.

Trekking through parts of Afghanistan where even today only the suicidal would dare to set foot without an armed convoy, Goes wandered north into Kafiristan, the homeland of pagans who had not yet been converted to Islam. The blue-eyed, fair-haired Kafirs living in these isolated valleys were said to be descendants of soldiers who had marched into India with Alexander the Great in the fourth century BC. These people being wine-drinkers, unlike the Muslims, Goes happily surmised that he had come upon one of these mythical Christian enclaves. His spirits lifted by this encouraging discovery, the Jesuit pressed on, skirting the northern reaches of Tibet on his voyage to Cathay. During the many rigorous months, two years in fact, that it took him to reach the Great Wall, Goes variously was forced to perform a European dance before the 12-year-old king of East Turkestan, found himself caught up in horrific scenes of civil-war carnage in the Hindu Kush, and was threatened by the maharajah of Kashmir with being crushed under the feet of an elephant. Disregarding these annoyances, on he marched, moving by night to avoid an encounter with the Tartar bandits who made a habit of spreading terror along the caravan routes.

On Christmas Day of 1605 Goes, the first European since Marco Polo to set foot in China, rode into Su-cheu, having failed to save a single soul on his crossing or to lay eyes on a fellow Christian, Nestorian or otherwise. Two years later, while still in the Chinese city, the valiant Jesuit gave up his own soul in obscure circumstances and was buried in a grave now long-forgotten, laid to rest by a young Chinese convert sent by the Jesuit Fathers whose mission was already established in Peking.

The death of Goes was embroiled in controversy, arousing strong suspicions of foul play on the part of the Muslims with whom the Jesuit had shared part of his journey and in whose quarter of Su-cheu he spent his final months. 'The hypothesis of poison . . . receives some confirmation from their action [the Muslims] after his death,' says the Jesuit chronicler Cornelius Wessels.

> Though not a scholar, Goes was a man of talent and a sharp observer. He kept an elaborate journal, in which he accurately noted down distances, roads and their condition, places and countries. But the same journal had recorded in its pages the sums of money advanced by Goes to several of his fellow travellers. This must have been known to them, for no sooner had he died than they possessed themselves of all his belongings, and as if by pre-concerted action first threw themselves on the diary.[1]

In a world immersed in treachery and intrigue, as was seventeenth-century Asia, this would have been a perfectly plausible sequence of events. Much later, the more factually documented murders of Western and mainly British explorers on trans-Himalayan missions became a prime incentive for employing native agents. With a dash of camouflage, these men ran a far smaller risk of coming to grief at the hands of fanatical Oriental potentates. Goes was nonetheless extremely lucky to have escaped persecution or worse on his voyage. The priest was determined that under no circumstances would he deny his Christian faith. 'That as a European he might not at once have to meet opposition,' writes Wessels, 'he donned the garb of a Persian trader and let his hair and beard grow. That he was a Christian he neither might nor would conceal, as is sufficiently apparent from the name, Abdullah Isai (servant of God), which he adopted.'[2]

Exploring Central Asia in disguise was a device pioneered by Goes, and it is one of several ways in which Goes's adventure, as well as the later travels of his Catholic brethren, is relevant to the story of the Indian Pundits. Hardly had the dust settled on Goes's epic journey than another Jesuit in disguise was making his way toward the lush valleys of Kumaon province, west of Nepal, at the foot of the mountains that demarcated the northern limits of Hindustan in what is today Kashmir. Antonio de Andrade was 44 years old when in 1624 he rode out of Agra, fired like his predecessor by tales of Christians living in seclusion in Tibet. In Delhi he joined a party of Hindu devotees starting off on a pilgrimage to a sacred temple in the Himalaya. This was as good a subterfuge as any Andrade was likely to find, so, adopting a Hindu disguise that even his Jesuit coreligionists in Delhi failed to penetrate, he negotiated to link up with the caravan, taking with him a Christian companion and two servants.

The Hindus turned out to be more astute, or at least more mistrustful than the Jesuits of Delhi. Andrade's expedition came within a whisker of ending in tragedy only several days' march from the Moghul Court. The Jesuit spent a few anxious days when the Hindus, taking note of Andrade's unusual mannerisms, snatched him from the caravan and blatantly accused him of being a spy. Andrade had been unmasked, but fortunately not undone. The priest was forced to admit that he was neither a Hindu pilgrim nor a travelling merchant, but thanks to an almost miraculous stroke of luck, he managed to persuade his captors of his bona fides as a man of God, albeit an alien divinity. It apparently made little difference to the Hindus whether the Muslim and Buddhist inhabitants of Tibet were converted from one religion to another. Once satisfied that espionage was not on the Portuguese missionary's agenda, they allowed Andrade to rejoin the caravan.

After a terrifying journey across collapsing snow bridges, and inching their way along rock walls hundreds of feet above the swift-flowing waters of the Ganges, Andrade and his party at last reached Badrinath, the holy Hindu temple perched 10,500 feet above sea level in the Garwahl Himalaya. Here Andrade bid farewell to his Hindu travelling companions and struck out for Tibet, turning a deaf ear to death threats from the rajah of

Srinagar, whose messengers had presented him with orders to turn back. He pushed on, sinking in snow drifts up to his shoulders on his ascent to the high passes. 'The intense cold numbed their hands and feet and faces, so that Andrade, hurting his finger against something, lost part of it,' says Wessels.[3] Andrade's body was so paralysed with cold that only the intense bleeding made him aware of his loss.

At last, one fine afternoon Andrade found himself gasping for breath on the summit of Mana Pass, with the Tibetan plateau laid out in bleak magnificence before his snow-blinded eyes. It was August 1624, and after a steep descent into the upper Sutlej river valley, Andrade became the first European to enter the Tibetan town of Tsaparang, situated at 15,800 feet above sea level, roughly the height of Mont Blanc. The wandering Jesuit returned to India bearing tales of red hat and yellow hat lamas, who wore necklaces made of human bones and used skulls as drinking vessels to remind themselves of death, along with a litany of doctrines and ceremonies that suggested a closer link with Christianity than Islam. None of these theories held water, of course, but they were sufficient to persuade the local Tibetan chieftain to lend his support to the Jesuits' proselytising work. The mission established at Tsaparang was abandoned a few years later as hopeless, and within a decade of Andrade's arrival the Jesuits' presence in Tibet had withered to little more than a memory.

A trickle of Portuguese missionaries continued to ply the routes of the High Himalaya to Tibet well into the eighteenth century, in pursuit of converts and imaginary secret Christian communities. Their adventures, along with those of later Franciscan friars, were undeniably heroic achievements of great single-mindedness. But their exploits bore little consequence for another generation of explorers whose missions were undertaken in the name not of God, but of Empire.

A few hours on a steamy June afternoon in 1757 were all it took to seal the fate of the Indian subcontinent for the next two centuries. Sir Robert Clive, commanding a force of 3,000 British and native troops, joined battle with the Nawab of Bengal at Plassey, a small village and mango grove near Calcutta. The nawab, Siraj-ud Daula, had deployed a superior force of 50,000 men, including French artillery, in the field. The motive for the battle, at least from the British side, was the nawab's attack on Calcutta the previous year, in which some of the British defenders had been cast into the city's infamous Black Hole, whence a few were never to emerge alive. It was the pretext Clive was after to dethrone the nawab and take possession of the rich and fertile region of Bengal in the name of his employer, the East India Company.

The Bengal army opened hostilities with a sustained artillery barrage from the French gunners, a bombardment as ineffective as it was furious, until at midday a monsoon downpour on their poorly protected powder stores forced the nawab to retire his forces from the battlefield. Clive lost no time in launching a vigorous counter-attack. A general rout ensued; Clive's troops scattered the panic-stricken Bengalis across the plains, pursuing them for 6 miles and picking up forty abandoned cannon along the way. The final tally was more than 500 Bengali troops killed, while Clive's losses numbered only twenty-two. Among the enemy casualties was Siraj-ud Daula, who had been taken prisoner and stabbed to death by accomplices of Mir Jafir, the turncoat chieftain whom Clive now enthroned as puppet Nawab of Bengal.

Plassey was the battle that launched Britain on its imperial conquest of India. It was a resounding triumph for British arms, for, as well as crushing the nawab's forces, Clive drove the remnants of his enemy's allies, the French, out of northern India, thereby leaving the field free for Britain's subjugation of the subcontinent. The sixty-year reign of George III, who was an imperialist by vocation, being the first British monarch since Queen Anne to be born in England, oversaw a swift expansion of East India Company rule in India. The Honourable Company steadily extended its dominion from a foothold in Bengal across a vast swathe of territory, stretching south from Delhi for nearly

2,000 miles and across the Bay of Bengal to Ceylon. The acquisition of new lands by definition creates new frontiers and these need to be defended. The imperial power must know what lies on the other side of its borders, for the purposes of defence and also in planning further expansion. In the early nineteenth century British India, preceded by its colossal paraphernalia of bullock carts laden with ammunition and stores, winding columns of red-coated infantry, gaggles of bureaucrats and a host of camp-followers, was slowly advancing toward the most formidable natural barrier on Earth, the mighty Himalaya range.

Like the early Jesuits, the British set off on their trans-Himalayan voyages with a deep sense of mission. These were not casual explorers, fortune-seekers or reckless adventurers. But it was not religious faith that carried them over the high mountain passes. For men like Goes the motivation was Christian evangelism at its purest and most enterprising. The driving force behind the early British and Indian exploits that carried on into the late nineteenth century was a more complex affair. They were inspired, or more often than not officially commissioned, in the name of scientific research, or in response to military imperatives, or not least of all to secure new trade routes for British India.

Colonel William Lambton, an infantry officer whose early life remains almost a total mystery, was the man who breathed life into the scheme for a scientific mapping of India, a task that was originally intended to cover the southern peninsula of India, from Coromandel to the Malabar coast, and that over the next decades crept its way up to the flanks of the Himalaya. Lambton's plan was launched in the very early years of the nineteenth century as the Great Trigonometrical Survey of India and christened as such in 1818 by Warren Hastings, the Governor-General of Bengal. What a grand undertaking this was destined to become. For nearly three-quarters of a century, Lambton and his successors to the office of Superintendent laboured to construct this basic yet essential instrument of imperial expansion. The immediate task of the Great Trigonometrical Survey was the accurate determination of the position of important points, to form the basis for geographical and other surveys and maps.

Before Plassey, the only reputable map of India was, ironically, the work of a Frenchman, the renowned map-maker Jean Baptiste Bourguignon d'Anville, whose native country at the time posed the most serious threat to British expansion on the subcontinent. D'Anville was a cartographic prodigy who engraved his first map at the age of 15. His map of India appeared in 1852, a document modelled solely on reports from French explorers, traders and missionaries, for in his lifetime d'Anville never set foot outside Paris.

Lambton's venture was conceived on a far grander scale. The Trigonometrical Survey, whose successor, the Survey of India, is today headquartered in rolling woodland in Dehra Dun on the approach to the Himalayan foothills, employed an extensive staff and came to hold a vast collection of measuring devices to carry out the surveyors' work.

The project was submitted with the approval and recommendation of his [Lambton's] commanding officer, Colonel Arthur Wellesley, later to become the Duke of Wellington, to the consideration of Lord Clive, who was then governor of Madras. Thus the Government was readily convinced of the necessity for a survey to be undertaken with the object of furnishing a basis for the geography of the peninsula, and for connecting the local surveys that were being commenced in the newly acquired provinces, with those of other portions of the Madras presidency that had been completed or were in progress.[4]

Lambton's original tools were a theodolite, zenith sector and steel chains, or more accurately folding steel rods. The instruments were to suffer misadventures of their own even before they were landed at Madras. The French captured the theodolite, en route from England, on the high seas and carried it off to Mauritius. A volley of sharp diplomatic notes persuaded 'the chivalrous French governor' of this island enclave to send the instrument on to its destination, along with 'a complimentary letter to the Governor of Madras'.[5] The chains, meanwhile, had been previously sent to Peking as a gift with a British diplomatic embassy, but this common piece of ironmongery was unceremoniously spurned by the Chinese Emperor. The set was handed over to the mission's astronomer, who carried it back to Madras with the zenith sector. There were further misfortunes in store for the Survey's theodolite. During a morning's routine surveying work, the 3-foot instrument met with near disaster. While it was being hoisted to a high pagoda on the plains, the bearing rope snapped and the instrument slammed into the wall with a violent crash, distorting the delicate optics badly enough to render the system useless. Never admitting defeat, Lambton took the instrument to pieces, and after six weeks of ceaseless labour in the steaming tropics, he succeeded in restoring the mechanism to its original shape using wedges, screws and pulleys.

Within two years of its creation, the Great Trigonometrical Survey team had got to work in earnest. In its simplest form, without taking into account the curvature of the Earth or three-dimensional measurements, the work consisted of laying out a network of triangles, each drawn from three points of reference and then stacked alongside one another. The chain of triangles can be protracted in any direction across a landmass for the purpose of measuring distance. In the case of the Trigonometrical Survey, this took the form of a Great Arc of the Meridian, tracing a line some 1,600 miles up the spine of the Indian subcontinent.

Lambton succumbed to the hardships of life in the Indian wilds in 1823. He was 70 at the time of his death, itself a testimonial to the man's iron-willed determination to see a job through. In little more than twenty years of ceaseless work, Lambton completed the triangulation of 165,342 square miles in the peninsula of India, much of it unknown territory. He was remembered by his loyal servants and a small cadre of scientific followers, but otherwise the first Superintendent of the Great Trigonometrical Survey passed out of men's memories. Not so the Survey's second Superintendent and veteran surveyor, Sir George Everest, the man whose name will always be associated with a mountain that he neither discovered nor set foot on. Everest's character was without doubt cast in the same mould as his predecessor's in that, despite their very different characters, both were men of extreme determination and single-mindedness. The stern, patriarchal surveyor, whose flowing white beard bestowed on its wearer an almost biblical countenance, through twenty years of toil and suffering earned the accolade of 'creative genius'. For Clements Markham, President of London's Royal Geographical Society, 'he had completed one of the most stupendous works in the whole history of science. No scientific man had ever had a grander monument to his memory than the Great Meridional Arc of India. The whole conception of the Survey, as it now exists, was the creation of his brain.'[6] Writing in 1871, Markham cited as examples of Everest's achievements the replacement of Lambton's network method with a gridiron system, the switch from rods to parallel compensation bars for measuring base lines (duly tested by Everest himself in London at Lord's cricket ground), and the design of triangulation towers.

A stiff upper lip was a gross understatement in Everest's case. In the monsoon season of 1823, the year Everest took charge of the Survey, he reported being struck down by 'a smart attack of bilious fever, owing to too much labour of computation'. His condition rapidly deteriorated a few days later as he was suddenly seized with 'an uneasy sensation in my loins'. There followed a violent pain in all his bones, accompanied by a bout of typhoid fever. In the course of a few days the symptoms grew worse and he was deprived of the use of his limbs. 'My mind became affected almost to delirium, dreadful paroxysms took place, in which my limbs were violently and involuntarily agitated. My skin peeled off, my nails gave way, the most frightful and hideous dreams disturbed me at night.'[7] For six months afterwards Everest could only lie on his back, unable to sleep for more than three hours at a stretch. Yet he carried on with his surveying work, for 'now or never, the question was to be decided whether the Great Arc should be carried through to Hindustan [in the Himalayan foothills] or terminate ingloriously in the valley of Berar [central India, between the Deccan and the Ganges plain]'.[8]

In 1876 the Survey produced a map on a scale of 96 miles:1 inch, displaying a web of triangles snaking their way across India, with an extension of secondary lines fixing the peaks of the Himalaya to the extreme north. By that year British India had been ruler of the Punjab for three decades, having vanquished the Sikh ruler Ranjit Singh, a mixed blessing as the government was soon to find out. For this acquisition included the unruly North-West Frontier belt of tribal land that was teeming with hostile Pathan tribes, and the British army was soon to have to cross this no man's land as it prepared to fight the second of three wars that England waged with Afghanistan during the period of the Raj. In the lands that lay west of the Khyber Pass, borders were ill defined and often non-existent. This posed an uncomfortable state of affairs for Britain, with evidence piling up of a steady Russian advance toward Afghan territory and Tsarist designs on India itself. As for the lands north of the Himalaya, the English possessed only the sketchiest knowledge of likely invasion routes, the feasibility of supply lines, whence and to where the mighty rivers of Asia flowed, or even the precise location of the Tibetan capital of Lhasa. 'It was inevitable that within a decade of Plassey, its officers [the East India Company's] were vitally interested in the Himalayan states whose frontiers marched with its north-eastern borders,' writes George Woodcock. 'Aggressive rulers in these states might form a threat to territory. Friendly ones might offer the promise of profitable trade.'[9]

The age of trans-Himalayan travel began to swing into high gear with the advent of the Great Trigonometrical Survey in 1800. While the great Pundit explorers belong to the second half of the nineteenth century, and more properly to the Great Game era of espionage and high intrigue, a handful of Englishmen were to be found wandering through jungles and over high passes beyond the confines of British India in pre-Survey days. One such early voyager was George Bogle, a 28-year-old servant of the East India Company. Warren Hastings, who had recently arrived in Calcutta, so greatly admired this young Scotsman that he plucked him from his humdrum routine as Assistant Secretary of the Board of Revenue to take a diplomatic mission into Tibet. The purpose of this embassy was to conclude a 'general treaty of amity and commerce' with Bengal's northern neighbour and open a commercial route through Bhutan. Bogle was endowed with just the nature required to negotiate a passage through the warlike hill tribes of Bhutan and treat the great political–spiritual leaders of Tibet with the requisite diplomacy. Hastings recognised these qualities in his protégé and he chose Bogle as his envoy 'for the coolness and moderation of temper he seems to possess to an eminent degree'.[10] Hastings saw an opportunity to expand British influence in a region that could open a valuable trade route into China. There was an urgent need to restore the East India Company's balance sheet to health. The Company's finances were in a parlous state because of massive expenditures made in combating the disastrous Bengal famine of 1769–70. It was also one year on from Britain's annexation of Cooch Behar, a small principality bordering on Bengal, which the Company had brought under its sovereignty as part of an agreement to send military assistance to enable the Rajah to beat off a Bhutanese invasion. It was Tibet's peace overtures on behalf of Bhutan that inspired Hastings to exploit this opportunity to send Bogle as his plenipotentiary to Tibet and Bhutan.

The party that set out from Calcutta at the height of the hot season in May 1774 was comprised of Bogle, the East India Company surgeon Alexander Hamilton and a swollen entourage of servants, plus one rather ambiguous character named Purangir Gosain. Gosain, or more properly 'the Gosain', rather than a surname is a Bengali term for holy man. The word derives from the Sanskrit *goswami*, and is applied to Hindu religious mendicants in general. This young Hindu quasi-priest was of a class of wanderers who could travel unchallenged throughout India and Tibet, recognised as they were as spiritual seekers on a pilgrimage to some holy shrine or site in the mountains. Two months before Bogle's departure, the Gosain had arrived in Calcutta as representative of the Panchen Lama of Tibet, who was revered as a spiritual leader just below, or for some on an equal footing with, the Dalai Lama himself.

The Gosain did not travel equipped with the classic trappings of the later Pundits – he affected no disguise, carried no surveying equipment secreted in his saffron robes, nor was he on the British Government's payroll. Yet any one of the great Pundits of the next century might have considered himself an incarnation of Purangir Gosain, who in many ways fulfilled the role of precursor to the celebrated company of native explorers. Accordingly,

> Many of them [early explorers] took advantage of their immunity from interference to become traders, specialising in light and valuable items, and often accumulating considerable fortunes under the guise of devotion to religion. Their freedom of travel gave them opportunities to act as spies and envoys, and many of them became double or even multiple agents, making their services available to several rulers.[11]

So here we have an embryo of the Pundits, embodied in the figure of an equivocal Hindu guide-cum-go-between who was to lead a party of Englishmen deep into uncharted trans-Himalayan territory.

Bogle carried in his baggage a private commission from Hastings with a detailed brief, mostly of personal interest to the Governor-General. It was a most bizarre shopping list that Hastings delivered to Bogle in the guise of a 'private commission'. Among the particulars detailed in his order, Hastings requested Bogle to bring back some carefully packed fresh ripe walnuts for seed, as well as one or more pairs of goats that produced the highly prized Tibetan shawl-wool, along with curiosities that might be acceptable to refined English society. Most revealing of the primitive state of imperial geography in the late eighteenth century was a request to ascertain what countries stood between the Tibetan capital of Lhasa and Siberia. Nearly two centuries after Sir Francis Drake had circumnavigated the globe, and with British redcoats fighting insurgents in the far-away wilds of the American colonies, what lay north of the Himalaya remained an almost total enigma. In all, the private commission consisted of nine specific instructions. But there was a tenth, and a most intriguing item, added almost as an afterthought, which appeared on the document below Hastings's signature. Bogle was instructed to explore the Brahmaputra with a view to determining the river's course and navigability, as well as to give information on the countries it traversed on its course to the Bay of Bengal.

The mystery of the Brahmaputra was later to turn into the siren's call that launched some of the Pundits' most heroic exploits. The romantic enterprise of searching for a river even captured the imagination of Rudyard Kipling, who used this device in *Kim*, his classic account of the Great Game, to send his hero into the shadowy world of Himalayan espionage. Extraordinary explorers like Kintup spent years toiling through unknown terrain at great risk to life and limb, in an attempt to resolve the mystery of whether the great Tsangpo and the Brahmaputra were at some point linked together. This was the great enigma that kept British geographers intrigued into the twentieth century. The eccentric adventurer Colonel Frederick M. Bailey in 1913 led a daring expedition into the Tsangpo Gorge, the deepest chasm on Earth, to attempt to lay to rest once and for all the debate over what became of this river after it ran off the Tibetan plateau. A decade later, the no less intrepid botanist–adventurer Francis Kingdon-Ward managed to penetrate deeper into the gorge than any of his predecessors. Although he found it humanly impossible to navigate the last few miles of this canyon, which at one point was only 15 feet across and several thousand deep, his findings were taken as conclusive that the Tsangpo and the Brahmaputra were one.

Bogle's cavalcade met with some resistance in its attempt to cross the mountain border into Bhutan, a country that even today allocates its tourist visas with the parsimony of an eye-dropper. Bogle and Hamilton spent weeks trekking about the hills outside Tassisudon, the country's ancient capital, in anticipation of a report from the Gosain, who had raced ahead to negotiate arrangements for their visit to the Bhutanese ruler, the Deb Rajah. It was only through the Gosain's persistent efforts that the party was eventually allowed to proceed to Tassisudon, a large town crowded with one-storey wooden houses sprawled under the shadow of golden domes of Buddhist shrines and lamaseries. Bogle was lodged for several days in 'one of the better houses near the palace', when the royal summons finally arrived. The British party had to jostle its way through a street crowd of some 3,000 ogling Bhutanese who had never before laid eyes on a Westerner, before being hustled into the Buddhist monarch's throne room. 'The Deb Rajah again urged Bogle to return to Calcutta, but the Scotsman dug in his heels, using the expectation of letters from the Panchen Lama as an excuse to stay in Tassisudon and to find out what he could in the meantime about Bhutan, its people and its possibilities as a source of trade.'[12]

There is a curious phenomenon in Asia, by which Westerners will perceive certain events to be going disastrously wrong, while to the natives they merely represent a problem that needs to be directed to the right channels in the appropriate manner. While the European frets and stamps his feet in despair at the impending calamity, a sequence of behind-the-scenes machinations is quietly set in motion and, before long, the crisis is past history. So it was with Bogle's petition to be allowed to proceed through Bhutanese territory into Tibet. One day in late August the Deb Rajah's attempts to dissuade Bogle from carrying out his mission suddenly ceased. In a face-saving gesture, he informed the envoy that the Panchen Lama had agreed to the mission entering Tibet. Unbeknown to Bogle, it was the skilful diplomat the Gosain himself who had applied a gentle measure of arm-twisting on the Tibetan Lama to persuade him to receive the

British delegation. After waiting another six weeks in Tassisudon for an unexpected outbreak of civil war to subside, Bogle began his march to the north, accompanied by Hamilton, the Deb Rajah's representative, a Tibetan envoy sent by the Panchen Lama, a Kashmiri trader recruited by Bogle, and a long train of servants, porters and pack animals.

Bogle put the Company's request for a trade agreement to the Panchen Lama, who listened courteously and thanked him for his gifts (dried fish, biscuits and assorted English victuals that were not likely to excite his host's palate), while he in turn presented Bogle with some silks, purses of gold dust and silver talents, and then wished him a safe and pleasant journey back to Calcutta. And with that, Hastings's emissary and his party wended their way back home across the mountains to Bengal. Bogle failed to secure for his employer a trade route to Tibet and China, but his mission was not entirely lacking in achievement. He carried back to India the first detailed written description of the Tsangpo, which he came upon after an exhausting descent from 16,000 feet above sea level, an elevation higher than any point in Europe. If nothing else, Bogle opened a line of dialogue with Tibet, a foot in the door that 130 years later would take the form of a steel-tipped boot, when Sir Francis Younghusband marched a British expeditionary force into Lhasa to impose a trade agreement at bayonet point.

The next two years found the assiduous Gosain on an almost non-stop sprint between Calcutta and the Tibetan hierarch's palace in Tashilunpo, keeping open the lines of communication with that country. Bogle had by now settled into life as a desk-bound Company servant, albeit with the high rank of Collector, giving him jurisdiction over commercial dealings with foreign powers. In 1776 Hastings decided to test the temperature of the water once again by dispatching Bogle's companion Alexander Hamilton to Bhutan and hopefully into Tibet to renew the diplomatic assault on the Panchen Lama.

It was the Gosain who delivered the news that was to condemn Hamilton's efforts to failure. The Hindu go-between reported that the Emperor of China had already sent an envoy of his own to

Tashilunpo. Under these circumstances, the Panchen Lama was not about to risk invoking the displeasure of his powerful neighbours by simultaneously playing host to a group of Englishmen. Plans for a third journey came to a sad end with Hamilton's death.

China's political manœuvring served only to strengthen Hastings's resolve. For reasons of economic necessity and sheer doggedness, the Governor-General was determined to keep up the pressure on Tibet. Bogle was recalled from his desk job to lead another mission in 1779, an endeavour that was doomed to tragic failure when the following year Bogle unexpectedly followed his friend Hamilton to the grave. Hastings was a man of tenacity, one not to be daunted by these dark omens. In 1783 he assembled a fourth mission under the command of his kinsman by marriage Samuel Turner, an East India Company army officer. Turner succeeded in negotiating a territorial treaty with the Deb Rajah in Tassisudon, and after a three-month sojourn in Bhutan he was granted permission to enter Tibet, thanks to the good offices of the ubiquitous Gosain. Here Turner made a remarkable discovery.

As had been suspected for years, the Chinese were systematically extending their imperial hegemony over Tibet, and therein lay the explanation for the several cold-shoulder incidents with the Panchen Lama. But Calcutta had always tacitly acknowledged that the Ch'ing dynasty rulers in Peking believed they had the right to treat Tibet as their back yard. Chinese expansionism stood as an impediment to Britain's commercial ambitions in Tibet, but far more worrisome was the appearance of a new peril, the growth of Russian influence in High Asia. Turner was told by high-ranking officials that Tsarist operatives were putting unwelcome pressure on Tibet to open up its northern regions to their camel caravans.

There is no sign that either Turner or the Tibetans in Tashilunpo regarded the Russians as the kind of threat they became long afterwards in the mind of Lord Curzon. But that was before the Tsarist armies had made their drive southward into Central Asia, before the great mysterious cities of Bokhara and Samarkand had fallen into their hands, and before their power, extending to the Pamirs, stood divided only by Kashmir from the western marches of Tibet.[13]

The spectre of a Russian pincer movement against British India, initially through Tibet to the north and later via Afghanistan on the North-West Frontier, was to focus the minds of English politicians and generals for the following century and a quarter. The Russian menace, unearthed by Turner in its embryonic stage, was also destined to become the leitmotif of the trans-Himalayan exploration carried out by the Pundits.

Hastings threw in the towel with the last Turner expedition. None of the four voyages, put together at considerable expense to the East India Company, had been allowed to travel to Lhasa, and two of them had turned back even before reaching the Tibetan border. For the moment, Tibet looked to remain a closed shop, increasingly under Chinese domination. There would be no more official missions. Hastings pondered his dilemma of how to prise open that Tibetan door and establish a British trading route to China. Within six months of Turner's return to Calcutta, he had devised an alternative strategy. The Gosain's star was suddenly catapulted into the ascendant. The Company's perennial middleman was selected to try his luck at leading a trading party of merchants into Tibet. The caravan would be made up of Indian traders, without any Europeans in the ranks. As would be expected of the knowledgeable Hindu, the mission was a resounding success.

It is a great pity that we have no description of this tireless emissary. One could well envisage him a forerunner of Kipling's corpulent, effervescent spy Hurree Chunder Mookerjee (himself modelled on the distinguished Pundit Sarat Chandra Das), toddling about the Himalaya with his blue and white umbrella, quoting Herbert Spencer to the world at large while he dreamt of membership of the Royal Society. At the other extreme, he might have fitted the mould of the enigmatic lama (who turns out to be a Frenchman) in James Hilton's *Lost Horizon*, an ascetic whose quiet gaze radiated an unfathomable oriental wisdom. It is recorded that the Gosain was called upon to serve the Company in several more minor exploits. He then vanishes without a trace and we know nothing of his fate, a fitting finale for so cryptic a figure.

The honour of being the first Englishman to set foot in Lhasa fell to Thomas Manning, a cerebral Chinese scholar who sauntered into the Tibetan capital in 1811, disguised as 'a Tartar gentleman'. By this time the Company had had its fill of costly, unproductive missions. Thus Manning's petition for government backing for his plan to cross China via Tibet fell on deaf ears. Manning was endowed with a short fuse and he spared no invective in condemning what he saw as official short-sightedness and ignorance on the part of Calcutta bureaucracy. In the end, it was this very failure to secure government backing that enabled him to reach his destination. The Chinese were unlikely to have been taken in by the ruse Manning pretended to effect, but, while Tibet's Mandarin overlords were certain to halt another delegation from Calcutta at the border, Manning the independent traveller was for some unexplained reason granted permission to visit Lhasa. Apart from establishing a precedent for future exploration – and almost a century was to pass before another Englishman set foot in Lhasa – Manning's journey did nothing to advance British interests in Tibet. He returned to Calcutta a disillusioned man, having failed to achieve his objective of entering China. But at least he came back alive, which is more than can be said for several unfortunate souls in the next wave of British explorers to venture across the Himalaya.

CHAPTER 2

Mad Amirs and Englishmen

The golden age of Pundit exploration covered a relatively short period, beginning roughly in 1864 when Nain Singh made his first attempt to cross into Tibet directly from his home in the Kumaon village of Milam, and ending with Hari Ram's last journeys up the Brahmaputra some thirty years later. As was the case with the taming of the Wild West or the Spanish conquests of Mexico and Peru, major historical episodes have a way of influencing the world far out of proportion to the space they occupy in time. There is usually a 'softening-up' process paving the way for these events, as was the case with the great American wagon trains loaded with settlers migrating westward, and the voyages of Columbus that put the New World and its riches on the map. The Pundits' immediate prototypes were a collection of Englishmen, or more accurately Europeans, including an odd-ball family from Munich, some acting in an official capacity and others as freelance adventurers, who journeyed over the Himalaya seeking trade opportunities for the Company or suspicious signs of Russian activity, or simply in search of horses to purchase. It was the fate that befell some of these intrepid explorers that triggered the Survey's decision to employ native spies, rather than take risks with the lives of vulnerable Europeans. There was also the loss of face, inasmuch as the British were almost powerless to mount a punitive expedition to these far-flung regions to redress the outrage.

'The preliminary arrangements for our journey across the Himalaya having been effected, I left Bareilly [northern India] in the end of October, 1819.'[1] So describes William Moorcroft at the beginning of an epic five-year journey that was to take this remarkable veterinarian–explorer deep into trans-Himalayan territory, making him the first Englishman to enter the legendary oasis city of Bokhara in what is today Uzbekistan. Moorcroft was the first person to qualify and set up practice as a vet in England and was so highly regarded in his profession, counting among his clients members of the royal family, that he was appointed Superintendent of the East India Company's Bengal stud. It was in this role that Moorcroft was commissioned to acquire horses to improve the quality of the British cavalry's breeding stock. The Public Stud was instituted to raise horses for the use of cavalry within British India, instead of depending on outside supply. Moorcroft had nothing but contempt for this enterprise, dismissing as useless the Company's efforts to put together a body of mares 'for the most part unfit for the purpose'. The stud was composed of breeds from India, Arabia and England. 'From the discordance of such a motley assemblage, as constituted that in question, expectations of success could be indulged only by minds so sanguinely intent on the accomplishment of ends, as to overlook the fitness of means,' he reports in a memorandum to the government. 'And the slow progress of improvement arises in great measure from this originally vicious composition.'[2] Moorcroft was convinced that the best foreign horses for military purposes were to be found in the countries north of the Oxus.

In spite of availing themselves of camels and elephants up to the Himalayan foothills, Moorcroft's entourage would have passed through the hills almost unnoticed compared with some of the full-scale expeditions of the day. A classic example was the embassy to Afghanistan assembled in 1808 by the Honourable Mountstuart Elphinstone, on which occasion 'it was determined that the mission should be in a style of great magnificence'.[3] Elphinstone departed from Delhi with what resembled a small army in train, made up of a secretary, two East India Company assistants, a surgeon and an infantry captain and seven officers commanding an escort of 450 mounted cavalry and infantrymen. The party that set out from Bareilly eleven years later was made up of Moorcroft's friend George Trebeck, acting as draughtsman and surveyor, a Mr Guthrie who was attached to the East India Company's medical service, Ghulam Hyder Khan, a native of Bareilly and a 'stout soldier and faithful companion', and the very compelling Mir Izzat Ullah, 'a native gentleman of talent and information' who a few years previously had travelled the route Moorcroft now proposed to follow. There was to have been a fifth member of the party, an unnamed English geologist and mineralogist who had joined them at the outset but was soon sent back by Moorcroft, whose past travels had endowed him with a finely tuned awareness of potential troublemakers. 'His conduct towards the natives was so exceptionable, that I was obliged, at a very early period, to decline his assistance,' writes Moorcroft.[4] Truly an example to be emulated by some of today's expeditioners.

More than five years later, on the morning of 25 February 1825, Moorcroft was able to exclaim: 'It was with no slender satisfaction we found ourselves at the end of our protracted pilgrimage, at the gates of that city [Bokhara] which had for five years been the object of our wanderings, privations, and perils.'[5] The weary travellers were received by the Amir, who was summarily depicted as 'a selfish, sensual and narrow-minded bigot'. A few years later 'murderous' would have to be added to his list of character traits, in respect of the fate of two unfortunate Englishmen. What transpired in that punishing sixty-four-month Central Asian journey is a tale that Moorcroft was not destined to recount in person. The travellers' spirits were riding high on their successful return journey to India, then with terrible swiftness the mission was overwhelmed by calamity. Moorcroft died in mysterious circumstances at Andkhui in northern Afghanistan, while leading the horses he had bought for the Company back to the stud farm at Pusa, some 400 miles south-east of Delhi. The fact that there were no traces of his remains, apart from 'an autograph scratched on a smoke-blackened wall of one of the caves in the Buddhist monastic complex at Bamiyan',[6] kindled the inevitable legend that Moorcroft did not die in Afghanistan, but had instead made his way to Lhasa, where he lived on for another ten years. Apart from a story picked up by two French missionaries who happened to be in the Tibetan capital in 1846, no proof has ever been put forward to corroborate this tale. Moorcroft's comrade Trebeck succumbed to a fever a few weeks later, and this tragedy was followed by the demise of the surgeon Guthrie, a victim of slow poisoning. So we are left with Moorcroft's journals and the later writings of Mir Izzat Ullah to tell the story of their pioneering deeds beyond the Himalaya.

Izzat Ullah was in many ways a template for the later Pundits, in that he was a native Indian, recruited by the Government to carry out exploratory work in territory beyond British India's ill-defined frontiers. Sir Charles Metcalfe, British resident at the Moghul court in Delhi in the early nineteenth century, employed Izzat Ullah as a confidential Persian translator and personal assistant, the sort of man one could discreetly send into the bazaars on intelligence-gathering missions. Izzat Ullah came highly recommended to Metcalfe's staff, and by no less a personage than the Honourable Mountstuart Elphinstone, who graciously referred to this servant of the Raj as 'a very intelligent native of Delhi'. Izzat Ullah had served as chief 'munshi', or native headman, on the Kabul mission in 1808. His fluency in Persian and Turkish served his employer well on that enterprise. Elphinstone was impressed by the courage Izzat Ullah showed on his later travels to Bokhara, the city of his forebears, where he was sent by Moorcroft to ascertain the possibility of obtaining horses for the Bengal Cavalry.

Moorcroft acquired his first taste for adventure in 1811, eight years before he was to embark on his epic trek to Bokhara. In that year, the vet-cum-explorer, along with his fellow traveller, a 19-year-old Anglo-Indian bearing the extravagant name of Captain Hyder Hearsey, plus the customary multitudinous retinue of guides and porters, marched out of Pusa. The demons that drove Moorcroft to pursue his wanderings across Central Asia were implanted on this first journey to the Empire's untamed north-western territories. Eight months and 1,500 back-breaking miles later, after a largely routine trip, Moorcroft was back in Pusa with little to show for his efforts. He had had no luck obtaining suitable breeding stock in this region on the upper reaches of the Ganges, but a chance meeting on the way home in the bazaar of Gwalior, about 50 miles south of Agra, definitively ignited his budding sense of wanderlust. There Moorcroft came across one Ahmad Ali Khan, an Indian merchant who calls to mind an image of Kipling's scarlet-bearded horse trader Mahbub Ali.

> From a lifetime of experience on the road hawking northern horses round the Deccan [southern part of India], he was able to explain to Moorcroft the once strong ebb and flow of the great northern horse trade. He recalled how, as little as fifteen years ago, Afghan merchants went north to buy horses at Bokhara. For the first time the name of that legendary desert city far away beyond the wrinkled mountains of Afghanistan and the fabled Oxus river appears in Moorcroft's official correspondence.[7]

Within weeks of returning to Pusa, and thence onward to Calcutta for a debriefing with the Company's officers, Moorcroft was already making feverish preparations for his second journey in search of breeding stock, while also looking for ways to secure the lucrative Tibetan shawl-wool trade for India.

Moorcroft and Hearsey set out on their second expedition disguised as Hindu pilgrims, under the assumed names of Mayapori and Hargiri. It was to prove to be a singularly unsuccessful gambit, but they now laid their plans as more seasoned Himalayan travellers, shedding most of the cumbersome entourage of bearers and bullock-carts that would have slowed them to a snail's pace on the arduous and highly uncertain road that lay ahead. They had good reason for wanting to be on their way quickly. Moorcroft had not secured government backing for his venture into virtually uncharted territory. Hence the idea was to make good their escape as swiftly as possible and then present the Bengal Government with a fait accompli. There were grievous concerns in Calcutta that the journey of an Englishman travelling in disguise and without permission through the territories of Nepal was bound to give umbrage and excite suspicion on the part of the ruler of that Himalayan kingdom, with whom Britain would shortly be at war.

Their objective was Bokhara, reputed to be the home of a magnificent breed of horse that was ideally suited to the stud's requirements. Here we come across a prelude to the Pundits in the guise of Moorcroft's trusted Izzat Ullah, as well as a young Indian guide with the party named Harkh Dev, who was trained to take 24-inch paces every step of the way and then transfer his figures at intervals 'either to the notebook which Hearsey kept tucked in the folds of his robes or to Hearsey's fingernails', presumably noted with a fine quill pen.[8] Thus were laid the foundations of Great Game intrigue.

In spite of the recurrent attacks of diarrhoea and dehydration that left him toiling his way up to the frontier a shivering wreck, Moorcroft could reflect with optimism on the first stage of his trip. The little caravan managed to struggle across the Niti Pass east of Kamet, the towering sentinel that guards the entrance across the great Zanskar Range into western Tibet. In doing so they achieved a Himalayan record, being the first Europeans to set foot on the 16,628-foot summit pass. Moorcroft also broke new ground for the Survey by being the first Briton to reach the western shores of Tibet's holy Lake Manasarowar, in the summer of 1812. No foreign traveller would visit any part of the great transverse watershed separating the Indus and Sutlej rivers from the Tsangpo until the Pundit Nain Singh explored the area more than fifty years later.

The return journey turned out to be a less happy affair. Tension between India and Nepal was mounting over repeated Gurkha encroachments into British territory. Given the natural paranoia that news of two Englishmen traipsing in disguise around the country was bound to trigger, once Moorcroft and Hearsey reached Kumaon, some 50 miles north of the British frontier, they were quickly taken prisoner by a detachment of Gurkha troops.

The Government of Bengal, while angry that Moorcroft had ignored Company warnings not to undertake a journey that would be 'replete with danger to that gentleman [Moorcroft]', managed to rise to the occasion when the said gentleman became the victim of mistreatment by impudent foreigners. While under arrest, Moorcroft had managed to dispatch a local goatherd in disguise to India with letters alerting the Company of their plight. The response was not long in coming. 'Intelligence was received about the perilous situation in which Mr Moorcroft was placed and the Governor-General dispatched a letter to the Rajah of Nepal requesting him to issue orders . . . for his release and safe conduct back to the Company's territories.'[9] The King of Nepal was obviously not yet prepared to provoke Britain into an open conflict, so seventeen days after their detention the orders came for Moorcroft and Hearsey to be allowed to continue their journey back to India. To judge by the contradictory memoranda issued in the wake of Moorcroft's safe return, it is obvious that, although he was in line for a stern rebuke, the Government was highly pleased with the report their wayward servant had brought back.

Moorcroft, the report states, made a 'very interesting report of a trade carried on by the Russians in the neighbourhood of the Company's Provinces on the North-West and Northern Frontier'. The Company expresses acknowledgement of a 'Map of information collected and digested under circumstances of great difficulty and personal inconvenience and of which otherwise we would have remained entirely ignorant'. However, it remained that the 'Government of Bengal would not have given assent to the journey had they known of it in time'.[10] The letter continues that, although his aim was the improvement of the stud, Moorcroft was overstepping his remit in undertaking such a journey. For his part, Moorcroft responded with an appropriate measure of remorse, expressing his obligation for the securing of his release and regret at having 'been the occasion of so much trouble to Government'. He refuted the charges made by the King of Nepal that he went through the Gurkha country without the permission of the Nepal Government and in a dress different from that ordinarily worn by Europeans. 'It is not possible for them to bring the slightest proof of my having in a single instance acted with impropriety. It was customary in the time of the Hill Rajahs for persons of all ranks and countries to traverse their territories in the disguise of Pilgrims and this practice has not changed since their expulsion.'[11]

Moorcroft did not realise his dream of reaching the fabulous city of Bokhara on this trip, but his resourceful agent Mir Izzat Ullah did. While Moorcroft and his 'reduced' company slogged northward, driving before them a train of yaks laden with the accoutrements befitting the pukka sahib traveller, the multi-lingual forerunner of the Pundits was off in the wilds of the Himalaya, reconnoitring routes through Kashmir to Turkestan and Bokhara. Izzat Ullah departed from Attock, the fortified city astride the Indus at the gateway to the North-West Frontier, in August 1812. He left with a sense of great relief after spending several months in detention in that city, a prisoner of the tribal chieftains who were not satisfied with his story of being an innocent trader. It took him sixteen months to traverse the high passes, desert plateaux and treacherous mountain routes that led to the great Silk Road caravan cities of Yarkand and Kashghar. Moorcroft had harboured serious misgivings about sending his agent abroad on so risky a mission, bearing letters from his employer that would immediately blow his cover as an innocent native trader. Izzat Ullah was running a great risk, apart from the perils of the road.

For one thing the mysterious and sensitive bazaar network of Muslim Asia would not overlook the fact that this man, the friend and servant of a European, had already been on a political mission to the previous ruler of Afghanistan. Moreover he would be carrying letters from Moorcroft to some of the rulers of the lands through which he passed that might well have compromised him with others along the road. Moorcroft was uneasy about this and not only on Izzat Ullah's behalf. He later confessed to the Board that he had been guilty of what he called many irregularities in 1812, and this was certainly one of them.[12]

But for Moorcroft, Bokhara represented a trophy to be acquired at any price. By now he was becoming something of a practitioner in after-the-fact tactics. He was aware that in the wake of his escapade of the previous year, the Bengal Government would be in no mood to grant permission to send a British subject abroad in the Company's name. He nonetheless dutifully went through the motions of addressing a letter to Calcutta requesting permission to dispatch his native emissary to Bokhara. He added, in a letter to his superiors, the hope that the Board would not object to Izzat Ullah's mission. It would not really have made any difference if it had, for Moorcroft's letter was not received in Calcutta for another two months. 'Five days before it was even written and several weeks after the scheme was hatched at the Delhi residency, Mir Izzat Ullah, with all his preparations completed, had set out into the unknown.'[13] Moorcroft was certain that the horses he sought were to be found in the markets of that great Uzbek desert city, and Izzat Ullah's findings were to endorse that conviction.

Izzat Ullah arrived in Bokhara on 1 April 1813, where he set about compiling copious notes in his journal, describing in minute detail all that passed before his attentive eye, from the number of families living in the Jewish quarter to the style of turban worn by the Amir Meer Hyder, a man 35 years of age, 'tall and well made, naturally of a fair and ruddy complexion, his incessant labours in the administration of justice, his night vigils and frequent fasting have made him pale and wan'.[14] On a more relevant note, he was able to furnish Moorcroft with precise data as to the days of the city's horse fairs, the going rates for breeding stock, as well as details of the breeds brought in by Cossacks, Turkomans and other traders. Izzat Ullah was also the source for the information on Russian movements in that unexplored part of Asia that Moorcroft was later able to pass on to Government. The Persian brought word of intense Russian trading activity, with gigantic caravans of 4,000 to 5,000 camels making the four-month journey between Bokhara and the Tsar's dominions once a year. In fact, it emerged from his observations that Russia was Bokhara's principal trading partner, with an exchange of items ranging from copper and iron, to fine goods like silk and spun yarn.

By the time he entered the gates of that walled city, Izzat Ullah had covered a greater distance than any of the Pundits who were to follow in his footsteps, give or take several degrees of longitude and latitude. One cannot help but be humbled by the courage and fortitude that drove him on his way against sandstorms, blizzards, the menace of highwaymen and detection, as he made for the caravan cities of Asia and beyond. From Attock, he tramped eastward to Srinagar, across what is today the embattled state of Kashmir. After a rest-stop of several days, he departed Srinagar on 13 September. He began to suffer the effects of altitude, marked by breathlessness, palpitations and nausea, as he trekked upland toward Leh, lying at a dizzying 11,500 feet above sea level. So little was known about altitude sickness in those days that Izzat Ullah was convinced that his illness was caused by drinking the local water. He claims that the symptoms vanished once he switched to tea, arguably a very early documented instance of a placebo at work. This leg of the journey took him twenty-one days to complete, averaging at best 7 miles per day against the rarefied high altitude air. 'The actual distance between Srinagar and that town [Leh] is only 120 kroh [130 miles], but the natural difficulties of the road compelled me to travel slowly,' he complains.[15] Leh, today part of Indian Kashmir, is the main town of what Izzat Ullah called 'Tibet', and is still known as 'Little

Tibet', Ladakh sharing as it does the vast plateau that spills down from the. Chinese annexed territory. Izzat Ullah's record bears testimony to the extraordinary paucity of knowledge about the mysterious land of the lamas. What he tells us in 1812 is that the Tibetan capital Lhasa was a 'well-known city', which he estimated would take two months to reach, travelling 650 miles south-east from Leh. He accurately identified it as the residence of the 'head of the Lamas' (Dalai Lama), but 'whose name is not known'. What Izzat Ullah did pick up from bazaar informants was that for the past fifteen or twenty years this head of the lamas, in consequence of troubles with the Gurkhas, had placed himself under the protection of the Emperor of China. Peking's grip on Tibet had obviously not slackened since the days of Bogle and the other late-eighteenth-century emissaries.

In his guise as a trader, Izzat Ullah was able to ascertain some valuable insight for Moorcroft into the workings of the shawl-wool traffic between Tibet and Kashmir, a subject that held such a fascination for his employer, not to mention the Government in Calcutta. 'An export duty of four rupees per load is levied on shawl-wool taken to Kashmir,' he notes in his journal. 'No duty is charged on this article when brought into Leh from the surrounding districts. Eight hundred horse-loads of shawl-wool are exported to Kashmir annually . . . The wool from which shawls are made is the short soft substance on the bodies of goats, growing below the hair.'[16] If Government were to try to grab a piece or all of this trade for the Company, they would do well to consider the political, as well as commercial sensitivities involved. Izzat Ullah reports, 'The Ruler of Kashmir is careful not to make any hostile demonstrations against Tibet from fear of the loss of revenue he would suffer from any disturbances of the trade of shawl-wool which would cause the stoppage of the manufacture of shawls and deprive him of the yearly revenue of ten lakhs of rupees [one million rupees, a huge fortune in those days] that he derives from this source.'[17]

As the clouds began to thicken with the arrival of the first autumn snows, Izzat Ullah tucked his journal into the sleeve of his sheepskin-lined robe and headed off on a nearly 300-mile trek northward to Yarkand, close to the western limits of the Chinese Empire. It was the depths of winter, with the snows quickly piling thick on the passes that separated the famed market cities he was determined to visit in order to lay the groundwork for Moorcroft's later journey. Izzat Ullah picked up a small caravan on the road from Kashghar to Chinese Yarkand. It was here that he made the unexpected discovery of jade quarries situated, according to his notes, half a mile between the Karakoram Pass and Yarkand. The existence of a source of valuable gemstones was undoubtedly one of the arguments later put forward by Moorcroft to procure Government consent for a third journey. It was on their way up a pass called Ikezuk that they ran into serious trouble. A blizzard was in full blow and had all but obliterated the trail over the pass. The small party, half-blinded by the driving storm, was forced to battle its way inch by inch up the hillside. The snow, Izzat Ullah later recalled, lay in places to a depth equal to the height of a man 'and occasionally twice that depth'. Ever the resourceful traveller, Moorcroft's scout recruited a gang of about one hundred Kirghiz at the lower altitudes to make the trail passable for the caravan. They were sent tramping up and down the trail, pressing down the snow till it presented a hard surface. Once over the pass, Izzat Ullah sprinted to Yarkand in thirty-eight days, a truly astonishing feat when taking into account that the crossing was made in mid-winter, skirting the menacing wastes of the Taklamakan Desert in north-western China, whose name translates as 'he who enters does not return'. Return he did, enduring illness and imprisonment, among other hardships, and by a route that today would stretch the limits of the severest Foreign Office travel advisory: Khotan, Samarkand, Balkh, Herat, Kabul and home to India, where he arrived on 16 December 1813.

Moorcroft was to be found in those days at Pusa, looking after the stud farm while anxiously awaiting news of his loyal servant's return. Izzat Ullah's report left no doubt in his mind that the best parent stock was to be found north of the River Oxus, and moreover that this would very probably be his last chance to acquire the horses he sought, for he was already approaching 50. But it was not until six years later, at age 52, that Moorcroft set out on the journey that was indeed to be his last in this life. The intervening years were a period of planning, preparations and above all angling for permission from the Board permission that, after the Gurkha wars, was finally forthcoming in mid-May 1819.

Moorcroft obtained leave of absence with full salary, which was all the Government support he was to receive. But even this financial support was withdrawn when it was learnt during his two-year stay in Ladakh that Moorcroft was negotiating commercial treaties on his own responsibility. 'The credit and good with which he aimed, no less, to open up trade between British India and Central Asia were supplied by two Calcutta firms. The risk was his own and that of a young companion, George Trebeck. The letter to the Amir of Bokhara for which he asked the Governor-General was not granted.'[18] The journey was overshadowed by an air of doom from the outset, as the gallant band of travellers set off from Calcutta on a wing and a prayer, with no hope of being bailed out if they met with disaster.

Izzat Ullah and Ghulam Hyder Khan, fresh from the Gurkha campaigns, were the two Indian veterans of Moorcroft's previous expeditions who volunteered to accompany the English vet on this, his great enterprise beyond the Oxus. The Persian translator also took along his brother and son, who found themselves more in the role of nursemaids than disciples when the venerable Izzat Ullah started to show the signs of years of cumulative fatigue, after eighteen years in Government service. He nearly dropped with illness on the march, having succumbed to debilitating bouts of diarrhoea and fever that were brought on most likely during their crossing of the rainswept Himalayan foothills.

Moorcroft faced a major crisis in Kabul, that breeding ground of British catastrophes, when tensions began running high over the Afghan warlord Habibullah Khan's threat of imposing customs duties on the party by force, and even of attacking and plundering their caravan. Servants began to desert and even the stalwart Izzat Ullah, fearing the worst, ordered his son to return to the safety of India. Once they were out of Kabul, their dilemma was far from over. The little party was virtually taken prisoner by Murad Beg, the sinister Afghan ruler of Kunduz, the city that nearly two centuries later was to become the last northern bastion of the Taliban. This despot was holding Moorcroft and the others to ransom, and after several days of desperate haggling the sum being demanded for their release was whittled down to a manageable figure. But things were not so straightforward in this world of Afghan intrigue and Murad Beg, like a cat tormenting its prey, was not prepared to release his quarry so easily.

> Once again, morale among the little party slumped and in nobody more than Izzat Ullah. He had been showing uncharacteristic signs of loss of nerve whenever things went wrong for the last twelve months. The unhealthy reputation of Kunduz had terrified him, all the more when two strangers in the serai, whom Moorcroft tried to relieve with medicine, died of yellow fever. Then . . . Izzat Ullah's servant succumbed to the same complaint and the Mir himself began to exhibit similar symptoms. He could take no more. He begged in tears to be relieved of his post, so that he could return to India and his family while there was still time. It was a bad time to be without him, but his demoralisation seemed so total that he would probably have been more of a hindrance than a help in the near future. Moorcroft wrote him a typically generous testimonial, paid him his travel expenses and watched him set out with a few of the others for Kabul on 19 October.[19]

Moorcroft expressed his hope that in recognition of the knowledge gained by Izzat Ullah of 'the political condition of various countries touching upon the British Territories and of others more remote, but which are not without a great prospective interest in the present and possible future relations of the British Government' his servant might find employment, perhaps as honorary consul in some salubrious posting like Lahore, should his health be restored.

Moorcroft's caravan began its uneasy departure from Kunduz in late October on the final 300-mile stage of its trek to Bokhara. The apprehension shared by the travellers was well founded, for it soon became apparent that Murad Beg had not yet finished toying with his victims. The party was shortly intercepted on the trail and ordered back to Kunduz, where a few days later a frightened and dispirited Izzat Ullah was also brought into the city. For a second time in a month the hapless Moorcroft was forced to bribe his way out of trouble and possible wholesale murder at the hands of this deranged potentate. As soon as they were set free to continue on their way, with promises of no further harassment, Izzat Ullah resumed his journey home to India. He never made it. Weakened by fever and exhaustion, the faithful servant of the Raj died miserably two months later, in February 1826, while en route to the North-West Frontier town of Peshawar.

If one were to seek a single factor distinguishing the later Pundits who were trained and employed by the Great Trigonometrical Survey from Mir Izzat Ullah and others of his generation, it would be tempting to conclude that the former were made of sterner stuff. Certainly men like Nain Singh, Sarat Chandra Das and Kintup suffered hardships and misfortunes well beyond those experienced by Izzat Ullah, and not once did they flag in their duty. There was never a question of allowing any tin-pot Amir to bully them into turning back from their mission. In a way it was fortunate for Izzat Ullah, or more accurately for his descendants, that he had not undergone professional training as an agent of the Survey. The Government bestowed a good deal more generosity on his surviving relatives than was the case with many of the retiring Pundits whose professional activities, if revealed to British India's neighbours, might have provoked some serious diplomatic embarrassment.

Izzat Ullah's son sent a somewhat syrupy letter to Charles Metcalfe, Resident in Delhi, reminding him of his father's many years of devoted service to Moorcroft and to British Government interests.

> He was despatched on a monthly pay of 4,000 rupees for himself and messengers towards Multan for the purpose of gaining over and transmitting intelligence respecting the chiefs of that country. Having accomplished this he was recalled, and afterwards proceeded with the Honourable Mr Elphinstone on the mission to Kabul, and having performed his duty heart and soul, returned to Delhi. He remained attached to [Council member] Mr Seton and yourself until you deputed him to Turkestan where he suffered many hardships, among others that of remaining some months a prisoner at Attock. Thence he proceeded to Yarkand and was presented to the King, to whom he represented the justice and prosperity of the Honourable Company's Government. It is now seven years since our father was placed with Mr William Moorcroft on his travels in Turkestan. It is impossible to describe his labours, sufferings, and devotion in this expedition. They will be found in the letters of the aforesaid gentleman . . .

Sparing no efforts to ensure himself and his descendants a government pension, he rolled out letters from supporters like Elphinstone, who two years after his own journey had recorded in a memorandum that Izzat Ullah was head munshi on the Kabul mission in 1808 and spoke Persian and Turkish. Elphinstone also noted that Izzat Ullah was employed by Moorcroft on a journey via Kashmir, Ladakh, Kashgar and Yarkand, as far as Samarkand, and thence through Bokhara to Kabul, 'of all which he has written a very intelligent narrative'.[20] A letter from Metcalfe to Delhi, written in 1814 in the wake of the second journey to the north-west, alludes to Izzat Ullah's service under him as 'head of the office of Northern Intelligence', a reference linking Izzat Ullah to perhaps a more shadowy role than that of Persian translator. Without too much procrastination or excessive generosity, the government determined, 'in consideration of his general character and services', to grant Izzat Ullah's surviving sons a pension of

150 rupees per month, 'being a moiety of the salary which he received from Government', for the support of his family.

It took some considerable time for the news of Moorcroft's death to reach Calcutta, but when the sad event was finally confirmed, the Board issued an unemotional memorandum verging on dismissiveness of the English vet who had given the best years of his life, and finally his very existence itself, to the Raj. 'Moorcroft had collected much valuable information and may justly lay claim to the title of an ardent and enterprising traveller. His political views are characterised for the most part by zeal rather than by sound judgement.'[21] And then, as if having absent-mindedly omitted some dignitary's name from an after-dinner toast: 'We regret extremely the decease of this indefatigable traveller.'[22]

Not long after Moorcroft's and Izzat Ullah's deaths, the Government of India would have cause to contemplate with horror the consequences awaiting Englishmen who fell foul of bloodthirsty and duplicitous Central Asian rulers. The setting was Afghanistan, for more than a century the tinderbox of conflict between British India and a succession of anti-British despots. The outrages commenced in 1842, during the ill-fated British occupation of Kabul. The warlord Akbar Khan, the favourite son of Amir Dost Mohammed, who had been deposed by the British when they marched into the Afghan capital, incited his followers to rise up against the infidels. As a result of this rabble-rousing, the British envoy to the city, the adventurer Alexander Burnes who had attempted to negotiate an alliance with Dost Mohammed, was the first high-profile figure to fall victim to the mob. On 2 November of that year the Afghans torched the Residency and hacked Burnes to pieces, along with two British officers and all the sepoy guards inside. Next came the turn of Sir William Macnaghten, the Government's caretaker administrator, who had arranged to meet Akbar Khan for truce talks at a spot by the banks of the Kabul river, a quarter of a mile from the Residency. No sooner had Macnaghten alighted from his horse than he was brutally slaughtered in the presence of the Amir's son. These two murders were a prelude, and as things turned out quite a minor one, to the treacherous massacre of 16,000 British troops, their families and camp-followers, who had agreed to abandon Kabul on Akbar Khan's solemn assurances of safe conduct to India.

Scarcely had the British bones that lay scattered across the Afghan plain been picked clean by vultures than some 900 miles to the north two Englishmen knelt under the executioner's sword in the central square of Bokhara. For Colonel Charles Stoddart and Captain Arthur Conolly, the prospect of imminent beheading must have come as a blessed relief. Both officers had spent many tormented months in a pit filled with vermin, into which they had been thrown by the Amir Nasrullah, who suspected his captives of spying for the British. This bigoted tyrant had unleashed a reign of terror as soon as he mounted the throne in 1826, starting with the blinding and murder of his brother, a potential rival for power. Cruelty and depravity were the spice of life for this detestable creature. 'In addition to his harem . . . he enjoyed the services of forty to fifty degraded beings in this city where all the horrors and abominations of Sodom and Gomorrah were practised.'[23] Stoddart had been sent to Bokhara to put Nasrullah's mind at ease over British designs on his neighbour, Afghanistan. Conolly could lay claim to being the first to coin the phrase 'Great Game'. In a letter Conolly sent in 1837 to his friend Henry Rawlinson, British political agent at Kandahar, he wrote: 'You've a great game, a noble one, before you.' A month later he wrote again: 'If only the British Government would play the grand game . . .'. Soon afterward, Conolly set off for Bokhara on a freelance rescue mission to determine the fate of Stoddart, who had been languishing for three years as the Amir's prisoner.

Arthur Conolly should have known better. The East India Company cavalry officer was one of the Great Game's most skilful players. For a man of Conolly's experience, allowing himself to walk into Nasrullah's trap was a fatal error of judgement. In 1829, at the tender age of 22, Conolly could be found riding across Central Asia with his Indian guide, both wearing the disguise of travelling merchants. His objective was to spy on Russian movements in the region of Khiva. Conolly never made it to that city of intrigue, having been waylaid and held captive by highwaymen on the road. But further along in his journey, 'with a mixture of apprehension and excitement', he succeeded in entering the gates of the bustling Afghan city of Herat. 'Herat was then governed by the greatly feared Kamran Shah, one of the most ruthless and brutal rulers in Central Asia.' The British agent somehow managed to elude the attention of the Amir's secret police and was able to carry on to Kandahar, on a route that took him through 'bandit-infested country where, he was warned, the slave-raiders removed their captives' ears to make them ashamed to return home, and thus less likely to escape'.[24] Conolly's reconnaissance mission took him across Persia and Afghanistan, from Tabriz in the mountains of Iran to the north of British India. Only this was not a solo crossing. Here we encounter the picturesque figure of the 'Newswriter', in this instance one Syed Keramal Ali, a contemporary of Mir Izzat Ullah and, like Moorcroft's faithful 'translator', a progenitor of the Pundits.

It is doubtful that Conolly could have penetrated these remote and dangerous parts of Central Asia had it not been for the knowledge and resourcefulness of his Persian-speaking servant. Conolly engaged Keramal Ali's services in Tabriz as soon as Sir John Macdonald, British resident in that city, had sanctioned the plan to travel overland to India. The Indian came highly recommended, as being 'much in the esteem of the English', although little else is known about him apart from his being a native of the holy city of Benares, today called Varanasi. Conolly was fully convinced that Russia was contemplating an attack on British India, via Persia and Afghanistan to the Indus. 'We no longer fear France,' he wrote in a memorandum to Government. 'But to destroy *her* power, we gave strength to another nation, which now threatens India more closely than France did. Russia is now to us nearly what France was twenty-three years ago, only she is a great step in advance of what that power was, for France intrigued to *gain* influence over Persia, while Russia *has* it, completely.'[25] The Board acknowledged that Government's knowledge of Russia's military designs on India, as well as its trade with countries of Central Asia, was limited. 'As Mr Conolly was inclined to penetrate some of the countries with which our acquaintance was most imperfect, Sir John [Macdonald] recommended him to do so, and promised to solicit Government to grant him pay and allowances from the date of his departure,' states an official memorandum of the day.[26]

Conolly's high regard for his Indian guide comes through loud and clear in his dispatches to Calcutta. 'He was so esteemed that Sir John Macdonald proposed to send him on Secret Service to Khiva, but eventually he determined to accompany me. During the journey he was zealous in his endeavours to procure information, was exposed to some risks, and suffered much in health.'[27] Conolly, though he claims to have endured 'great pecuniary loss on the journey', went so far as to request that his allowances be transferred to Keramal Ali for his services. 'It was chiefly owing to the ability of Syed Keramal Ali that I was aided from a predicament which otherwise prevented my journey and the best part of the information which I had the honour to submit to Government was collected by him.'[28]

Here Keramal Ali disappears from sight. His name is not encountered again in official dispatches. Hardly surprising, as the loyal Indian was rewarded for his reconnaissance work by being appointed Newswriter at Kandahar, on a salary of 150 rupees per month, 'until some better situation falls vacant'. One could hardly imagine a more hazardous job than that of spying for the British in that volatile Afghan hotbed of intrigue. Conolly was satisfied that he had done his friend a just service. But what a tragedy that Keramal Ali was not around ten years later, to be sent out on reconnaissance work that would have enabled him to forewarn his employer of the peril he faced by marching straight into the butchering arms of the Amir Nasrullah.

Keramal Ali became part of a fledgling cadre of native agents who were employed by the British at diplomatic posts in various rough spots across Central Asia. The Newswriters, a euphemism for informants on the ground, were contemporaries of the elite corps of Pundits. The network of Newswriters was not confined to the trans-Himalayan region, for the British espionage services were at a loss to determine where the Russians might be planning to launch their feared strike on India. One of the major listening posts was the Iranian city of Meshed, which at the height of Great Game fever in the late nineteenth century was receiving regular reports on Russian troop movements from Newswriters in fifteen locations, as far afield as Bokhara and Tashkent. 'The Consul's first and foremost job in Meshed was the gathering of intelligence about Russian activity in Central Asia and monitoring the Russians' moves towards India. Much of the Russian military activity was based in Tashkent, but a consulate there would have been useless for intelligence gathering, by being too conspicuous and under constant observation.'[29] Meshed was teeming with unofficial British spies, most of whom were local traders looking to supplement their income, men able to mingle undetected with the thousands of religious pilgrims who streamed into the city from the surrounding khanates. By this time most of these places had fallen under Russian influence, if not outright occupation, hence presented a superb opportunity to collect information on Tsarist troop activity in Samarkand, Bokhara, Merv and even Baghdad. Little if anything is known about these men, apart from the fact that they were playing an extremely dangerous game in which several who had been unmasked paid the ultimate price for their efforts. The local Russian authorities were well aware of these Indian traders skulking about the bazaars, and eventually got so fed up that in 1893 they expelled the lot of them from Tashkent, a key military outpost. 'This was a setback for the Indian intelligence service, which did indeed employ some of these traders more or less openly as reporters.'[30]

The British authorities were notoriously slow to grasp the fact that it was open season all year round on any white face spotted north of the Himalaya or west of the Khyber Pass. Years after the deaths of Moorcroft, Conolly, Stoddart and other courageous servants of the Raj, British surveyors and political agents were still to be found roaming the fiefdoms of Central Asia, risking their health as well as their necks to expand the Government's store of cartographic and military knowledge. Curiously, the straw that broke the camel's back was the murder not of a British but rather of a German subject, albeit one who had been sent into the field with Britain's blessing.

The Schlagintweits were five German brothers, each with a penchant for exploration and travel, who were born in Munich between 1826 and 1837. One spring morning in 1853 the eminent German scientist Baron Alexander von Humboldt approached his Embassy in London with a request: to petition the British Government for support in granting three of the Schlagintweit brothers, Hermann, Robert and Adolf, permission to organise a Himalayan scientific mission that would take them through British territory. Von Humboldt had already secured an undertaking from the German Government to pay the Schlagintweits a stipend of £5,200 a year for three years of expeditionary fieldwork. The Germans took Von Humboldt's proposition to the Royal Society. After reviewing the useful work that had already been carried out by the Schlagintweits in the Alps, that august body bestowed its endorsement on the project. After all, had not Germany during Victoria's day been embraced as one of the family, ever since 1840 when the English queen had married her charming cousin Prince Albert of Saxe-Coburg Gotha? The Royal Society would later have cause to regret its decision.

The Schlagintweit brothers set sail from Southampton on the steamer *Indus* in September 1854. A little more than a month later the three Bavarians landed in Bombay, where they stocked up on provisions, and engaged six servants and twenty camels for the journey ahead. Armed with compasses, theodolites and other surveying instruments that their coolies transported on long bamboo sticks, they set off on an 18,000-mile trek that was to rank as one of the more ambiguous enterprises in the annals of Himalayan exploration. The heat was so unbearable for these natives of Munich, accustomed to the Alpine climate of Bavaria, with daytime temperatures hovering around the 100° F mark, that the Schlagintweits would send their camels ahead at sundown, while they snatched what sleep they could before setting out after their caravan an hour or two before daybreak.

Six months later, alternating their mode of transport from horse to camel according to the roughness of the terrain, the trio rode into Calcutta, the capital of the Raj. Here at last was chilled beer to sip in the cooling breeze of the fan-pulling *punka wallah*, an imperial bastion of civilisation in which they could comfortably plan their assault on the unexplored reaches of the Himalaya. Soon afterward, the almost forgotten luxury of rail travel awaited the saddle-sore travellers, as Adolf and Robert boarded the overnight sleeper heading into the heart of Bengal, while brother Hermann made his way toward the Buddhist kingdom of Sikkim, first taking the narrow-gauge Toy Train that zigzags up through lush tea plantations to Darjeeling, in all a journey of 350 miles.

Hermann ran into trouble straightaway. He trudged through ferocious rainstorms in a region that gets some of the worst of the monsoon, only to find his plans to enter the lower reaches of Sikkim thwarted by the Sikkimese Government, which had had its fill of foreign 'botanists' and 'geologists' snooping about this politically fragile kingdom. Hermann was left with no recourse but to send his assistant Abdul, 'being a native', into the forbidden territory on a surveying mission. Hermann eventually managed to explore vast swathes of India's north-east frontier, later retracing his steps across the subcontinent in a broad westerly arc through Simla and up to the Ladakhi capital of Leh. Robert joined his brother in Ladakh and together they proceeded northward to the remote Nubra valley that lies at the foot of the Karakoram range, below the Khardong La, the world's highest mountain pass with an elevation of 18,500 feet above sea level. Hermann and Robert amassed a vast itinerary of observations and measurements from their journeys, all of which was minutely recorded in a journal of nearly 2,000 pages, before returning to Europe early in 1857, a fortuitous time to be departing India, as events were soon to bear out. The report tells us that two of the celebrated future Pundits, Nain Singh and his older cousin Mani Singh, were employed for two summer seasons by the Schlagintweits, in Turkestan and Ladakh, as a forerunner to their later grand exploits under the Survey. The Indians left Adolf in Peshawar in January 1857 to return to their village in Kumaon. However, it was Mani who found out through the bazaar grapevine and then revealed to the world the fate that befell the German on his solo trip to Yarkand. Adolf, a former lecturer in geology at the University of Munich, was 28 years old when he arrived in the turbulent capital of Chinese Turkestan, which was then under the rule of a degraded debauchee, the Amir Wali Khan, who had just emerged victorious from a bloody power struggle for the throne.

In spite of his youth and lack of experience, Adolf quickly acquired a flair for exerting authority with the natives, a talent that filled him with an impulsive self-confidence that may well have been a major factor in his tragic end. When rallying his bearers for the climb up the 17,000-foot Traill's Pass in Kumaon, Adolf discovered that the men had no idea of where they were going, and even less inclination to venture up the treacherous glacier. Adolf cast about for the most effective tactics to persuade his group of vacillating porters to do the climb. He finally induced them to carry their loads up the mountainside by promising to sacrifice three goats on top of the pass, which was eventually performed in strict observance of Muslim sacrificial ritual. But some of the men were so terrified by the howling wind that raged across the barren, ice-clad summit that Adolf found himself struggling to revive them from fainting fits. At another stage, he found himself playing a cat-and-mouse game with Chinese guards at the Tibetan border, when he was taken prisoner and placed under armed escort, with orders to return straight to India. On the first night, he managed to escape his captors under cover of darkness, but he failed to make good his escape before the Chinese caught up with him in the woods. Adolf then changed tack and, 'by liberal use of money', he persuaded his guards to turn a blind eye as he proceeded north to Gartok, the Tibetan trading station first made known by Moorcroft on his 1812 journey. He later crossed Ibn Gamin, a 22,260-foot peak that, for lack of documented evidence to the contrary, took him to the greatest height yet reached on any mountain.

Adolf entered Yarkand in August 1857, by which time the astonishing news of the Sepoy Mutiny that had broken out three months earlier was already buzzing through the bazaars. Russian agents stationed in Yarkand would not have taken pains to discourage any rejoicing over the dreadful tales of massacres of British soldiers and their families at the hands of Indian insurgents. The Muslims of Central Asia fully sympathised with the rebellion, in particular because one of the sparks that triggered the mutiny was a protest over orders to use lard for greasing the sepoys' rifle cartridges. By all means, the Russians reasoned, let the natives bear witness that the British had lost control of their own native troops, who made up the backbone of the Empire's defence forces. As for Adolf, German he may have been, but this mattered little, since he had arrived from British India travelling as an agent of the British Government. Adolf's position was rendered even more exposed by the fact that Yarkand at that moment happened to be standing off a siege by the Turks. The last thing the German geologist anticipated was to be conscripted by the Chinese and forced into taking part in the city's defence. After the siege was lifted Adolf decided that Yarkand was, after all, not a healthy spot to be visiting, so he slipped out of the city in disguise and joined the Turks on their desert march south-east to Kashgar.

Adolf's fatal mistake was to unwittingly step out of his disguise when he came across a group of Rajput prisoners who had been caught up in the siege of Yarkand. It was no secret that these Indians were being taken to the slave markets of Central Asia, or in the case of those of slight market value, to be executed. Adolf was overcome by a sense of outrage at this injustice against subjects of a government whose unstinting generosity he enjoyed. The Turks' suspicions were roused, and then very soon confirmed when Adolf suddenly took it upon himself to intercede on the

Indians' behalf, begging for their lives to be spared. The exact circumstances in which Adolf met his doom are not known, but by all accounts a dispute arose and the Turks hacked him to death on the spot. Within days, the bazaar rumour-mill was alive with hushed reports pinning the guilt for this atrocity squarely on Wali Khan. The depraved Amir went to great lengths to protest his innocence, according to a dispatch brought back to India by Robert Shaw, a British agent who had spent three months in Kashghar. The Amir went so far as to claim that he had arrested and personally put to death Adolf's murderer, lamenting that disgrace must attach to his country for this outrage. But for those accustomed to Wali Khan's duplicitous ways, this was evidently a case of he 'doth protest too much'.

The Schlagintweits were naturally distraught over the loss of their young brother, whose death was never avenged. But they, and not to mention the Royal Society that had championed the Germans' enterprise, would have cause for even deeper distress when they pondered some of the reports by eminent geographers of the day that cast serious doubts on the value and accuracy of the Schlagintweits' findings. 'Unfortunately their contributions to Indian and Himalayan geography were of little value,' Colonel R.H. Phillimore sums up in his official record of the Survey of India. Phillimore quotes the distinguished Victorian Scottish cartographer Keith Johnston, who 'could make nothing of their map of Central Asia', and sent Andrew Waugh, appointed Surveyor-General and Superintendent of the Great Trigonometrical Survey in 1843, a rough sketch made 'in a fruitless endeavour to reconcile the positions given by the Schlagintweits with those of former observers'. Phillimore goes on to say that the surveyor James Walker found their positions 'north and north-west of the Hindu Kush . . . much too far to the westward. If I were engaged upon a map of those countries, I should not pay any attention to them.' Captain (later Colonel) Thomas George Montgomerie, the man responsible for raising the corps of Pundits, added his voice to the chorus of derision. He deemed their chronometrical longitudes to be 'of but little value, the usual precautions . . . having been neglected. Leh had proved to be no less than nineteen miles in defect of the Great Trigonometrical Survey value of latitude.' Montgomerie added that, with regard to the position of places in Garwhal, Kumaon and Ghari Khorsum, as well as in Ladakh, 'the longitudes given by the Schlagintweits in these regions, being all affected by a westerly bias, cannot be safely adopted'.[31]

The Indian Mutiny was one of history's most extreme instances of a colonial administration falling foul of the subjects who were assumed to be securely under its control. Once the British had re-asserted power over the seditious territories that had joined the uprising, the Government had to devise a policy to decide where, how and above all *by whom* future trans-Himalayan expeditions were to be carried out.

CHAPTER 3

Enter the Pundit

Pundit is the popular Hindi term for a sage, or more accurately a man learned in Sanskrit lore. The word is taken from the Sanskrit *paita*, signifying 'learned' or 'scholar'. This is not to be confused with *Pandit*, an honorific Indian title, as in Pandit Jawaharlal Nehru. The highly entertaining Anglo-Indian dictionary *Hobson-Jobson*, published in 1886, gives a contemporary reference to the origin of the expression in connection with the British spy network.

> Within the last thirty or thirty-five years the term has acquired in India a peculiar application to the natives trained in the use of instruments, who have been employed across the British Indian frontier in surveying regions inaccessible to Europeans. This application originated in the fact that two of the earliest men to be so employed, the explorations by one of whom acquired great celebrity, were masters of village schools in our Himalayan provinces. And the title *Pundit* is popularly employed there much as *Dominie* used to be in Scotland.[1]

Today the average Indian would be inclined to associate the word
Pundit with a less romantic meaning. The image of a popular
Toyota saloon, called the Pundit, might come to mind, or
perhaps the title of a book on the 2004 India–Pakistan cricket
test match.

During the years he served as espionage agent for the British, he
was known only as 'No. 1', or more often than not, 'the Pundit'.
By the time he was about 35, this headmaster of a village school
in the Himalayan foothills had relinquished his real name, and
indeed his very identity, vanishing like Kipling's bazaar urchin
Kim into the twilight world of the Great Game. Nothing is known,
or more accurately nothing was ever revealed about Nain Singh's
early life, prior to his recruitment into the Great Trigonometrical
Survey of India, along with his cousin Mani Singh.

Both men were Bhotias, people of Tibetan origin whose
ancestral homeland straddles India's border with Nepal. They
worshipped Nanda Devi, the giant Himalayan peak that casts its
25,645-foot shadow over their little village of Milam. The Bhotias
are a hardy race of nomadic stock, people who move with agility
and confidence across the treacherous high passes separating
India and Nepal from Tibet. They can easily pass for natives of
either country, they are for the most part fluent in the local
Tibetan dialect as well as Hindi, and they are capable of enduring
extreme hardship in what is one of the world's most inhospitable
regions. In 1862, Captain Montgomerie was keen to interview
men with these very qualifications.

'In carrying out my plan for exploring beyond the frontiers of
British India by means of Asiatics, I have always endeavoured to
secure the services of men who were either actually natives of the
countries to be explored, or who had at any rate the same religion
as the people, and who had been in the habit of travelling or
trading in the said countries,' Montgomerie wrote in a report to
the Royal Geographical Society in London.[2]

Montgomerie estimated that roughly 1.4 million square miles
of unexplored land north of the Himalayan and Karakoram

ranges was accessible from British India. Conversely, this implied that the same vast unmapped area could also serve as access into British territory. By the early 1860s the Survey possessed a fairly reliable set of data on some 40,000 square miles of this area. This still left a blank on the map similar in size to India. Walker sadly acknowledged that the Government had only the vaguest notion of the position of major cities like Lhasa, and that the strategic question of whether the Tsangpo and Brahmaputra were joined at some point remained an irritating enigma. Gilgit, Chilas and Chitral, strategic outposts of the North-West Frontier, were totally unexplored. Yarkand was later proved to be 100 miles out of position on the Survey's map. Central Tibet was a total geographical mystery, while the city of Shigatse was the only point on the Tsangpo to have been mapped with any accuracy.

The Government of India considered three options for putting this colossal swathe of *terra incognita* on the map. The Government could dispatch a mission of British officers over the Himalaya. This might have been the first choice, however past experience had shown that it could also be a counter-productive enterprise. The hostility of the Chinese authorities that held sway over Tibet, not to mention the unknown Russian military presence to the north, quickly rendered this a stillborn strategy. The idea of sending an army column to escort a party of explorers and surveyors was likewise out of the question. Calcutta had given strict instructions that the frontiers of independent states were not to be crossed by British surveyors, and the 1,500-mile mountain border with Tibet was closed by standing order of the Emperor of China. The Chinese position was even more explicit, in that any 'Moghul, Hindustani, Pathan or Feringhi [unbeliever]' found in Tibet would be put to death. Then there was the third option, 'that efforts be made to train intelligent natives of the border, accustomed to come and go between Tibet, Turkestan and the British territories, in the use of instruments by which they might fix the position of the chief cities, the courses of the great rivers and mountains'.[3]

Nain Singh came to the Survey's attention through Major
Edmund Smyth, the Government's education officer in Kumaon.
In a letter to Walker in 1861, Smyth sang the praises of two
Bhotia teachers in his district who, in his opinion, were
eminently suited to the task of surveying. 'I think I can get just
the kind of men you want,' Smyth wrote. 'The men I would send
are Bhotias, who have a thorough knowledge of the Tibetan
language and spend every summer of their lives in that country.'
For the pilot expedition Smyth recommended one of his local
schoolmasters, Nain Singh.

> He was with one of the Schlagintweits for two years, and was
> taught to read certain instruments, and trusted to take
> observations. He is one of the best natives I know, and
> thoroughly honest and trustworthy. These Bhotias are just the
> people for your purpose, as they are allowed by the Tibet
> authorities to go to certain parts of Tibet for the purpose of
> trade and having this advantage, would not find much
> difficulty in going beyond these limits.[4]

Nain Singh was in deep financial distress because of certain of
his father's 'social misdeeds', in the Survey's diplomatic language.
What had happened was that his father, Amar Singh, had at an
early age eloped with a married woman. He was at the time
already married to a village girl, so this constituted a double crime
of adultery and desertion, an offence serious enough for him to be
excluded from the family inheritance. To worsen matters, Amar
Singh contracted marriage twice more in his lifetime, thus putting
himself in a state of penury. The Pundit's chief motivation, at least
at the outset, was to rid himself of the debts his father had
incurred. His teacher's salary was insufficient to cover these debts,
so General Walker's approach was the answer to his prayers. As a
native employee he drew a salary well below that of a British
Survey officer, but considerably in excess of what he had
previously been earning as a headmaster. Walker was impressed by
Nain Singh's abilities, particularly his remarkable fluency in Hindi,

Persian, English and Tibetan. It was thanks to this ability to converse with natives of almost any origin that Nain Singh was later to become chief trainer of subsequent Pundits.

Walker, who was about to retire to England, did not hesitate to act on Smyth's recommendation. He paid a visit on the young teacher and made him an offer to take on a mission for the Survey in unexplored parts of Tibet. The schoolmaster jumped at the opportunity to exchange his humdrum routine for a bit of adventure. Nain Singh, and shortly thereafter Mani Singh, were placed in the eager hands of Captain Montgomerie, who instructed them in the art of espionage.

Montgomerie devised a bold scheme that must stand as one of history's cleverest pieces of spycraft. Nain and Mani Singh were taken to Survey headquarters at Dehra Dun. From the moment of their arrival at the walled compound on the city outskirts, the Bhotia cousins were put through a training course that lasted nearly two years. Kipling's hero Kim passed his exam in 'elementary surveying' in six weeks, and 'with great credit'. The Singh cousins were put through a far more rigorous training programme, for apart from basic surveying techniques, Montgomerie wanted his fledgling Pundits to be competent in reconnaissance work: how to use the sextant to determine latitudes, the pocket compass for taking bearings, the basics of astronomy for night navigation, the use of a thermometer for measuring heights and how to keep accurate records of the terrain and distance covered. Storing the quicksilver for the thermometers presented a sticky problem. It was difficult to carry and needed to be protected from the wind. Nain Singh himself came up with the answer. All Tibetan pilgrims carry a wooden drinking bowl, and so by acquiring one with a deep bottom he managed to transport his quicksilver, which he later stored in a coconut shell before reaching Lhasa. A reserve supply was kept in wax-sealed cowrie shells.

Recording the ground which the Pundit would cover each day, an indispensable task for subsequent map-making, was addressed by one of the most ingenious contrivances of Montgomerie's entire bag of tricks. Tibetans count off their prayer beads while chanting a holy mantra, the most famous one being the six-syllable *Om mani peme hung* (Hail to the Jewel in the Lotus). Their rosary, or *mala*, is composed of 108 beads. Tibetan Buddhists deem this number to be sacred for a variety of deeply esoteric reasons. Nine and twelve are said to have spiritual significance, and nine times twelve is 108. There are said to be 108 lies that humans tell. There are believed to be 108 Upanishads, or texts of wisdom of the ancient sages. And so on. But 108 is an awkward number as a base for mental calculation. Montgomerie had eight beads removed to leave a mathematically convenient one hundred, without risk of the missing beads being noticed. The Pundits were taught to slip one bead every hundred paces, so that each circuit signified ten thousand paces. The Tibetan rosary has one larger bead, and this was slipped to record a completed circuit. The Tibetan prayer-wheel contains a scroll on which is inscribed the sacred six-syllable mantra. Each turn is believed to launch one recitation of the mantra into the heavens, thus bestowing merit on the devotee who spins the wheel and blessings on humanity. Montgomerie envisaged another use for this instrument. The Pundit would need somewhere to stash his notes with the record of his daily route. The ideal place was the copper cylinder of the prayer-wheel. Later, the Dehra Dun spy workshop began assembling prayer-wheels that could also hold the Pundit's compass. Sextants and other large pieces of equipment were concealed in the false bottoms of their travelling cases, and on more than one occasion the Pundits sweated out some anxious moments with Tibetan customs officials.

To ensure as high a degree of accuracy as possible when measuring distance, the Pundits spent months learning to take a pace of the same distance, regardless of the terrain they happened to be crossing. Montgomerie had their feet tied with a cord measuring what he considered to be the ideal stride for each Pundit. In the case of Nain Singh, this worked out at 33 inches, therefore 1,920 paces would equal 1 mile. This was one of the useful artifices that Kipling's Hurree Chunder would later impress upon Kim. The teenage spy-in-training learnt that 'a boy would do well to know the precise length of his own foot-pace, so that when he was deprived of adventitious aids he might still tread his distances'.[5]

To complete the trappings of high intrigue, the Pundits were given code names consisting of numbers, designations or initials. The first one, Nain Singh, was given the dashing *nom de guerre* of *No. 1*, or simply *The Pundit*, or even *The Chief Pundit*. His cousin Mani Singh became *GM*, a reversal of the two first sounded letters of his name. The cryptic pseudonyms were often devised from the final and initial letters of the English form of name. Some reports referred to Mani Singh as *The Second Pundit*. The remaining members of the Singh family who later joined the Survey went under the code names *GK* for Nain's brother Kalian Singh, and the celebrated *AK*, Kalian's cousin Kishen Singh, who happened to be Mani Singh's brother.

Montgomerie was encouraged by the initial results of his work, which showed the two young trainees to be good pupils as well as schoolmasters. 'They were found to be very intelligent, and rapidly learnt the use of the sextant, compass, etc., and before long recognised all the larger stars without any difficulty.'[6] The Pundits were to be given a small monthly field allowance of sixteen to twenty rupees, with the promise of a bonus, to be determined by the value of the information they supplied.

Spymaster Montgomerie had given a great deal of thought to ways of protecting his Pundits from detection, a basic concern for any espionage agent prying in forbidden territory. It was decided that the Survey's agents would travel in disguise as Tibetan holy men on pilgrimage. The flowing ochre lama robe was an ideal vestment for concealing small instruments and bits of paper, which they would have to carry on their journey.

By 1865, Nain and Mani Singh had passed out as fully-qualified operatives of the Raj intelligence service and were now ready to embark on their first trans-Himalayan mission. They knew this meant that in a few days the world would be quite a different place for them, far from their families, the security of the classroom and out of reach of the rule of British law. Nearly forty years later, Kipling was to sum it up thus: 'We of the Great Game are beyond protection. If we die, we die. Our names are blotted from the book. That is all.'[7]

Captain Montgomerie's plan was to send his two Pundits through Nepal to Lhasa. He instructed them to carry out a route survey from Tibet's holy Manasarowar lake, and from there to follow an easterly course along the road that Montgomerie knew from hearsay existed between the great commercial centre of Gartok and the Tibetan capital. After completing their survey work, the Pundits were to trace an arc westward to Manasarowar, and from there to make their way back to India. In all, a journey, as it turned out for Nain Singh, of 1,500 miles, or 2.5 million paces on his rosary. Montgomerie held out high hopes that the route would define the unknown course of the Tsangpo (which was erroneously believed to flow from Manasarowar) to beyond Lhasa. Montgomerie admits that the Survey lacked any factual data on Lhasa's precise location. 'The position of Lhasa . . . was only a matter of guess, the most probable determination having been derived from native information as to the marches between Turner's 1783 expedition to Tashilunpo and Lhasa,' he writes in his expedition report. 'In fact, the route from the Manasarowar lake to Lhasa, an estimated distance of seven or eight hundred miles, was alone a capital field for exploration.'[8] Even here, Montgomerie's information was well wide of the mark, for the distance between the two points is less than 500 miles.

The Pundits set off on their journey carrying two large sextants, two box sextants, prismatic and pocket compasses, thermometers for taking air temperature and altitude and a pocket chronometer, all of which were concealed in the false bottoms of their cases. Nain Singh had also been given what was described as a 'common watch', later to play a curious role in the expedition. Their first expedition proved to be an abortive mission, leaving Montgomerie to ponder the wisdom of his scheme. The Singh cousins attempted to travel from their native Kumaon roughly 70 miles north-east across the Himalayan passes to Manasarowar. The route was not practicable, which resulted in a great disappointment for the two fledgling Pundits. However, before venturing beyond the Kumaon district, they happened across some Bhotias who, by virtue of residing in this region, enjoyed the status of British subjects. It emerged over the fire that the Pundits' two clansmen had been robbed while trading in Tibet's Chinese-controlled territory near Gartok. This was by no means an unusual occurrence in those lawless parts, but this one presented the Pundits with a possible excuse for penetrating into deepest Tibet. When the Bhotias heard that the Pundits were intending to go to Lhasa, they implored them to act as their agents, known as *vakeels*, in order to recover what they could of the money that most certainly had been whisked away to the capital. This struck Nain Singh as a ready-made pretext for continuing on their travels. He sent his cousin Mani back to confront Captain Montgomerie with this piece of news and to await fresh instructions. He pondered developments so far: a failed mission at the outset, but here was just possibly a plausible excuse for his two agents reaching Lhasa, only this time via Nepal. The Nepalese Government had always maintained relations of some sort with Tibet. Traders from both countries were continuously crossing one another's territory, unhindered by the authorities. Why not send them under that same guise in the company of other traders? Their story would be that the Pundits, themselves of the Bhotia race, were acting on behalf of their countrymen to recover money stolen by the Tibetans, who were usually regarded with suspicion by the Nepalese.

Nain and Mani Singh returned to Dehra Dun and by early January they were once more on the move, this time off on the 450-mile trek to Kathmandu. Most future expeditions got underway in the summer months, the purpose being to leave an escape route open for the agents before they were hit by the worst of the Tibetan winter. But despite it being midwinter, this journey was to take them due east in reasonable comfort through the jungles of the Nepalese Terai. It took them three months to reach Kathmandu, averaging 10 to 15 miles per day, much better going than they would achieve in the days ahead on the 300-mile trek to Lhasa across the high Tibetan plateau. The Pundits found it quite easy to mingle among the bazaar traders, and, having gained their confidence, they began to make discreet enquiries about the most feasible route to Lhasa. The direct caravan route had become almost impassable because of the early arrival of the winter snows, so they were recommended to travel via Kirong, a major trading centre between both countries. This would require a crossing of the notorious No La, a 16,600-foot pass that descends to strike the Tsangpo, about midway between Lhasa and Manasarowar. Nain and Mani Singh hired four servants for the onward journey, and, once inside Tibetan territory, they found it expeditious to slip out of their disguise as Bhotia traders and don the dress of Bisahiris, people from the Indian valley of that name north-east of Simla, and give out that they were on their way to buy horses and at the same time to do homage at Lhasa's holy shrines. They assumed the character of Bisahiris, because it was well known that hill people, since time immemorial, had been allowed to travel freely to and from Lhasa.

The next leg of the expedition failed to get off to an auspicious start. No sooner had the Pundits reached Kirong than they were stopped and subjected to a search by Chinese guards, who, despite the Bisahiri cover, took an uncomfortable interest in the purpose of their journey. Their baggage was subjected to a thorough search. 'Fortunately the instruments,' recounts Montgomerie, 'which had been ingeniously secreted in a false compartment of a box, escaped detection. But still, though nothing suspicious was seen, the plausible reasons given for the journey did not satisfy the jealousy of the Chinese authorities.'[9] The Pundits had not planned for this eventuality, and hence were unprepared to resort to the trusted device used by future agents when running foul of the Tibetan or Chinese guards: namely, a reasonable bribe. Unfortunately, this contrivance had not yet been included on the syllabus of Captain Montgomerie's spy school. Nain and Mani Singh found themselves in the depressing situation of once more having to turn back, at least as far as the Nepalese border village of Shabru. Here Nain Singh summoned up his courage to go and plead their case to one of the local high officials, who was artfully won over by their story. The official was persuaded to write a letter to the Kirong governor pledging that the two men were no impostors. Armed with this letter, the Pundits returned toward Kirong filled with optimism – until they came across a traveller who happened to reveal to them in conversation a few things about the governor. The Pundits learnt, much to their dismay, that the official they were going to see had been a personal acquaintance, in a previous posting near Manasarowar, of Nain Singh's brother Kalian. Proceeding onward carried too great a risk, for the governor was almost certain to realise that the Pundits were travelling under false pretences. So back they went to Kathmandu, reaching the Nepalese capital on 10 April.

The dilemma required a strategic decision. Throwing in the towel was alien to the Pundits' character, as will be seen in the extraordinary adventures of some of Nain and Mani Singh's successors. The Pundits revisited their old haunts in the bazaar to enquire after some promising way to get to Lhasa. After a while, news of two reasonable possibilities began to trickle from the grapevine. There was a good chance of attaching themselves to the camp of a *vakeel* who was putting together an expedition to the Tibetan capital. There was also a Bhotia merchant about to set off, who could conceivably be persuaded to take another traveller in his caravan. The *vakeel* was approached, but, in spite of some initial encouragement, in the end he took the view that it was better not to be found in the company of suspicious individuals like the Pundits. Their luck fared no better with the Bhotia. The merchant was intending to take the Kirong route and almost assuredly would cross paths with the governor, so that plan had to be scratched as well. Almost in desperation, Mani Singh tried striking out on his own. This, too, ended in failure. His health broke down on the trail and in that state he feared for his life on the unsafe roads. The surprise return of Mani Singh to India elicited some rather unkind words from Montgomerie, who suspected the Pundit of lacking determination. But at least his older and more experienced cousin Nain Singh was still out there, seeking a route to Lhasa. This he finally found, thanks to the Bhotia merchant, a disreputable character as it turned out, named Dawa Nangal. The merchant promised the Pundit safe passage to Lhasa, avoiding the Kirong governor, provided Nain Singh advanced him one hundred rupees to cover travelling expenses. The Pundit was an educated headmaster, but wiliness was not one of his qualities. Agreeing to go on ahead with one of the merchant's servants while the Bhotia himself remained behind 'for a few days' to tidy up some business in Kathmandu was an unwise move, for that was the last time he laid eyes on Dawa Nangal. Nor was he to obtain any recompense from the merchant's brother, whom he met on the road. Nevertheless, Chung Chu proved himself to be a better man than his brother, for he ultimately succeeded in getting permission for the Pundit to travel onward, after which, now having changed his disguise for that of a Ladakhi merchant, complete with pigtail, Nain Singh managed to join a large caravan travelling, as good fortune would have it, to Manasarowar. However, his mentor was taking no chances. He knew full well the penalty for anyone caught assisting a foreigner to enter Tibet. He therefore had the Pundit give him a written declaration to the effect that, should he be found out during his stay in Lhasa, it would be at the penalty of the loss of his life. This, Chung Chu assumed, would suffice to get himself off the hook.

All the while, the Pundit was engaged in making observations and surreptitious surveying. Keeping a record of his paces was not always an easy affair. At a point within five days' march of the holy city of Shigatse, where Nain Singh was to top up his expedition funds, which were at a low ebb, by teaching local shopkeepers the more advanced Hindu method of book-keeping, travellers were frequently transported by boat down the Tsangpo. Nain Singh told his companions that it was his custom to travel by land, and was thus able to keep track of his paces. At Shigatse, the Pundit took up lodgings in two rooms he thought well suited for night-time observations of the stars, so as to determine latitudes.

There was little relief in store for Nain Singh when, after several exhausting weeks on the trail, he finally reached Lhasa. Shortly after his arrival, he found himself engaged in conversation with two cunning Kashmiri traders who quickly saw through the Pundit's disguise. There was no way for Nain Singh to keep up his pretence, for the Kashmiris dominated trade in Ladakh and were well acquainted with the mannerisms of those people. When they heard the Pundit's tale, the two men seemed to take pity on him and even offered to advance him a small loan, on the security of the watch he had been given by Montgomerie, which he agreed to hand over. For someone engaged on a mission of high espionage, Nain Singh could at times behave like an innocent soul, and this was one of them. A few days later the Pundit was suddenly reminded of the letter he had given to Chung Chu, when just in time he spotted none other than the Kirong governor strolling down the street. To drive home the point, he then observed a crowd of people gathering anxiously in a square, where a Chinese was being led in chains by Tibetan guards. The Pundit learnt that the prisoner had been convicted of inciting a quarrel between two monasteries. As punishment for his crime, the man swiftly went under the executioner's axe, right before Nain Singh's terrified eyes. For a few days thereafter, the Pundit moved into a more secure residence and rarely showed his face in the street. But the tension had grown too great for him to bear, and when he found out that his Ladakhi companions were about to set off for the Tandum monastery and thence to Manasarowar, he signed on to the caravan and made good his getaway from Lhasa.

Midsummer found the party at the crossroads between Gartok to the north and the road leading south to India. This was where the Pundit took leave of his companions. His watch had fallen into the hands of one of the traders, but as Nain Singh lacked the funds to redeem it he asked the merchant to hold it at Gartok till he was able to return to reclaim his property. On 26 June, after eighteen months on service, Nain Singh was safely back in India, where Mani Singh awaited his return. The adventure was not quite over. Nain Singh then sent his cousin up to Gartok with money to redeem his watch, and this the younger Pundit duly accomplished, as well as carrying out a route survey between Dongpu, the place where Nain Singh had been forced to leave off, and Gartok. Both men set off for Survey headquarters at Dehra Dun, where they arrived on 26 October 1866, with a most remarkable tale for Captain Montgomerie.

Captain Montgomerie, who with his flowing black beard and penetrating gaze resembled not so much a spymaster as a fire-and-brimstone early American preacher, could rest easy that his idea of dispatching native agents on trans-Himalayan expeditions, with the years of attendant training involved, had been a success. Montgomerie acknowledged that reading the sextant at night without arousing suspicion 'was by no means easy' for Nain Singh. The Pundit had initially taken his nightly readings by the light of a kerosene hurricane lamp. But the contraption had been so admired by some curious officials during his brief sojourn at Tandum monastery that he had allowed himself to part with it, if only to keep in their good graces. From Tandum onward he was forced to make do with a common and far inferior oil wick lamp.

Summing up the initial results of the exploration, Montgomerie heaped plaudits on his Pundits for having provided 'a great number of meridian altitudes of the sun and stars . . . including a number of observations at Lhasa, Tashilunpo and other important places'. The venture had been an elaborate route survey, extending over 1,200 miles, which defined the road from Kathmandu to Tandum and the whole of the Tibetan road from Lhasa to Gartok. The two explorers had also fixed the course of the Brahmaputra from its source near Manasarowar (laying to rest the notion that the river flowed from that lake) to Lhasa. Montgomerie was most pleased with Nain Singh's altitude readings, which determined the height of thirty-three previously uncharted peaks and passes.

Latitude observations were taken with the Pundit's large 6-inch radius sextant. 'At any one point', Montgomerie's expedition report reads, 'the results deduced from a variety of stars differ *inter se* so very little, that it is not too much to say that the mean must be true within a limit of a minute.' Thanks to the Pundit's courageous efforts, the Survey now possessed reliable data on the precise locations of Kathmandu, Lhasa and other major centres. It was the first time that any member of the Survey had got away with using his instruments in Nepal and Tibet. Montgomerie remarks, 'There is no doubt but that the Pundit is a most trustworthy and excellent observer.' Furthermore, Montgomerie sympathised with Nain Singh's hardships in traversing the Tibetan plateau. 'Between Manasarowar and Tandum monastery the average height of the road must be over 15,000 feet, or about the height of Mont Blanc. Between Tandum and Lhasa its average height is 13,500 feet, and only for one stage does the road descend so low as 11,000 feet, while on several passes it rises to more than 16,000 feet above the sea. Bearing in mind that the greater part of this march was made in mid-winter, it will be allowed that the Pundit has performed a feat of which a native of Hindustan, or of any other country, may well be proud.'[10] Montgomerie was seeking perfection, as was evidenced by his somewhat pedantic complaint that, on several gruelling mountain crossings, the Pundit had to shorten the length of his pace from 33 inches to 31 inches. 'It may be remarked that more bearings to distant peaks would have been a great addition to the Pundit's route survey, but the recognising of distant peaks from different points of view is a difficult matter, and only to be accomplished after much practice. The Pundit's next survey will, no doubt, be much improved in this respect.'[11]

While at Lhasa, Nain Singh had overheard some intriguing tales of vast gold mines located in a remote area of Tibet, while Mani Singh had come across similar stories during his stay in Gartok, which placed the mines east of that city. Here indeed was a tempting prize worth going for, if only the precise location of these mines could be ascertained. When Captain Montgomerie was told of these gold fields, he immediately began putting together a second expedition, only this time a third Pundit, Nain's brother Kalian Singh, code-named GK, was brought in and trained as a back-up to Mani Singh. Ever since the second Pundit's untimely return to India, Montgomerie had doubted Mani's trustworthiness. Apart from the lust for gold, the Survey was anxious to fill in a large gap on the map between Gartok and Ladakh, a tract of high-altitude land astride the rugged Zanskar range. The Pundits were also instructed to search for the eastern branch of the Indus, as well as to 'explore up to the gold and salt mines east of Gartok', and as far beyond as they could get in that direction, with a view to gaining some knowledge of the unknown lands between the Gobi Desert and Lhasa.

Reports of fabulous gold deposits in certain parts of Tibet had made up the country's folklore since the days of the Greek historian Herodotus, who, on his travels north of Kashmir in the fifth century BC, claimed to have seen giant gold-digging ants. 'There is found in this desert a kind of ant of great size – bigger than a fox, though not so big as a dog. These creatures as they burrow underground throw up the sand in heaps . . . The sand has a rich content of gold . . .'[12] These were terrible creatures, able to smell the approach of humans who came to fill their bags with nuggets – which the ants coveted – and who were lucky to return home alive, with the ants in full pursuit. There is nothing to suggest that Montgomerie put any store by this 2,500-year-old traveller's tale, at once amusing and chilling, but the reports of large deposits of gold in Tibet were enough to set his antennae flying about. By the spring of 1867, the Survey office at Dehra Dun was abuzz with preparations for the next Pundit expedition.

In mid-July a group of Tibetan officials arrived at Dehra Dun, bearing the customary announcement that the treacherous 18,570-foot Mana Pass, 100 miles north-east of the Survey office, was open to the seasonal traffic of traders. Montgomerie thanked them for the good news and hastily assembled his little band of 'traders', all of whom were to assume the disguise of Bisahiris, for the journey to Tibet. This party consisted of eleven men, twelve donkeys and one pony to transport their surveying equipment, provisions and spare clothing. The men were all armed to the teeth with weapons they had acquired at Badrinath, the last Indian staging post below the pass, since they had been forewarned that the hills were teeming with robbers waiting to pounce on passing caravans. Despite the dire warnings, the two Pundits and their companions made the crossing unmolested, arriving at the banks of the Sutlej in early August. They made the river crossing on a 76-foot iron suspension bridge said to have been built by Sekundar Badshah, the local name for Alexander the Great, in the fourth century BC. The locals took great pride in this historic relic, lubricating the chain links every year with clarified butter. One more towering pass, the 19,220-foot Bogla, remained before Gartok, which they studiously circumvented lest the local officials should take an unhealthy interest in their onward journey.

The sight of the Indus filled the Pundits with pleasure after weeks of trudging drearily across Tibet's arid tableland. But their joy was short lived. The entire party was stopped at an encampment called Giachuruff on the river embankment. The headman came forth to question them about who they were and the object of their journey. This man, Gopa Tajam, was not taken in by the story that they were Bisahiri merchants who had come solely to sell coral and purchase the highly prized shawl-wool to sell in India. With frightening accuracy, he proceeded to rattle off each man's true land of origin. It was no great feat to see through their disguise. It could be put down to an intelligence failure that the Pundits had not been made aware that this part of Tibet was closed to Bisahiris, who the previous year had introduced smallpox to the country.

Nain Singh stuck to his story and in time he managed to bring the headman partially round to his version, enough at least to obtain permission for a few members of the party to proceed onward, on condition that a hostage was left to ensure their return by the same route. It was decided that Mani Singh, whose nerves were shattered by the physical and now mental hardships they had suffered on their crossing of the Himalaya, was to be left behind with the headman. Soon after getting under way, Nain Singh dispatched his brother Kalian, along with one servant, to the Indus to carry out a route survey as far as he could get to the river's source.

A freak snowstorm in late August held the party up at the base of the 18,760-foot Chomorang Pass, on the far side of which, after tramping many miles across snow, they came to the fabled Thok Jalung gold fields. Nain Singh records that the vast camp pitched on the desolate plain gave off a reddish brown colour, and as he drew closer he could make out the eerie sound of men and their families singing as, bent over their shovels, they dug up the earth, their voices carrying on the wind across the bleak wilderness. Had the Pundit come upon Herodotus' 'ants'? In parts of ancient Asia, certain races and tribes were known by the names of animals, such as snakes, horses and wolves. It is not beyond the realm of plausibility, yet it would require a stretch of the imagination to assume that the lowly gold diggers of Thok Jalung, in their crouching attitude, might easily have been described as 'ants'.

A middle-aged figure in a red robe and brown felt Chinese hat emerged from a tent to greet the Pundit when he marched into the encampment, which was located at 16,330 feet above sea level. This was Yudak Mingmar, the chief (roughly the equivalent of a modern site manager) of the mining camp. Mingmar had a weakness for fine Indian tobacco, of which the Pundit had fortunately taken along a plentiful supply for just such occasions. However, Nain Singh was reminded that he and the other 'Bisahiris' were taking a considerable risk by travelling in Tibet, their people having been declared *personae non gratae* for allegedly having brought disease to the local population. Being a kindly man, in the Pundit's description, the chief advised him to get on with whatever business had brought him to Thok Jalung and to make haste to depart the camp. Mingmar called Nain Singh into his tent to press him further on the purpose of his visit. The chief sat on a pile of embroidered cushions surrounded by bales of shawl-wool, packages of tea, strings of dried yak meat, several old matchlocks and a sword. Beside him sat a small box with paper and ink, and two cups, one for tea and the other for *chang*, the traditional fiery local brew. Mingmar sucked incessantly on a silver Nepalese hookah, observing his guest in the gloom of the black yak-hair tent, and then he got to the point: how did a humble Bisahiri merchant, he smiled, come to own such a fine bejewelled box, such as the one the Pundit carried with him? What was inside this box? Nain Singh had rehearsed his answer: the box had been purchased at auction and was used to carry his coral. The chief took the box and examined it closely. He had heard of these Indian auctions and was visibly impressed. He returned the box to Nain Singh, fortunately without discovering the large sextant that was concealed in its false bottom. Mingmar was nevertheless uneasy about having the Pundit and his party wandering about the camp. There was too great a risk of the chief being arrested for showing hospitality to a proscribed visitor. Nain Singh was therefore told he would have to abandon Thok Jalung on 31 August. The Pundit's undercover skills served him well during the five days he had to spend discreetly exploring the gold mining camp. He was able to determine the precise location and dimensions of the pits being dug, and the extraction methods, which were crude in the extreme, with diggers damming up a water channel that turned the camp into a quagmire, and then using this to wash the soil and collect whatever nuggets passed through the pits. Nain Singh reported 'large yields' of gold, with one nugget weighing in at an estimated two pounds. He also picked up stories about gold fields strung out along the northern edge of the Brahmaputra, all the way to Lhasa.

Tibet had been looked upon as a potential source of bullion, apart from being the natural gateway to the markets of China, since the days of Warren Hastings. Now the British had an accurate picture of where the ore was located, how it was mined and in what quantities. The Tibetans were selling gold to China along trade routes that had been in use since time immemorial. Establishing a road link from the mining sites to British India was a much more problematic affair, to say nothing of the political obstacles this involved with the authorities in Lhasa as well as

Peking. It is fair to say that these considerations, namely how to open up Tibet to trade for wool, tea and of course bullion, came into play in the run-up to the 1904 Younghusband expedition.

Nain Singh left Thok Jalung on the appointed day and retraced his steps to Giachuruff, where he found a much relieved Mani Singh. Kalian Singh returned shortly after to report that he had traced the Indus for a considerable distance, although not all the way to its unknown source. Kalian had come close to disaster at the hands of armed highway robbers, who attacked his party and seized one of the expedition thermometers and the coconut containing the supply of quicksilver. Kalian, a large and intimidating man, rushed to the rescue and yanked one of the robbers round by his pigtail, at which point the thief and his accomplice took flight.

Montgomerie's second mission, on which the Pundits were away for six months, turned out to be a highly rewarding undertaking. The three Survey agents mapped some 18,000 square miles of unexplored territory, with route surveys taken of eighty summits. They traced the course of the Sutlej, the longest of the five rivers that traverse the Punjab, through Tibet to the border of British territory. The position of Gartok was confirmed. The Pundits also defined the courses of the two upper branches of the Indus from near their sources into Ladakh, proving that the eastern branch is the true course of the Indus. To round off their remarkable work, the Pundits discovered a hitherto unheard of range, the Aling Gangri group, south of the Ladakh mountains. 'Altogether the Pundit and his brethren have, as I predicted, improved very much in the art of fixing distant peaks,' a proud Captain Montgomerie was able to proclaim to the Royal Geographical Society.[13]

Nain Singh's further adventures confirmed his position as the most celebrated of the Pundits, though when he was called back into service in 1873 he was nearly 50 years old and travel-weary. Montgomerie instructed the Pundit to accompany a mission to Yarkand, and in a sense this was also to be his final act as acting head of the Survey, for he returned to England that same year. He was replaced by Colonel (later General) James Thomas Walker, who in the following year sent the Pundit on a mission to Yarkand under Sir Douglas Forsyth. The explorer Forsyth had specifically requested Walker to depute two Pundits from the Survey, whom he planned to send from eastern Turkestan across the Gobi Desert, through Tibet and back down to India. In the end he got three: Nain, Kalian and now Kishen Singh, whose remarkable adventures were later to earn him a distinguished place in the annals of the Survey.

Nain Singh acquitted himself well on the Yarkand mission, which was to be his final bow, earning the praise of such Establishment luminaries as Sir Clements Markham, who served as Secretary of State for India and later as President of the Royal Geographical Society.

The journey performed between July 1874 and March 1875 by the Pundit Nain Singh, of the Great Trigonometrical Department, is the most important, as regards geographical discovery, that has been made by any native explorer. For the first time the great lacustrine plateau of Tibet has been traversed by an educated traveller, who was able to take observations and describe what he saw. Thus a great increase has been made to our scanty knowledge of Tibet.[14]

Stealing into Tibet in the dead of night along with his four attendants, all disguised as lamas, Nain Singh summoned up every ounce of strength he could muster for the crossing, fully aware that this was to be the last great exploit of his long career. During those eight months, the Pundit moved at a slow pace, 'as all his baggage was carried by sheep, 20 to 25 lb each', and thus they plodded on for more than 1,000 miles over the frozen plateau, across gold fields that had until then remained undiscovered, mapping lakes and mountain peaks and taking nearly 800 astronomical observations for latitude and elevation. 'The eastern extremity of the Pangong Lake was settled, a system of numerous lakes and rivers was discovered, the existence of the vast snowy ranges of the northern Himalaya was clearly demonstrated, several peaks were fixed, thirty miles of the Brahmaputra was discovered, and the Tawang route from Tibet to India was surveyed.'[15]

Once back in India, the Pundit retired from the Survey, following which his identity was revealed to the world. Markham praised Nain Singh as 'the greatest scientific traveller that India has produced'.[16] In spite of the Government's notorious underfunding of secret service budgets, in this case it felt obliged to open its hand to a unique individual. Nain Singh was provided with a generous pension, enhanced with the grant of a village of his own. Five years before his death at age 56, Nain Singh, who was made a Companion of the Indian Empire, became the only Pundit to receive the highest honour of the Royal Geographical Society. He was awarded the Society's coveted Patron's Medal 'for his great journeys and surveys in Tibet and along the Upper Brahmaputra'.

CHAPTER 4

All in the Family

'In the reports of the Survey this man is simply called AK, in conformity with a long-standing custom of suppressing the names of the explorers while they are still strong and vigorous, and liable to be again employed in work of this nature.'[1] With these words, General James Walker, late Surveyor-General of India, commenced his address to a packed audience at the Royal Geographical Society in London, on a biting December evening in 1884.

Nain Singh had executed some of the boldest adventures in Tibet since Marco Polo's crossing of the plateau in the thirteenth century, on his fabled voyage to the Chinese emperor's court. But even after the Pundit had hung up his rosary and prayer-wheel, there remained a colossal expanse of Tibetan territory still to be explored, particularly to the north and east. By 1878, Britain's second invasion of Afghanistan, triggered by Russian intrigues at the Court of Kabul, was only a matter of months away. To the north, the Tsar's forces were rapidly descending toward Tibet's frontier. An air of urgency prevailed at Dehra Dun headquarters. The Survey's officers perceived an immediate need to build up their file of reliable intelligence on what could (and in 1903 would) become a battlefield on the roof of the world.

Kishen Singh had performed admirably on the Yarkand mission, having thrown himself with great enthusiasm into his route surveying two days after marching from Leh. He was constantly found mapping the ground covered during the daily march, while at night he busied himself with his theodolite, taking frequent astronomical observations for latitude. Expedition member Captain Henry Trotter, who later drew up the official report for the Great Trigonometrical Survey, had great praise for the young Pundit and his ability to keep up a 'continuous route survey the whole way'. Security became an issue once the party reached Shahidulla, about 250 miles south of Kashghar. The British explorers decided that, from that point onward, all open surveying or display of instruments on the road was to cease, for they were embarking on a voyage into the unknown.

Shahidulla is a strategically important centre on the way to the Karakoram passes on the main route north from Ladakh. This short cut to India via Ladakh was, in fact, in regular use until the Chinese closed the borders soon after the Communist takeover in 1949. At the time of the British mission, caravans would often rest and graze their animals in the fertile valley near Shahidulla until conditions were favourable to cross the Sanju Pass leading to Yarkand. Shahidulla controlled the route north across the Sanju Pass from where a caravan could head north-west to Pishan and Yarkand or north-east toward Khotan. The pass makes for difficult crossing, although it is possible to take laden yaks across outside the winter season. But the area had never been mapped and it was necessary to do so, for this was a natural route for trade from India, or invasion of British territory. The job fell to Kishen Singh to take observations quietly with a small pocket compass all the way to Yarkand, making rough but tolerably correct road survey by day and night. The Pundit was able to fix the position of some neighbouring bazaar towns, and he accompanied a small party of mission explorers on an excursion to the north of Kashghar, making a traverse survey of the road.

He then accompanied one of the Survey officers beyond Yarkand and bravely returned on his own over 100 miles of terrain that had never previously been surveyed. Continuing on past Khotan through notorious bandit country, the Pundit was able to report back on some gold fields he had come across about 160 miles east of that city, thus demonstrating the initiative and fortitude the Survey was seeking in a worthy successor to Nain Singh.

The result was that, in the spring of 1878, Walker dispatched Kishen Singh to Tibet with orders to strike across the great Tibetan plateau and head north to Mongolia, leaving it to the Pundit to find the most practicable route. Agent AK, as he was now known to his Survey superiors, was instructed to make his return by a parallel but different route, in the hope of opening up new ground for moving goods as well as troops, should the need arise, across this territory.

Kishen Singh, who was 28 years old, departed from Dehra Dun equipped with the standard panoply of undercover gear: a 9-inch sextant for taking latitude observations, a Tibetan tea bowl as a mercury trough, a prismatic compass for taking bearings on distant hills, a pocket compass for route bearings, a rosary for counting his paces, a prayer-wheel for secreting his field notes, an aneroid barometer and some boiling-point thermometers. The Survey dug into its pockets to provide the Pundit with funds to purchase provisions at Lhasa, where he was to commence his explorations in the guise of a travelling merchant.

The Pundit AK, who had gained his initial field experience on the Forsyth mission to Yarkand, was briefed by Nain Singh about what to expect on his first solo exploration under Survey auspices. He was warned to avoid attempting to cross into Tibet via Nepal, where the border guards were on high alert. He worked out that the most sensible route would take him north from Darjeeling, through the western edge of Bhutan, a country with which the British had traditionally enjoyed cordial relations. This was the tried and tested itinerary that had been followed by earlier British explorers, from Bogle to Manning. It took the Pundit five months to reach Lhasa, where first he laid in a stock of provisions, and then made his way to the bazaar to make enquiries about joining the next caravan for Mongolia. The caravan would provide him with the cover he needed to make an anonymous crossing of this vast expanse of territory in safety.

Kipling once remarked, 'all the hours of the twenty-four are alike to Orientals'.[2] One is tempted to add that the Asian concept of months and indeed years bears little resemblance to our frantic obsession with 'maximising' time, and our embedded fear of 'wasting' it. So it was that Kishen Singh came to spend an entire year in Lhasa, unruffled by this delay to his trip to Mongolia. What had happened was that in the market he had met the leader of the first caravan heading toward Mongolia, but the man was unable to give him a definitive date for its departure, saying only that it would probably leave Lhasa in February, some five months away. There was a sound reason for not setting a precise date for the caravan's departure: the road ahead was crawling with robbers, who also had spies lurking in Lhasa. If the highwaymen knew when the caravan was scheduled to move out, it would be no trick to position themselves to attack it on the road. 'In November, the caravan leader sent for the other traders and the Pundit and begged them to excuse him from going to Mongolia on account of his being under a heavy debt of five hundred *kurs* (equivalent to the colossal sum of 77,000 rupees) which he must liquidate before leaving the city. After four months' further delay he gave up the idea of conducting the caravan and the explorer had no alternative but to wait for another.'[3] Meanwhile, the Pundit occupied his time making secret survey measurements of the city and brushing up his Mongolian language skills, while compiling a detailed sketch of Tibetan religious customs. Finally, in early autumn a caravan from Mongolia wended its way into Lhasa. Half the camels arrived unladen, as they had been brought in for the return journey to Mongolia, which, the Pundit learnt, was to take place more or less immediately. Agent AK knew this was his chance to cross the exposed plains without having to battle his way against the winter storms. In September 1879, he started northward with around one hundred other traders, the majority Mongolians and the rest Tibetans, all armed with spears, matchlocks and swords. Scouts rode ahead to give warning of approaching danger, the column kept close order and the marches were always made by day, starting at sunrise. A four-man guard of two Mongolian and two Tibetan sentries kept watch over the camp at night, as the traders huddled close to the smouldering fires.

Sixty miles north of Lhasa, the caravan began lumbering up the 15,750-foot Lani La Pass, which issues onto the world's highest plateau, the Chang Tang (which translates simply as 'the northern plain'), occupying the greater part of Tibet. Here in the thin atmosphere the caravan by necessity slowed its pace, averaging at best 13 miles a day. The Pundit described this mournful region as one 'abandoned to wild animals', no sign of human habitation being passed for almost 250 miles.

They never heard them coming. Like a force of nature the mounted bandits, fully 200 of them, swarmed down from the hills in the early hours, when the camel-drivers were readying their beasts for the day's march. The still morning air erupted with the clash of steel and the cries of the wounded, but after a fierce engagement the robbers realised they had met their match in the tough Mongolian and Tibetan traders who were prepared to defend their possessions to the death. The gang of freebooters was driven back into the hills, carrying with them most of the goods the Pundit had assembled for barter, as well as his baggage animals. Fortunately, his box of surveying instruments survived the attack. AK was devastated by the loss of his merchandise but, being a Pundit to the core, he was determined to break away from the caravan, which was taking a different route, and press on northward to the Gobi Desert.

Christmas of 1879 found Kishen Singh with his servant marching into the village of Hoiduthara, penniless and with precious few goods to his name that he might offer for sale. He had no choice but to take up employment at the home of a

Tibetan from Gyantse, a man of property and influence. The Pundit spent the winter looking after the Tibetan squire's camels in return for food and lodging. When spring began to signal its arrival in March, AK took his leave of the Tibetan to resume his voyage and route mapping.

Kishen Singh's travails were far from over, however, for after a three-month interlude at a Mongolian nomad tent encampment called Yembi, where AK raised 200 silver rupees from the sale of the goods he had accumulated at Hoiduthara, his servant ran off, taking with him most of the Pundit's money and newly acquired horses. Kishen Singh had feared some act of treachery, for the servant was complaining endlessly about the Pundit's plan to venture into the heart of Mongolia, a land he believed to be inhabited by Muslims who were at war with the Emperor of China.

The situation could hardly have appeared more desperate, yet the Pundit was firmly committed to going on at whatever cost. He again entered into service, this time spending five months tending ponies and goats for a local farmer. Once he had accumulated enough funds to resume his journey, he started off on the road, resigned to begging his way when the money ran out.

In January 1881 he joined a party of traders, and together they headed across the high passes that descended into fertile pastureland only 4,000 feet above sea level, a tropical paradise compared with the barren wasteland he had had to endure, and the lowest altitude he had encountered since leaving Darjeeling three years earlier.

After a delightful week marching through lush alpine meadows and rolling hills, Kishen Singh found himself at Sachu, a major trading post that had been visited by Marco Polo. There the Pundit spent several restful days negotiating his passage north with a party of traders. Bad luck seemed to be AK's constant travelling companion, for no sooner had he left the town than he was stopped on the road by the district governor's men. It was destined to happen sooner or later, and now Kishen Singh found himself under arrest as a suspected spy. He was fortunate to escape with his life, but he was kept under surveillance for seven months until a lama he had befriended along the road, a cleric of great influence in the region, happened into town and secured the Pundit's release, taking him under his wing as a servant. The Pundit accompanied the lama to his monastery and there he sat for two months, waiting for his wages that would take him back to Lhasa.

Despite his misfortunes, Kishen Singh had performed a large number of route surveying tasks on his journey. He was now bent on getting back to India without delay, as can be seen by his covering a remarkable 450 miles of rough terrain in twenty-five days to reach the large town of Darchendo on the Chinese–Tibetan border, following, as General Walker had instructed, a different route homeward. Darchendo was the seat of the French Catholic mission in Tibet and luckily AK retained a letter of introduction to the French missionaries, given to him by Walker in case the Pundit's route happened to take him in that direction. Here it looked as though AK's luck had taken a turn for the better. 'The Bishop kindly assisted the Pundit with a present of money, and advised him to take the direct route back to India via Batang,' Walker stated in his report. The bishop also sent a letter to one of his priests who was in India at the time, informing him that the Pundit had reached Darchendo in good health. 'This information was most welcome,' says Walker, 'as four years had elapsed since any communication had been received from him, and most distressing rumours had recently reached his family, that he had been seized by the authorities at Lhasa and had had his legs chopped off in order to put it out of his power to make further explorations.'4

As might be expected, getting home was not to be a cut-and-dried affair for Agent AK. It was his misfortune, when heading westward for the Yalung river crossing, to arrive at the village of Nagchukha in mid-February, with the Tibetan New Year celebrations in full swing. The arrival of a foreigner at that time of year, when nobody had cause to be on the road, could have

Captain Thomas George Montgomerie, the man responsible for raising and training the Corps of Pundits. *(Courtesy of Royal Geographical Society)*

The impenetrable Tsangpo Gorge. *(Courtesy of Royal Geographical Society)*

Map illustrating the journey of the Pundit Nain Singh through Great Tibet. (*Courtesy of Royal Geographical Society*)

Pundit Nain Singh, the first Pundit. *(Courtesy of Royal Geographical Society)*

Pundit Kishen Singh.
(Courtesy of Royal
Geographical Society)

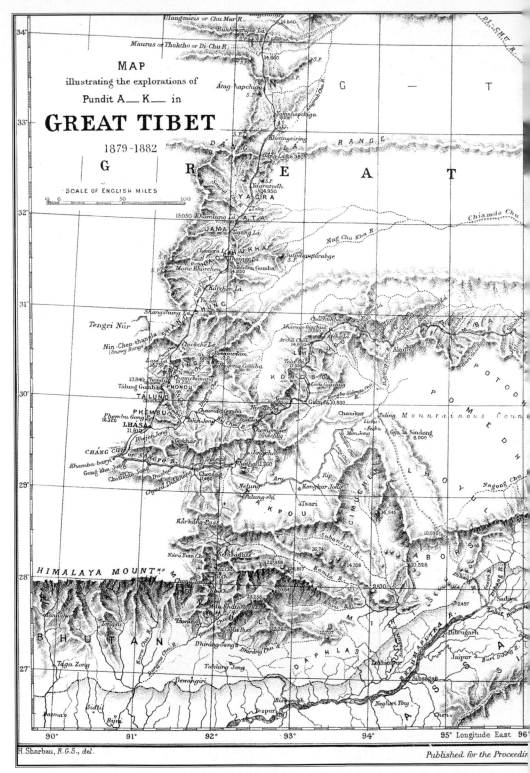

Map showing route followed by the Pundit Kishen Singh. *(Courtesy of Royal Geographical Society)*

Map showing routes of Sarat Chandra Das. *(Courtesy of Royal Geographical Society)*

Right: Pundit Sarat Chandra Das astride a yak. *(Courtesy of Royal Geographical Society)*

LHASA

G

Daibung Gamba
Radung Chu
Sing-donkar
Toilung Chu
Sena Mo
Dechen Jong
Chumig gang
Norbu gang
Nethang
Songkar La
Gokhar La
Nam
Jang-tsi
Jang-ngaé
Tshe-bu-teng
Tse-kang
Char-shul
Jim-khar
Chaw Bridge
Toi-ta
Tongbu
Khamba-partshi
Tol La
Shesti-teng
Go-tu-lung
Dorje-tag ghats
Tag
Tso-mo Jong
TSANG PO
Tsong-ké
Samye Gamba
Ch—
Mabour
Nam-kar-Jong
Popadzong
Dugolagze
Cho
Toi Suduling
Long-bu-toi-Jong
Mendal-long
Yong-shon
Togu-cho
Sabar-cho
Norbu-tsang
Nyen Jong
Soljon Khamar
Nagri-tseng
Mango Ferry
Nyungar
Khamba La.
14500
Tamaibing
Yos-nam-gyaling
Tsa-sang
Shenak M
Sheak-shika
Torlung Shobal
Tsetang
(Chetang)
Pinduo
Ombu
Tag-tsan-bumba
Tib
Nedong-Jong
Re-Jhung
Palti Jong
Sharu teng
Dablung
Hang
Nagartse
14100
Tib La
Padang Jong
Yar-lung
Nujin Kang Sang S.P.
Kharo La.
16800
Gam-thang
Tharpa
puchow
San-ding
DumoTso
Ringlin
Yamdo Tso or Lake Palti
Tong-da
Shab-shi
Karmaling
Plain
29
Ralung
Talung
Ke-utag
Nyen-n
Kabu La
Nyang-tang
Loh bu Jong
Kan-me-do
Komi-bu-ja Cho
Cheng Khar
Kyan-patta
Nargm
Riwa tag Jong
U

E
OF
LHO
K
A
H
28

Pundit Sarat Chandra Das.
(Courtesy of Royal Geographical Society)

The Pundit Kintup.
(Courtesy of Royal Geographical Society)

The Potala Palace in Lhasa, residence of the Dalai Lama. *(Courtesy of Royal Geographical Society)*

Major Frederick M. Bailey, the adventurer who led an expedition to the Tsangpo in 1913, with the Maharajah of Bhutan. *(Courtesy of Royal Geographical Society)*

Above: Charanjit Kaur Mamik, Senior Librarian, Survey of India, Dehra Dun. *(Author's Collection)*

Left: Bust of Sir George Everest at the Survey Office. *(Author's Collection)*

Below: Surveying instruments at the Survey of India Museum, Dehra Dun. *(Author's Collection)*

only one meaning: the traveller had come to rob the village while its unsuspecting inhabitants were rollicking in the festivities. Kishen Singh now found himself a prisoner of the drunken villagers. It took several days to send a runner up and back to Darchendo to confirm that no theft had been reported at that place, so presumably the outsider was not a thief after all, and he was duly set free. His next misadventure came at Litang, described as a 'cheerless place' and one of the highest towns in the world, at 13,300 feet. The Pundit's arrival coincided with a smallpox epidemic in the district. By now he knew what to expect: he was put in quarantine for three weeks, during which time he was administered a native prophylactic consisting of a kind of snuff prepared from the dried pustules of smallpox victims. This potion induced a mild form of the disease that was intended to serve as a preventive against the full-blown variety. This delay was more than merely another of the many inconveniences the Pundit had been obliged to endure on the road. He was out of money, but, ever the resourceful explorer, Kishen Singh resorted to reciting sacred Tibetan chants from house to house, like a wandering minstrel. In this way he managed to scrape together about twenty rupees, enough to see him back to India, barring further mishaps.

It was now April 1882, and the Pundit found himself descending into low hill country toward Assam (in modern Arunchal Pradesh), the years spent on the arid Tibetan plateau fading into memory. Kishen Singh was euphoric over the approaching end of his ordeal. He reckoned he was only 30 miles from the British frontier, a two-day march at most. Then he received the bitter news from some local villagers that this route to India led into the land of the Mishmis, a ferocious tribe against which the British were obliged to send a punitive mission in later years. In fact, the Mishmi country was so dangerous that it was not properly explored until the early twentieth century. This was no place for an outsider to be loitering, so with great regret AK turned his face to the north for the return journey to Lhasa.

Agent AK's failure to bring his expedition to an end after four years on the road came as a blow to the weary Pundit. For the

Survey, it was a blessing in disguise. By mid-July, Kishen Singh had trudged back over the Himalayan passes and once more stood on the great Tibetan plateau, in a quarter that was 'of great interest to geographers, for it is the region of the water-parting between the eastern and western systems of rivers, and it constitutes an impassable barrier to the oft-asserted flow of the great Tsangpo river of western Tibet into the Irrawaddy'.[5] Kishen Singh's travel log, which explained in detail his various crossings of the river system for 200 miles, left no doubt in Dehra Dun that the Tsangpo merged not into the Irrawaddy but into the Brahmaputra, as had been maintained for some years by several eminent British geographers. More than forty years were to pass before the debate was scientifically closed, but Kishen Singh's findings provided crucial impetus for the Survey to carry on its quest.

After passing through Zayul on the road down to India, the Pundit reached the Shinden monastery, where there waited yet another unpleasant surprise. Zayul was in those days a notorious Tibetan penal colony, and Kishen Singh's ragged clothes and dishevelled appearance led the monks to believe that an escaped convict had stumbled into their midst. It was only with the arrival a few days later of an 'influential personage', whom the Pundit had happened to meet on the road, that the monks were persuaded to let him continue on his journey.

A final unpleasant encounter awaited the Pundit when he crossed the last mountain barrier before joining the road leading to Lhasa. He descended to a settlement nestled in an upland valley called Chomorawa, a nomad encampment where he found the people in great distress, dragging the carcasses of animals to a burial site. The beasts had succumbed to a deadly poisonous insect, a kind of wingless beetle about half an inch long with a black head and yellow body. The insects swarm about the pastureland, concealed under grass where they spread their poison so that animals grazing on the land become infected and rapidly spread the disease to others. Kishen Singh discovered to his horror that several herdsmen who had unknowingly eaten the flesh of these diseased animals had died of fever. Once they were infected, there was no cure, therefore the nomads took a prophylactic, catching and scorching some of the insects, which they then ate with salt to build up immunity, in much the same way that the Pundit had been given the dried pustules of smallpox victims to take as snuff.

At this place Kishen Singh left the Lhasa road and turned southward to the Tsangpo, 'which we may now without any hesitation call the Brahmaputra'.[6] Travelling as rapidly as his exhausted body could carry him, he reached Darjeeling on 12 November 1882, four and a half years after he had started out on his arduous travels, battling his way through heavy snows on the final stage of the journey. Walker describes the state in which the Pundit, along with his loyal travelling companion Chumbel, reached India: 'They arrived in a condition bordering on destitution, their funds exhausted, their clothes in rags, and their bodies emaciated with the hardships and deprivations they had undergone.'[7] Nonetheless, it was a triumphant return for Kishen Singh, who had miraculously brought back every piece of surveying equipment that had been issued him for the expedition, even his bulky 9-inch sextant, plus of course his valuable journals and field-books.

Walker saw fit to award Kishen Singh one of the two bronze medals 'for Asiatic explorers' that in the previous year had been placed at his disposal by the commissioners of the International Geographical Congress and Exhibition at Venice. More meaningfully, the Government of India rewarded the Pundit, who was only 32 at the time, with a grant of land in perpetuity, as had been done for Nain Singh. Thus Agent AK was able to live out nearly forty more years in comfort, reflecting on a life of adventure and accomplishment equalled by few.

Kishen Singh's journey to Tibet and Mongolia was a remarkable tale of fortitude, unmatched by any of his Survey contemporaries save the immortal Kintup. The Pundit carried out a continuous route survey, taking magnetic bearings and maintaining a measured pace, for nearly 3,000 miles. Even when moving across the steppe with his Mongolian companions, who would never allow a fellow trader to travel on foot, Kishen Singh was able to record the distance covered by counting the length of his horse's paces. Most of the routes he covered north and south from Lhasa, roughly 1,700 miles of territory, were entirely unknown to geographers. Walker confirms that the Pundit's misfortune of being confronted with the warlike Mishmis, 'though very distressing to him at the time', was most fortunate from a scientific point of view. 'It necessitated his surveying six-hundred miles of route over entirely new ground, which took him round the eastern basin of the Tsangpo river and enabled him to determine that that river certainly flows into India, not Burma, and is the source of the Brahmaputra, not of the Irrawaddy.'[8]

Further accolades were forthcoming from Clements Markham, the Royal Geographical Society's President, who recognised in Kishen Singh's journey remarkable qualities that rendered the Pundits deserving servants of the Raj. 'Let them [the British people] consider the skill, the endurance, the resolution, the patience, the capacity shown by this native gentleman,' Markham, in an outpouring of hyperbole, told a packed house in the Society's grand London premises. 'Had he been an Englishman he would have possessed the stimulus afforded by a liberal education, but . . . he was a comparatively uneducated man. Had he been an Englishman he would have looked forward to returning to his native land, where the applause of the public, the thanks of Parliament, the gracious approval even of the Sovereign would have awaited him. But what had that poor man to look forward to?' For Markham, it was above all a deep-rooted sense of honour that drove Kishen Singh on in the face of winter blizzards, bandits, penury and imprisonment, not to overlook smallpox epidemics and killer beetles. Markham had not the slightest doubt that General Walker's crowning success had been 'this marvellous journey of the Pundit AK', who was the general's 'own creation'.[9]

Walker's address to the Royal Geographical Society had rolled on well past the usual closing time on that December evening.

The hundreds of Society Fellows gathered under the auditorium's vast chandelier may well have begun to wonder about the chances of catching a hansom cab passing along windswept Kensington Gore at that hour. Markham summed up in a few words what was undoubtedly the chief merit, from the Government's point of view, of Kishen Singh's explorations. General Walker's paper had been chiefly addressed to 'the adventurous journey of the Pundit'. But there were other considerations that made it a valuable undertaking, namely the possibilities that this new route survey information afforded for opening up trade with Tibet. The Tibetans prized British broadcloth, knives and hardware, tobacco and indigo, not to mention tea. 'It is an instructive fact that within one hundred miles of Darjeeling is a people which drinks tea morning, noon and night, which uses practically no other beverage, and yet obtains its supply from districts of China 1,200 miles away.' Markham considered it an outrage that the richest part of Tibet was 'practically within a stone's throw [Kishen Singh might have had to suppress a grimace at that one] and the inhabitants, who are from the highest to the lowest keen traders, are debarred from intercourse with India through sheer ignorance and the tenacity of tradition'.[10]

Markham's indignation was heard in the India Office, 2 miles away across Hyde Park, where a policy was being formulated to bring the blessings of British trade to Tibet, peaceably or otherwise, and in doing so to ensure Britain's pre-eminence in a territory in which Russia was making felt its uncomfortable presence.

CHAPTER 5

Spies of the Wild Frontier

Kim, Kipling's masterpiece of Indian espionage, was set in the North-West Frontier, not in Tibet. It would be wrong to assume that the Land of Snow was the only country shrouded in mystery, as far as the Survey of India was concerned. From a commercial as well as a military point of view, the passes leading into Chinese Turkmenistan and Central Asia were of vital importance. Fully a year before Nain Singh set out on his great expedition across the Tibetan plateau, Montgomerie was training a Muslim agent to undertake a 400-mile journey northward from Leh, over the Karakoram range to Yarkand, the Chinese city today known as Shache. For obvious reasons, there was no question of dispatching a Hindu explorer to lands inhabited by fanatical Muslim tribesmen. Sending Survey agents into these regions posed an even greater political risk than the exploratory missions to Tibet.

When Montgomerie was carrying out his own research around Kashmir and Ladakh, he was struck by the possibility of organising a reconnaissance of the uncharted territories to the north of the Karakoram and east of Ladakh, mainly in eastern

Turkestan. He was loath to send European surveyors very far up the Yarkand road, which he knew would bring them within range of the Khirgiz robbers, always at large in that part of the world. 'While I was in Ladakh I noticed that natives of India passed freely backwards and forwards between Ladakh and Yarkand, and it consequently occurred to me that it might be possible to make the exploration by their means. If a sharp enough man could be found he would have no difficulty in carrying a few small instruments among his merchandise, and with their aid I thought good service might be rendered to geography.'[1]

The man recruited for Montgomerie's experimental voyage to Yarkand was Abdul Hamid, who was assigned the code name NA, and came to be known as the *Munshi*, a term of respect used to designate a person of education. The Munshi brought some route-making ability to the job, having been previously employed in the north of India. He was therefore acquainted with the use of basic surveying instruments and did not require to be put through the extensive Pundit training course at Dehra Dun. This was just as well, for Montgomerie was anxious to launch his experiment, and by the summer of 1863 he had the Munshi kitted out and ready to go, carrying the smallest pocket sextant, thermometers and general surveying paraphernalia obtainable. The Pundit was expected to travel light, for Montgomerie was keen to see him back in India early the following year with results in hand. After an initial test, surveying the road from Kashmir to Leh, which he passed with 'tolerable proficiency', on 12 June 1863, he was sent north, with instructions to march more than 400 miles over largely unexplored mountain terrain to Yarkand, and once there to fix its position, while taking daily survey measurements on his route. The Pundit joined a caravan bound for Yarkand in late August, and after thirty-one days' 'hard marches' over some of the most elevated country in the world, he reached the city on 30 September.

Montgomerie took every precaution to prevent the Pundit's instruments looking conspicuous. He was given a long wooden walking stick of the type that was in common use with

Himalayan traders along the narrow and often precipitous mountain trails. But this was a special staff, fitted with a large head cut flat on top to provide a convenient resting-place for his prismatic compass. The journey proceeded without mishap, but it was filled with the kind of solitude that few travellers are prepared to accept. For nearly three weeks, the caravan trudged across high mountain terrain without setting eyes on a village or cultivated field. The pack animals had to go without grass for twelve of those days, and the caravan's supply of grain was soon exhausted by the starving ponies. Numbers of beasts collapsed and died by the wayside.

Since the Munshi was travelling with a caravan, taking proper survey measurements on the road was out of the question. Montgomerie had foreseen this problem and told the Pundit to take hourly bearings of the road's direction with the naked eye and make notes of the time he spent on each march. It took the Munshi sixty-six days to cross the Karakoram range, half of which were spent at an elevation never below 15,000 feet. Montgomerie estimated that the mountains were at no point less than 400 miles across. To give some idea of the vastness of scale, he reckoned that, by comparison, it would take no more than three days to cross the European Alps, an accurate enough estimate.

The Munshi was fortunate on his arrival in Yarkand to come across an old acquaintance from India, Awaz Ali, who offered him hospitality in his home. This provided the Pundit with a secure rooftop observation point for taking night-time readings during the six months he was to spend in the city. All went well until late March, when the Muslim governor of Yarkand, whom the Munshi had befriended, summoned him to his residence to warn the Pundit that the city's Chinese overlords were growing wary of his activities. The governor advised him to send off his belongings with a southbound caravan so that he could himself discreetly beat a hasty and unburdened retreat from Yarkand within a fortnight. This he did, taking along Awaz Ali, who had no desire to be left behind to answer uncomfortable questions about his friend.

Foul play was ruled out following a detailed inquiry by the British authorities into the death of the Munshi and his friend Awaz Ali. The sad event occurred soon after they had descended the Karakoram Pass, the last great obstacle on the route to India. Both men had grown very weak and deteriorated rapidly, dying within a couple of days of one another only a short march from Ladakh, according to the story supplied by their travelling companions. It was said the victims had died of poisoning from eating wild rhubarb. It may in fact have been a case of cerebral or pulmonary oedema caused by exposure to high altitude, although this would be strange, since they had already reached lower ground before they died. None of the Munshi's equipment had been touched, though the others in the caravan had appropriated some of his saleable possessions. Montgomerie dismissed robbery as a motive for murder, since according to local custom the merchants would have made off with these goods whether the Munshi's death was accidental or otherwise.

The Pundit's expedition reports did not reach Montgomerie until early 1865, when he was preparing to return to England on leave. It was clear that the poor Munshi had achieved his expedition's objective, that is, he had accurately fixed the latitude and height of Yarkand, while the city's longitude could be fixed from the Pundit's route survey, not a very difficult task, as the journey was made almost along a vertical line on the map. Montgomerie found almost all the instruments in good working order. Of the books the Munshi had compiled, there was one of astronomical observations and another of the route survey, both written in English, plus two others in Persian, along with notes and sketch maps of several towns in eastern Turkestan. The Munshi had also made some notes about Russian movements in the region, a subject of much lively discussion in government circles. The maiden expedition by a Muslim Pundit ended on a tragic note, but this by no means put an end to the Survey's undercover work beyond the North-West Frontier.

The next Muslim Pundit to be sent abroad stands out as the greatest among his peers, not least for his valiant incursion into

Afghanistan at a time when British India had an anxious eye fixed on the turbulent events that were unfolding in the tribal lands beyond its western frontier. In less than a century, eighty years to be precise, Britain fought three wars with Afghanistan. Two of these, the bloodiest ones of 1839 and 1878, were undeniable acts of imperial aggression, while the 1919 conflict was in essence a month-long skirmish along the North-West Frontier that ended with the defeat and, ironically, the long-sought independence of Afghanistan. Britain's two invasions of Afghanistan were not launched for territorial gain. They were obviously cases of overreaction, but the campaigns represented more than a knee-jerk, panicky response to Russian intrigues with the Amir of Kabul on the diplomatic and commercial fronts. The fears of a Russian invasion were not unfounded.

There was no shortage of informed intelligence agents and army officers to warn of the approaching menace. Colonel Algernon Durand, brother of Mortimer Durand, the man who defined the western frontier of the Indian Empire between what are now Pakistan and Afghanistan, travelled widely in the northern territories beyond British India. He was able to report in 1900, a year before the publication of *Kim*: 'The Great Empire . . . is expanding in many directions. Central Asia is now hers. That her soldiers, and the ablest of them, consequently believe in the possibility of conquering India, no one who has had the chance of studying the question can doubt.'[2] Durand was convinced that the Tsar's troops were determined to gain a foothold on the south side of the Hindu Kush – the great range that spills into northern Afghanistan – which would have effectively paralysed the large numbers of British troops needed to hold the line against a possible Russian advance.

In the intervening years between the first two Afghan wars, the Survey of India had to face up to the fact that it possessed pitifully few maps of that country, not to mention of the unexplored khanates stretching north of the ill-defined Afghan frontier, many of which were now dotted with Russian military encampments. *Kim* was set on the North-West Frontier because, as late as 1901, as has been seen, the British were deeply concerned over a possible Russian advance through the mountain passes that straddle Afghanistan. Mahbub Ali, the horse trader who came from that 'mysterious land beyond the Passes of the North', warns young Kim, the future spy, of rifles making their way from Quetta 'to the north', and falling into the hands of India's enemies. But precisely where these arms ended up and in whose hands, even the wily Afghan merchant was unable to say. 'The Game is so large that one sees but a little at a time,' he tells Kim.[3]

On a February day in 1869, two Englishmen on an exploratory mission in Kashghar were sought out by a mysterious Muslim who had just arrived from India. The visitor turned up in a bedraggled state, looking every bit the exhausted traveller after months on the road in wildest Central Asia. The man told the two Englishmen, the explorers George Hayward and Robert Shaw, that he too was a British subject and, moreover, in the employ of the Great Trigonometrical Survey. If it were not too much trouble, he enquired, could one of the gentlemen kindly lend him a watch? It would also be helpful to know the day of the month, for after his long wanderings on the road he had completely lost track of time. These two tools, the Muslim explained, were essential in order for him to establish his exact position from the stars – an intriguing remark from someone who had just wandered in from months of wandering across the steppes. Was he a harmless eccentric, a madman, or perhaps an impostor with a hidden agenda? The Englishmen suspected the latter. The pair were being detained under house arrest by the Amir of Kashghar, no less nasty a piece of work than his opposite number in Bokhara. The charges were the usual ones of acting as spies for the British, given that Hayward and Shaw were unable to provide a convincing explanation for their presence in the country. But their suspicions regarding the Muslim visitor were far from the mark. For the man was Mirza Shuja, code-named 'The Mirza', the second Pundit to be sent abroad by Captain Montgomerie to explore beyond the Hindu Kush, Mustagh and Karakoram ranges.

The fate that the unfortunate Hayward was to suffer reinforced the wisdom of Montgomerie's strategy of training and sending out native agents. Hayward, whom the Government had tried to dissuade from going to Yarkand, was murdered in Gilgit less than a year later. The freelance explorer had foolishly dug his own grave by sending a letter to India denouncing the atrocities that had been committed by the Maharajah of Kashmir's besieging forces on the Gilgit garrison following its surrender. No sooner had this letter found its way into *The Pioneer* newspaper than Hayward's fate was sealed. The story goes that Hayward died valiantly, in the tradition of Stoddart and Conolly at Bokhara, only requesting a few moments of prayerful solitude on a hilltop before turning to face the executioner's sword. His death was glorified with true imperial pomp in the poem 'He Fell among Thieves', by that minstrel of empire Henry Newbolt:

> 'I have loved the sunlight as dearly as any alive.'
>   'You shall die at dawn,' they said.
>
> He flung his empty revolver down the slope,
>   He climb'd alone to the Eastward edge of the trees;
> All night long in a dream untroubled of hope
>   He brooded, clasping his knees.

The Mirza, who was in his mid-forties at the time he embarked on his great misssion, brought an unusually high degree of breeding and education to the ranks of the Survey's native explorers. A Persian by birth, he quickly acquired fluency in Pushtu, the language of the Pathan tribes of Afghanistan and the North-West Frontier, as well as English, which he taught to the family of the Amir Dost Mohammed during a sojourn in Kabul. Mirza Shuja had a long connection with the Survey, stretching back to 1838. He had first attracted the attention of Eldred Pottinger, a fascinating Great Game character in his own right. When a Persian army attacked Herat in 1837 this 26-year-old British Army officer, who was on a reconnaissance mission for the

East India Company, slipped into the besieged city in disguise and organised its successful defence.

After a three-year attachment to the Survey in Peshawar, the Mirza was put on a public works team. At the end of 1855, General Walker felt the time was ripe to recommend him to the Great Trigonometrical Survey, although he would need training in mathematics before he could enter the ranks as a fully-fledged agent. General Walker noted of his protégé:

He is well born and respectable and may seek information among Mussulman tribes who would not suffer the approach of Europeans. With a view to his future employment with exploring expeditions, the Surveyor-General [Montgomerie] asked that he should be taught to make all the observations such as observing for latitude, time, longitude, azimuth, magnetic derivation, base measurements, angles for heights and distances, barometrical heights, thermometrical heights, and climatic observations and recording them intelligibly.[4]

The Mirza remained at the Survey office until 1857, and after a training period that involved such mundane tasks as tower building and line cutting, he was then granted six months' leave to go to Kabul to recover some money of his, with which, as he stated, a merchant of Peshawar had absconded. On his return to India, the Mirza was given two years of formal survey training at Dehra Dun, and in October 1868 he was dispatched in disguise, with a small party of servants, to follow a route across the Pamirs, literally the 'Roof of the World', to Kashgar and Yarkand.

The Mirza's journey to Afghanistan got off to an unpromising start. The Pundit departed Peshawar in the autumn of 1867, intending to enter Afghanistan by journeying north some 150 miles through mountainous tribal territory into the Chitral valley, and from there to cross into Afghanistan's north-eastern province of Badakshan. His first attempt ended in failure when he was turned back by Afghan border guards. The Mirza then thought of getting a letter through to the Amir in Kabul, but his old friend

Dost Mohammed had died five years earlier and the new ruler, Sher Ali, was having enough trouble holding on to his throne to be bothered with providing a safe conduct pass for some unknown Pathan.

The Mirza's next move was to retrace his steps southward, past Peshawar, in the hope of crossing the frontier from the Kurram valley, but this also proved unsuccessful. Shifting himself and his small party of servants up-country once more, he tried to penetrate the valley of Bungush, north of Kurram. By now the valley was buried in snow, making the route impassable. To make matters worse, the countryside was alive with gangs of roving bandits and the Mirza was glad to escape with his life. The Pundit then followed the course of the Indus south to the city of Dera Ismail Khan, trying to get into Afghanistan by the adjoining Kakar valley, but here again he was thwarted by hostile tribes. At this point the Mirza was on the verge of despair. This was his maiden expedition for the Survey, yet his every move up and down the border had met with frustration and failure. He decided to mount one more assault on the border, which in fact turned out to be the last attempt but one. The Bolan Pass, after the Khyber, is the major trade route between India and Afghanistan. The Mirza would head for this pass, travelling upriver by steamer after having sold off his baggage animals. But, once there, the Pundit encountered the region in an ugly mood, with the tribesmen in a state of revolt. Finally, carried by the momentum of his quest, he resolved to try for Khelat, where the British had inflicted a signal defeat on the Afghans in 1839, by advancing through the less travelled Mala Pass. His determination at last found its reward. After a march of 244 miles he was deep inside Afghanistan, a land he discovered to be in total anarchy, owing to internal strife and the threat of Russian and Persian incursions. Anyone else might have been inclined to call it a day, but Captain Montgomerie's Pundits were stalwarts to the core.

There would be little opportunity for rest at Khelat. The reports coming into the city warned of a complete breakdown in law and order on the roads. It was imperative to make a start for

Kandahar before the warring tribes forced the Pundit into spending a fruitless winter at this remote spot in the Afghan hills. Almost everywhere there were outbreaks of fighting between the armies of opposing warlords. The Mirza made the acquaintance of a merchant from Kandahar, who agreed to escort the Pundit to that city, offering to hire out his donkey into the bargain, which the Pundit needed to transport his surveying equipment. In May 1868, the Mirza made his way from Khelat to Kandahar, with fighting raging across the country as Amir Sher Ali's forces struggled to put down the rebellious warlords. Once there, the Mirza could see that, the longer he delayed in Kandahar, the less likely were his chances of making a break for the relative safety of Kabul, 200 miles to the north, which was his gateway across the mountains into Central Asia. He would need to travel light, so some of his less compromising baggage was sent ahead to Kabul. But the plan backfired, for his bags contained a number of personal papers of a highly incriminating nature in the eyes of the district officials who had detained and searched the Mirza's bearer. It was only by attaching himself to a column of Sher Ali's returning army that he was able to escape arrest for spying, and complete his journey to Kabul.

By early summer, the Mirza was ready to depart from Kabul for his push northward over the Hindu Kush to Faizabad. This formidable range that cuts across the country in a north-easterly direction between Kabul and the Oxus was so named, according to the fourteenth-century Muslim explorer Ibn Battuta, because so many slaves brought from India died in the passage owing to the severe cold and snow. Later scholars say the term 'Hindu Kush' derives from a Hindu army that was lost in its attempt to cross into Turkestan by a pass now known as Dead Hindu. Whatever the origin of its name, the Hindu Kush lives up to its grim reputation. 'The country between Kabul and the Oxus appears to be in a very lawless state and slavery is rife,' states the Survey report received from the Mirza. 'A slave, if a strong man likely to stand work well, is in the Upper Badakshan considered to be of the same value as one of the large dogs of the country, or if a horse, being about the equivalent of eighty rupees. A slave girl is valued at from four horses or more, according to her looks, et cetera. Men are, however, almost always exchanged for dogs.'[5]

Violence and treachery were the order of the day in this part of the world. The Mirza's inexperience in the art of deceit nearly brought his travels to a disastrous end at Tashkurghan, a staging post between Bamiyan and Kunduz in the north-east of Afghanistan, along the road to Faizabad. One day, a strange-looking traveller in Asiatic dress, whom the locals all considered to be a European in disguise, approached the Pundit. He engaged the Mirza in amiable conversation, asking questions about his journey and speaking in Persian. But the stranger's perfect command of that language aroused certain suspicions, for the Mirza knew that no European could so effectively master the difficulties of Persian pronunciation. The Pundit held his tongue, revealing as little about his travels as etiquette would allow. After their meeting, the gossip that flowed round the bazaar left no doubt in his mind that the man had been sent by the local authorities to find out the real nature of his business. It was time for the Mirza to leave Tashkurghan.

He was fortunate to hear of a large *kafila* or camel caravan going to Kunduz, with an escort of more than one hundred armed horsemen to protect it against attack by the savage Khirgiz brigands who roamed the countryside. This would take him roughly halfway to the city of Faizabad, about 150 miles due west of the Wakhan Corridor. But once again, in Faizabad, as had been the case in Tashkurghan, the explorer found himself dogged by prying and threatening individuals, one of whom openly denounced him as an infidel spying for the British. The Mirza had no doubt that this man was in collusion with his servants. From the day they had marched out of Tashkurghan, the porters grumbled incessantly about the danger of meeting Khirgiz robbers on the road, nor were they happy about the cold days ahead as they advanced on the Pamir steppes. The Mirza was able to buy this pest's silence with a handful of gifts, and proceeded to make arrangements for his onward journey, enlisting the help of one Abdul Wahab, the son of a local *kafila bashi*, or caravan leader. In all, the caravan consisted of six of the Mirza's servants, plus another six he hired from the caravan, including guides. They started off on Christmas Eve, men and beasts pushing forward in a blinding snowstorm.

A few days later, the caravan wended its way into what is today the Wakhan Corridor, the elongated mountainous valley between the Hindu Kush and the Pamirs that was given to Afghanistan in 1893, essentially as a buffer to prevent Britain's and Russia's colonial empires meeting head-on. On the Mirza's first stop, at Patoor village, he took on a new guide, Peer Ali, who was experienced in winter crossings of the featureless Pamir range. For days they pressed on over the high mountains without any shelter for their night camps, apart from the dry-stone walls that traders had erected as a rude protection against the fierce winds of the steppes. The wind was so piercing that the men frequently had to shelter on the lee side of their horses as they marched along. Most of the Mirza's servants suffered from attacks of what they called *dum*, with nausea, headache and palpitations, all classic symptoms of high altitude sickness, which they believed was caused by a baneful wind. By the sixth night spent camping in the open, the men and ponies had fallen into a state of extreme sluggishness, rising in the morning literally out of a miserable bed of snow. The animals were suffering from shortness of breath, a situation that put the entire caravan at risk lest they be forced to a standstill in this desolate place. The local servants, however, had a procedure for relieving the symptoms, which was to bleed the horses' noses.

By early February, the weary and half-frozen caravan plodded into Kashghar in Chinese Turkestan, the northernmost point of the Mirza's explorations and the ominous spot where, eleven years before, Adolf Schlagintweit had been hacked to death by agents of the Amir. The Pundit was ushered into the presence of Kashghar's ruler, Yakub Beg, known as the Atalik Ghazi. He enquired uncomfortably whether the Mirza had any news of two

Englishmen (Hayward and Shaw) reported to be lurking about his territory, to which the Pundit of course professed ignorance. Hayward himself later noted, prophetically, that a foreigner entering the ruler's kingdom stood a good chance of being murdered. 'Even if allowed to go on, there was the strong chance that an Oriental despot accustomed to daily bloodshed, perhaps smarting under a defeat, might order the intruders' heads to be cut off, since he had done so before to men whom he took to be spies of the English.'[6] The Mirza was shown to his living quarters in the Amir's fortified residence, and with great difficulty he was able to take discreet meridian observations of the sun from one of the roofless houses in the fort.

The Mirza's presence in Kashghar was fodder for the suspicious instincts of nearly every official with whom he came into contact. One day, Yakub Beg sent the Pundit to pay a visit on the *Shagawul Dadkhwah*, or royal council of Yarkand. There a discussion was in progress over the nature and potential threat of several foreign powers, including British India and Russia. When the Mirza somewhat tactlessly pointed out to the assembled elders the vast military and trade resources of the British, one of the Afghan representatives rushed forward to denounce the Pundit as a Kafir (infidel) agent lacking proper respect for the Mohammedan lawgivers present. Fortunately, the Mirza summoned up a convincing rebuttal, enough to escape being stoned to death, which otherwise would have been his fate. As Montgomerie remarked in the official report of the Mirza's journey, 'Once the cry of Kafir is raised these bigoted Mohammedans are apt to act without further inquiry. The Mirza from that date did his best to avoid all public discussion lest he should get into trouble.'[7]

Although the matter was not openly discussed, the Mirza was effectively being held prisoner in Kashghar. Yakub Beg contrived by every possible means, short of torture, to extract the true purpose of the Mirza's visit to his domains, as merchants were never to be found travelling in these parts in midwinter. On one occasion, an official came to his residence carrying a compass and a sextant. His intention was to ensnare the Pundit with the crude ploy of asking him the use of these devices. Sensing a trap, the Mirza wisely pleaded ignorance.

From then on, it was one mishap after another. His frustrated attempt to wander into Kashghar's forbidden old quarter ended with more accusations of spying, and he was also prevented from visiting the Russian frontier, although he did manage to send to the border a local man, who returned with a well-detailed report of Tsarist troop strength in the area. At last, in early June, after keeping the Mirza under virtual house arrest for more than four months, Yakub Beg began to show signs of mellowing. There was no conclusive evidence against the Pundit, which under normal circumstances would not have stopped the ruler extracting the information he wanted by quite unpleasant means. But the likelihood that his guest was in the employ of the all-powerful and vengeful British Government rendered this an unwise course of action, at a time when Yakub Beg was struggling to keep the Russians at arm's length.

It took the Mirza only five days to reach Yarkand, his final destination on the route that had been set by Captain Montgomerie. Rather than stop at a public caravanserai, where it would have been difficult for him to take observations unnoticed, he went directly to the house of the *kafila bashi* who had guided him over the Pamirs. His main problem at this juncture was money, for most of the funds he carried had been spent in Kashghar on provisions, gifts and bribes. Fortunately, he came across an Afghan who was willing to lend the Mirza enough money to see him back to Leh, in exchange for a promise to remit some funds to the man's family in Kabul.

For once, the Mirza was not troubled by local officials conniving to burrow into his affairs. On the contrary, as soon as the news of his arrival reached the provincial governor, Muhammad Yunas, he was made a gift of food and regaled with praise for the British, as it was now an open secret that the Mirza was an agent of the Government of India. The governor, a man of a distinguished Tajik family from Tashkent, did not think it advisable to discuss this in public. The Pundit's only source of irritation, as had been the case since leaving Tashkurghan, was his quarrelsome servants. One of them had fallen in love with a Yarkandi wench, and he came to the Mirza with a demand for money so that he could remain behind and marry the woman. Otherwise, he threatened to divulge everything he knew about the Pundit's spying activities. The matter was resolved with as much cunning on the Mirza's part as insolence shown by the servant. The Pundit and his Afghan mentor explained to the man that, if he left the safety of the Mirza's camp and stayed alone in Yarkand, he would surely be dragged back to Yakub Beg and sold as a slave. At this the servant quickly sobered up, and a small sum of money changed hands as a goodwill gesture for his silence.

The Mirza had nothing but praise for Yarkand and its people, whom he described as good-humoured, honest and hospitable, a welcome change from the brutal Khirghiz tribesmen he had had to deal with in weeks past. When it came time to return to India, the Pundit linked up with a caravan 300 strong, many of its company being pilgrims on their way to Mecca for the Haj. By August he was safely back in Leh, whence he made his way to Kashmir and finally to Survey headquarters after a two-year absence.

The Mirza provided Montgomerie with a great deal of valuable data on the land beyond the Hindu Kush and the Oxus. But his fame was short lived. In 1872, Montgomerie dispatched the Pundit (along with his son-in-law) on a second mission, this time to Bokhara. After a safe journey north from Herat, the two men were treacherously murdered by their guides while they slept, somewhere on the lonely expanses between Maimama and Bokhara.[8]

Two of Montgomerie's Pundits had now met untimely ends. Yet the Survey's deputy superintendent, who had by now been promoted to the rank of major, was as determined as ever to push forward with the mapping of the northern territories. Montgomerie was particularly intrigued by the ranges of desolate mountains that lay between the Indus and the Hindu Kush, an area that might in the near future find itself disputed by the two great imperial powers of the region, British India and Tsarist Russia. It was around this time that St Petersburg began to deploy a markedly aggressive strategy of territorial expansion. First came the capture of Samarkand, turning Bokhara into a Russian protectorate, followed in swift succession by the construction of a permanent fortress at Krasnovodsk in Turkmenistan, the annexation of the Ily valley in Kazakhstan, and the dispatch of a trade mission to Kashghar to impose a commercial treaty on Yakub Beg. Himalayan politics suddenly became the Government of India's chief strategic priority.

'From 1840, if not earlier, political considerations dictated the pace and direction of exploration,' notes one Himalayan chronicler. 'This not only made life very difficult for the unofficial traveller but also shrouded in secrecy the efforts of those who had official blessing. . . . In the last thirty years of the [nineteenth] century when the direction of exploration swung away from Yarkand towards Gilgit and the west, this air of secrecy and intrigue deepened.'[9]

The Government was after reliable topographical data on this highly sensitive region, so spymaster Montgomerie was put on the case. From a geographical point of view, the most frustrating problem was that previous expeditions had mapped their separate portions with a high degree of accuracy, but the Survey was unable to fit the pieces together to form a 'reliable whole', in Montgomerie's words. The Survey needed to know how the tracts of explored land lay with reference to one another, and Montgomerie decided that the way to achieve this was by running a route survey straight through the heart of this territory to Faizabad, due north of Peshawar, thus fixing an axis on which to fit the outlying pieces of the puzzle.

Montgomerie sent his agents to scour the bazaars of Peshawar for suitable candidates, while he himself put out enquiries to his colleagues in an attempt to come up with someone of Pundit material. He eventually found his man. The Commandant of the Sappers and Miners corps referred him to a 'very intelligent sapper', a Pathan tribesman from the frontier who displayed a great deal of talent for the work. Montgomerie invested many weeks of training in his pupil, all for naught as it turned out, for shortly after the man had passed his preliminary route survey exam he was murdered in a tribal blood feud. A second Pathan was recruited and he too showed great promise, but before he could be sent abroad Montgomerie found it necessary to dismiss the man when certain unexplained facts came to light. Third time lucky, Montgomerie hoped, when he took on another Pathan sapper who was 'in every way' qualified for the job. This time there were no mishaps and by early August 1870 the Pundit, whose name was Hyder Shah, was ready to start.

This Pundit came to be known as the Havildar in the Survey records, a sepoy (native soldier) rank corresponding to sergeant. Other times he was simply called 'the Sapper'. He started from Peshawar with orders to follow a route northward through tribal territory to Chitral and Faizabad, in north-eastern Afghanistan. Once across the Malakand Pass, travellers ran a great risk of being attacked by bandits of the Kafir tribes who lay in hiding in the hills between the towns of Dir and Chitral. The Havildar was not reassured by the sight of hundreds of mounds of earth alongside the road, each with a small flag marker, the graves of those murdered by the Kafir tribesmen. Traders usually treated Dir as a staging post to wait for the arrival of other caravans so that they all started together on the journey north, sometimes with a party up to 200 strong to improve their chances of getting through in safety.

The Havildar's spirits were not buoyed when he learnt that all the traders for the northern route had already departed for Chitral. He went to the ruler of Dir, Ramatullah Khan, to beg his assistance, but was rebuffed. The Pundit tried bribery, laying before the ruler a richly embroidered gold lace scarf, with promises of more gifts to come. This had the effect of softening the potentate's heart. He agreed to provide the Havildar with an escort of twenty-five armed men, who proved their usefulness after a few days on the road when the party reached the village of Asreth, whose inhabitants, the Pundit reported, lived in abject dread of the Kafir bandits. The night spent at Asreth turned into an incessant exchange of small arms fire between the soldiers from Dir and the Kafirs, in which neither side suffered any losses apart from a night's sleep.

It was only a day's march to the safety of the first village in Chitral district, where the escort parted company with the Havildar. It was around this time that the Pundit picked up a report on the road concerning George Hayward's death, which provided the Government with the frightening details of this ill-fated explorer's demise. Hayward had been murdered at a place called Ushgoom ('Wurchagam', on Hayward's map), seven days' march north-east of Chitral. This had been the handiwork of Mir Walli, the son of the former ruler of Yassin. The Havildar actually came in contact with the murderer himself in Chitral, when he was summoned to the palace of Aman-i-mulk, the Chitrali *Badash* or ruler. 'On 4 September, the Badash of Chitral sent for me and gave me a seat on his right, between himself and Mir Walli,' the Havildar reports. 'After the ordinary inquiries the Badash then commenced to talk with some of his durbar [Court] officials who sat opposite to him, and while he was engaged thus I turned to Mir Walli and, in a quiet way, asked him what was the cause of the quarrel between Hayward sahib and himself.'[10]

The sinister Mir Walli proceeded to regale the Havildar with an elaborate tale of Hayward's mistreatment of his local servants, a situation that could not be tolerated, he explained. When Mir Walli remonstrated with the Englishman, the foreigner unleashed a torrent of abuse, claiming that this country belonged to the English and that he would behave in any way he saw fit. This caused Mir Walli to fear a more violent attack, so, logically, he went away and ordered sixty of his men to set an ambush for Hayward and his servants and to kill them all. 'This they did,' affirmed Mir Walli with indifference, 'killing Hayward sahib and seven of his servants.'[11] There were whispered reports in Chitral to the effect that Aman-i-mulk himself had instigated the murders. Not surprising, for the ruler was notorious for his evil acts, though to speak of them openly was to risk a lingering and painful death. In spite of his ruthless reputation, Aman-i-mulk treated the Havildar with civility, and, once the Pundit had laid at his feet what he considered to be an acceptable array of gifts, the party was given permission to march on toward Faizabad.

The Havildar and his servants were now travelling into Kafir country, and, to worsen their plight, they were confronted by the Nuksan Pass, which they would have to clear in a pre-dawn crossing to avoid being detected by the robber gangs. This posed a challenge approaching the level of serious mountaineering, with ice walls and crevasses threatening to bury or swallow them at every step. It was also the Havildar's first experience on snow. The report of crevasses in the Hindu Kush range came as a revelation to the Survey, leaving Montgomerie to surmise that the mountain passes were covered with previously unknown glaciers, and that others in all probability lay in the higher reaches. 'The above [the Havildar's report] is the first evidence that we have as to there being any glaciers in the Hindu Kush, nothing of the kind having been noted between Bamiyan and Pamir Kul, the most easterly point visited by the Mirza,' Montgomerie notes.[12]

Once across the frozen pass, the Havildar linked up with the route the Mirza had followed in the previous year, which to Montgomerie's delight completed a junction and connected both route surveys together. The Havildar descended the same trail that the Mirza had climbed going north, reaching Faizabad, the capital of Badakshan, in late September. The Pundit found himself carried forward by his own momentum and was all for advancing further, across the Oxus, but this plan was scotched by command of the Amir of Afghanistan, Sher Ali, who had ordered the road closed to prevent letters being sent through to his arch enemy Abdul Raman Khan by the rebel's supporters in Kabul. If the Havildar entertained any thoughts of flouting this prohibition, he was soon deterred when he witnessed the fate of one agent who had been caught attempting to get such letters through.

The unfortunate wretch was thrown from a high bridge into the swiftly churning rapids, never to be seen again.

The return journey commenced on 3 November. By that late date the Nuksan Pass was snowed in and closed to travellers. This meant they would have to tackle the Dora Pass, notorious for its intense cold and biting winds, which, if nothing else, helped to keep the road clear of snow. This was too much for several of the Havildar's servants to bear, and two of the men deserted on the spot. The Pundit later claimed that the two-day crossing was the worst hardship he had experienced in his life. The misery of the vicious winds and the loads they had to carry compounded the loss of the two porters, and there was also the threat of them falling victim to an attack by Kafir bandits at any moment. The Havildar made it back to Chitral in a state of near collapse, only to find Aman-i-mulk in a disturbingly changed mood. The Badash 'looked coldly on him', saying that in the Pundit's absence he had come to learn that he was a British spy. The words sent a chill down the Havildar's spine, recalling his host's reputation for extreme cruelty. But Aman-i-mulk had within his make-up a streak of cowardice, a trait shared by tyrants. If the Havildar was a British agent, any harm he came to might provoke the sort of trouble the Badash was unprepared to deal with. He had already got away with having caused the violent death of one British subject, and an Englishman at that. Better to send this man away and consider the matter closed.

The Pundit left Chitral in high spirits after his last meeting with Mir Walli, whom he found to be in great agony after having broken his leg in an accident. The Havildar reports that he could hear the scoundrel's bone grating when he moved, so that he was almost certain to be left with a limp that would betray his identity wherever he went, and perhaps one day would bring him to justice and the gallows.

Montgomerie's third Muslim Pundit had executed a 286-mile route survey over entirely unexplored ground. The Havildar's work accounted for about 13,000 square miles of *terra incognita*, checked by twenty latitude observations. He determined with accuracy the heights of the Nuksan and Dora passes, reckoning them to be 17,000 and 16,000 feet above sea level respectively. The Pundit determined the exact position of Chitral, its latitude being established by three astronomical observations. The course of the Koonur river near Chitral was also definitively fixed.

Montgomerie was exceptionally pleased with the results, exclaiming that the Havildar deserved all credit for his pluck and endurance. 'I am convinced, moreover, that his undaunted bearing on his return journey, when the chief had guessed his secret, was the means of preventing himself and party from being sold into slavery, or possibly from a worse fate,' Montgomerie wrote. 'The wily chief probably thought that his co-religionist, who showed such a bold front, did so because he was backed by something more than the few men he had with him.'[13]

The Havildar carried out two other missions for the Survey. In 1872 he was employed in making a route survey from Kabul to Bokhara, and in the following year he was sent on an expedition back to Faizabad, starting from Peshawar disguised as a travelling merchant. The latter journey was a comparatively uneventful affair, taking him to the Afghan cities of Jalalabad and Kabul, at which point he turned due north to trace a different and more westerly route to Faizabad. The Pundit made several crossings of the Oxus, a service of particular political significance, as this was to form the northern boundary of Afghanistan later agreed by the British and Russians. At the same time he explored large tracts of territory in and around Badakshan, on a 778-mile route survey that took him the better part of two years to complete. Five years after finishing his Survey work, the Havildar was taken ill with cholera at Jalalabad and died soon afterward. His work earned him a Royal Geographical Society obituary, in which his services were hailed as second only to those of the great Nain Singh.[14]

Montgomerie left India in 1873 in poor health, never to return. His position at the Great Trigonometrical Survey was filled by

Sir Henry Trotter, who took over the recruitment and training of Pundits. One more Pathan explorer was to be sent across the North-West Frontier, this time on three expeditions that were to prove a resounding success. This was Ata Mohammed, code-named the 'Mullah', the brother of an Indian sapper murdered in Swat in 1869. The Mullah's connection with the Survey was in fact to do with his brother's death, as Montgomerie had dispatched him to recover the murdered man's personal effects. This he accomplished, for his natural advantage as a mullah, in his case a learned man versed in Koranic law, was an ability to move about freely in the ungoverned tribal lands. This fourth Muslim in the line of Pathan Pundits was a well-educated man of Peshawar, versed in Arabic and experienced in survey work, having accompanied the Havildar through parts of Afghanistan. The Mullah's maps were drawn to such a degree of accuracy that they remained the standard reference work until after the First World War.

It has been said that the Mullah's three surveys were the most interesting of the Mohammedan explorations. What is beyond question was the man's resourcefulness in dealing with tight situations. To illustrate the point, on one occasion in the Yarkand district, while he was surreptitiously copying some bearings into his logbook, the Pundit suddenly found himself under the suspicious gaze of a Kirghiz tribesman. He quickly unrolled his carpet and knelt to say his prayers, after which he explained to the man that his compass indicated the exact hours of devotion. As a result of this subterfuge, the Kirghiz was so impressed that he had the Mullah write him a charm. By the time the Mullah returned from his fieldwork his fame had spread so wide that he had to repeat the exercise for a great number of the villagers.

For a time the Mullah came under the wing of the Havildar, travelling with the more experienced Pundit, who instructed the new recruit in the use of the prismatic compass. The Mullah accompanied his kinsman as far as Jalalabad on his 1873 expedition, at which point he struck out on his own up the Chitral river in late September, supported only by a young Pathan servant and a pony to carry a small supply of silks, textiles and other goods to substantiate his credentials as a travelling merchant.

On the first days of his travels the Mullah made the acquaintance of Mir Akhor Ahmad, the Governor of Shigar, a northern district of Jalalabad. The meeting was a fortunate one, for the Governor warned the traveller of dangers that lay ahead on the road, where bandits moved about more or less at will. This area had not yet come under British administration, hence the sanctity of the road – a principle that was rigorously enforced throughout the tribal territories of the North-West Frontier – was no safeguard. The Pundit was granted a passport to proceed as far as Asmar. The Mullah's cover story at this stage was that he was a timber merchant heading to this village to purchase stock that he intended to float downstream to Peshawar. The Mullah was also given a guard consisting of the local malik, or headman, and three Pathans, all armed with rifles, swords and pistols. The escort proved to be of dubious value, for no sooner had the party reached the limits of the Jalalabad district than they were set upon by a gang of about twenty robbers from a nearby village. The Mullah had stopped to take some compass bearings when he was taken by surprise, the brigands pouncing on his baggage train and quickly grabbing whatever weapons they could lay their hands on. He gave chase, but the thieves shouted back at him, with some irony, that they had been defrauded by a timber merchant from Peshawar and that this would make good their losses. The men may well have been working in collusion with the Governor of Shigar. To his joy, the Mullah's property was later returned to him in Chitral, thanks to the threatening intervention of a friend who knew the robbers' identity and their village.

The Mullah was not inclined to delay long at Asmar, whose Khan, or ruler, had a reputation for extreme piety, and also for summarily putting to death anyone to whom he took a dislike, usually with his own hands. The Khan would summon the

Mullah to his presence almost daily, requesting him to explain the meaning of Koranic verses that were beyond his intellect. The Pundit took no chances, and he never set foot in the palace without a loaded pistol secreted in his robes. This precaution would have been of little avail in the event of trouble, for the Khan himself was always surrounded by heavily armed retainers. The Khan, whom the Mullah described as being about 30 years old, with a 'very stern cast of countenance', had relations with neighbouring tyrants through marriage, his sister being the wife of the Chitrali despot Aman-i-mulk. The Khan's brother had the misfortune of being the younger sibling who, upon reaching his maturity and, in theory, a position to mount a challenge to his older brother's throne, was put to death.

A few weeks later, the Mullah heaved a sigh of relief to find himself back on his journey to Chitral, following the same road that had been taken by the Havildar in 1870. The road up the Lowari Pass leads to Shandur – which, at 12,500 feet, stands today as the world's highest polo ground – in the Chitral district on the border with Gilgit. In 1873 the Mullah describes it as resembling 'one continuous graveyard', so exposed was the road to hill bandits. The tops of the narrow defiles were lined with stone breastworks, behind which Kafir sharpshooters would pick off unsuspecting travellers at will.

Once safely inside Chitrali territory, the Mullah dismissed his escort and carried on with only his servant. He met with disappointment on arriving in Chitral, learning that the road to Yarkand via the Baroghil Pass, his next destination, had been closed since the governor of neighbouring Badakshan had chased his rival up the pass, which had now become his enemy's stronghold. But the Mullah again showed his resourcefulness by using a letter he discovered at a friend's house. It was a plea from a wealthy merchant, begging the ruler of Chitral for permission to travel north to recover some money he was owed, conveniently enough, by a timber dealer of Peshawar. The Mullah's plan was, letter in hand, to impersonate the merchant in the hope of being allowed to accompany a local slave trader named Inayat Ali, who was travelling to Badakshan. The stratagem worked, but the Mullah in reality had no wish to travel with the slave merchant. Now that the idea of his going to Yarkand by the Baroghil Pass had been set in train, he decided to bide his time in Chitral, waiting for a better opportunity to complete his journey, ideally once the pass was clear of winter snow. This came in March, when the Mullah left Chitral in the company of two servants and a sepoy. In the upper reaches of the Chitral district, the Pundit was greeted with the gladdening news that Mir Walli, George Hayward's murderer, had been killed in a territorial dispute with his cousin.

Passing though Wakhan, the Mullah was stopped and told that he could not proceed without written permission from the Mir. The Pundit was able to bring into play his considerable powers of persuasion, to convince the local authorities with his story of the defaulting timber merchant, and was thus allowed to carry on to Yarkand, which he reached in early June, following the same route as the Forsyth mission. By December 1874, the Mullah was back in Peshawar, bearing a report that was received with acclaim by the Survey. The last of the Muslim Pundits had made a detailed route survey along the entire road from Jalalabad to Yarkand, a distance of 380 miles, giving 'very valuable additions' to the Survey's geographical files. This mission also enabled the Survey to correct some errors found in the Havildar's reports in his 1870 exploration of Dir and Chitral. 'His [the Mullah's] survey is much more carefully executed than that of any of the Mohammedan explorers before employed by the Great Trigonometrical Survey,' states the official report. 'His route from Jalalabad to Sarhad (in Wakhan) shows 183 bearings with the prismatic compass, or one in every two miles, a very good performance indeed, considering that the country is thickly inhabited, and that throughout the whole of it the discovery of his employment would probably have entailed short shrift and sudden death.'[15]

The Mullah's route surveys made a worthy finale to the work of these remarkable Pathan spies. He was to resume his exploratory duties a year after his return to Peshawar, and again in 1878. On these occasions he surveyed unexplored portions of the Indus river and took measurements of unmapped mountain peaks, as well as following new routes in the Yassin region and surveying little-known areas of Kohistan. The Survey of India now shifted its attention to Tibet, and the hill station of Darjeeling was about to become the staging ground for espionage activity in the Land of Snow.

CHAPTER 6

A Learned Man of Chittagong

The Pundits were courageous, resourceful and tenacious servants
of the Raj. But for the most part, men of great intellectual stature
they were not – with one exception. Sarat Chandra Das was born
in 1849, the year in which Britain added some 150,000 square
miles of territory to its Indian empire with the annexation of the
Punjab, following the crushing defeat of the Sikh army. This
historic milestone was to have a major impact on the life of the
fledgling Pundit. The Punjab was at that time a frontier domain,
and the territorial limits of British India had now been pushed
right up against the volatile borders of Afghanistan and Kashmir,
with a small projection prodding Tibet's south-western underbelly.
By taking command, at least in nominal terms, of the North-West
Frontier, the Raj was also thrown into conflict with some of the
most warlike and hostile tribes in the world.

The trustworthiness of the native troops of what had now
become neighbouring Kashmir was untested, but would be put to
the test in less than a decade, in the fury of the Sepoy Rebellion.
British India's expansionist policies were greeted with hostility by
the Bengali soldiery. The annexation in 1856 of the kingdom of

Oudh, from which most of these men came, was one of the factors that ignited the powder keg. Fortunately for the Government, the sepoys of Kashmir, as well as the Punjabi ranks, remained loyal.

Almost overnight, Britain had acquired a large swathe of new borderland that needed to be explored, surveyed and defended. The rapid spread of British authority in India set off alarm bells in Moscow, which since the eighteenth century had been steering its empire on an expansionist course, mostly in the direction of British India and beyond that, to the warm water outlet of the Indian Ocean. 'After 1880 the local military initiative passed to Russia,' writes Lawrence James. 'For the next four years its forces fought a series of campaigns which put the finishing touches to the conquest of Turkmenistan. In January 1881 General Skobelev took the fortress of Gek Tepe, and in February 1884 Merv was occupied, bringing the Russian frontier to within 600 miles of India.'[1]

Chandra Das grew up under the shadow of the Great Game in its most turbulent years. Unlike most of his Pundit colleagues, some of whom were totally illiterate, Chandra Das was the son of a high-caste Hindu family from Chittagong, East Bengal, who saw to the education of its offspring with the typical enthusiasm of cultured Indian parents. Chandra Das was barely out of his teens when he was sent to that great seat of learning of the Raj, the Calcutta Presidency College, where he became a close friend and protégé of Sir Alfred Croft, the Bengal Director of Public Instruction, who guided the future Pundit in his geographical and literary work. Chandra Das's academic gifts gained official recognition at an early age, and he was later to go on to become a Tibetan language teacher to British surveyors. When he was 25, the Hindu was appointed headmaster of the Tibetan Boarding School in Darjeeling, which had recently been opened under the inspired orders of the Lieutenant-Governor, Sir George Campbell.

In modern society imperialism is a discredited creed, undeniably with some justification, but only some. Unfashionable it may be to mention the concepts of calling and duty, but men like Campbell epitomised that core of British administrators who with great devotion and sacrifice gave their talents to India, not to mention the best years of their lives. Britain stood alone among the European imperial powers in having colonialists like Major-General Sir George Roos-Keppel, the translator of Pushtu poetry and co-founder of Islamia College in Peshawar, or Olaf Caroe, the last British Governor of the North-West Frontier, who produced a learned treatise on 2,500 years of Pathan history. The Duke of Wellington himself, in 1800, founded the College at Fort William (Calcutta). As Charles Allen points out: 'A later Governor-General, Lord Hastings, had presided over the founding of the Hindu College, the Calcutta Book Society and the Calcutta School Society.'[2] Hastings was also a fluent Urdu and Bengali speaker. Indeed, the Pundits themselves put their necks on the line throughout their careers to safeguard the interests of the Raj. To be sure, the British set out to corner a rich and strategic market. But over the years, numerous strands of mutual respect and indeed a genuine fondness came to grow between both peoples, a relationship that today lingers in nostalgia, bereft of resentment on the part of former subjects as well as colonisers.

In Darjeeling, Chandra Das threw himself assiduously into the study of the Tibetan language, with which until that time he was only casually acquainted. It was a skill that was to stand him in good stead on his future missions. He also spent part of that period of his life visiting the great monasteries of Sikkim, the Buddhist kingdom in the Himalayan foothills north of Darjeeling. By that time, Chandra Das's prestige as a man of letters had spread to Gangtok, the capital of Sikkim, where he was feted at Court by the king, or Chogyal, and his ministers of state. He also spent some time at Pemayangtse monastery, Sikkim's ancient centre of religious teaching and the site at which the Chogyal traditionally received his enthronement. In the peaceful setting of the hilltop monastery overlooking Kangchenjunga, the world's third tallest mountain, Chandra Das expressed his desire to visit Tibet to Lama Ugyen Gyatso, a fellow teacher at the Darjeeling school who was also one of the 108 monks who, since the early seventeenth century, have sat at Pemayangtse. In 1878 Ugyen Gyatso obtained leave to take a journey to the north, travelling first through lush rhododendron forest, and steadily climbing onto glaciated terrain at several thousand feet above the tree line, with a bearing fixed squarely on Tibet. His brief was to persuade the country's political and spiritual leaders to ensure safe conduct for a visit by Chandra Das.

The Dalai Lama and his Government were in those days nursing a grudge against Britain for having recognised Chinese suzerainty over Tibet. In 1876 the Government of Calcutta signed the Sino-British Chefoo Convention, by which Peking granted Britain the right to send a mission of exploration into Tibet. When Ugyen Gyatso arrived in the Tibetan capital, he had a frosty reception from the Thirteenth Dalai Lama, who had two years previously taken charge of the affairs of state from the Regent, Thupten Gyatso. The Dalai Lama, now a man of 21, was obviously anxious to assert his power as the spiritual head of what he considered to be an independent nation. Sitting in the lofty throne room of his hilltop Potala Palace, the young Dalai Lama demurred over the request to grant permission for a visit by Chandra Das, a distinguished academic, yet all the same a servant of the country that for commercial expediency had betrayed Tibet's claim to political independence. The audience over, a frustrated Ugyen Gyatso picked himself up and trudged 175 miles west, across the rugged Tibetan plateau to Tashilunpo monastery in Shigatse, to plead his case before the Panchen Lama. Whether Tibet's second highest spiritual figure was more sympathetic to the British or simply wanted to exercise his own considerable powers of state, the outcome was a favourable response. Ugyen Gyatso returned to Darjeeling in triumph, brandishing an invitation for the 'Indian Pandit' to visit Tashilunpo, where his name had moreover been inserted as a student in the city's grand monastery. There is a certain irony in the fact that the Panchen Lama's invitation bore the honorific title of 'Pandit', while in fact Chandra Das made his journey very much in the guise of a 'Pundit'.

Chandra Das was promised red carpet treatment. He carried with him a *Lam-yig*, the crucial Tibetan safe-conduct pass that enabled him and Lama Ugyen Gyatso to travel from the Sikkimese–Tibetan frontier to Tashilunpo 'without delay or detention'. The document also offered them their choice of routes and commanded all District Magistrates and Collectors to help expedite the travellers with their baggage. In the event, this document was at best of ambiguous validity. The Government of India was jubilant over the prospect of one of its Pundits not only penetrating Tibet, but also going in with the official blessing of the host country's authorities. Calcutta's enthusiasm was suitably compensated. As his mentor Sir Alfred Croft noted in his foreword: '[Chandra Das] brought to India a valuable collection of Sanskrit and Tibetan manuscripts, having explored in the course of his travels the country north and west of Kangchenjunga, of which nothing was previously known.'[3] All well and good, but Chandra Das was less than happy with the Government's reluctance to enhance its praise with some financial support. Of all the Pundits, Chandra Das was well aware of how valuable a service he rendered the Raj, and the issue of pecuniary reward was a contentious one throughout much of his career. Reflecting on this first assignment to Tibet, he emphasised in his journal, quite astonishingly, that the journey had been undertaken at his own expense, 'the Government contributing not a rupee to it. As Deputy Inspector of Schools, I used to draw one hundred and fifty rupees a month. I got only a month's pay in advance, which I took with me.'[4] He set off on 17 June with a pocket sextant, a prismatic compass, a telescope and two hypsometers, instruments that determine altitude using atmospheric pressure as measured by the boiling point of water. Chandra Das had the extreme good fortune to be instructed in the use of these surveying instruments by none other than the legendary Nain Singh. There was some domestic bickering over the trip, as Chandra Das's wife was not happy about her husband, the family's breadwinner, traipsing off to distant Tibet with hardly a word of explanation as to the nature of his mission or when he was likely to return home. The

Pundit finally obtained his wife's consent by assuring her that Tibet was only a few miles' distance from Darjeeling.

They must have borne a striking resemblance to Don Quixote and Sancho Panza, the lanky Pundit on his quest accompanied by the corpulent monk, as they departed from their starting point at Dzongri, the frozen, windswept yak-herder encampment at 13,700 feet above sea level, which for present-day Western trekkers in Sikkim marks the end of the trail. Chandra Das had undergone the standard Survey of India metamorphosis and now figured as a cipher in the records, henceforth to be known as SCD, or 'the Babu', a term applied to certain persons of distinction. It was mid-June when the Pundit and the lama, along with their guide Paljor, whose services they had secured at Dzongri, and a handful of coolies, set off in dense fog, which made it impossible for Chandra Das to take observations by sextant and perform other basic surveying tasks. Northward they marched, their ears ringing with the crash of avalanches that exploded on the valley walls, as they climbed steadily upwards above 16,000 feet. They were forced to spend the nights in caves or any sheltered spot that afforded protection from the midsummer snowstorms raging across the eastern Himalaya. The weather cleared on the second day, but now Chandra Das was longing for the fog, to shelter his party from the fierce sun and blinding glare of the snow, 'which became doubly strong and unbearable under the midday sun. The lama and I put on our blue spectacles, while our coolies and guide painted their cheek bones below the lower eyelid with black to protect their eyes from the glare.'[5] In spite of the altitude and the deep snow that covered their path, they were making good progress. That same afternoon they trudged to the limit of the snowfield. The spot was marked by a stone cairn crowned with a cluster of Tibetan prayer flags flapping in the wind. Paljor turned with a broad Nepalese grin to proclaim that they now stood on the boundary of Nepal and Sikkim. Once they had descended to the Sherpa village of Kambachen Gyunsa, Chandra Das heaved a sigh of relief to find that his disguise as a Nepalese lama had achieved the desired effect. They were led to the house of a rich farmer, whose wife brought out the typical Tibetan tea, flavoured with butter and salt, for the travellers and the crowd of curious locals who had gathered round the fire in the smoky room. 'My lama cap and dress, and especially my Indian features, made the natives take me for a *Pal-bu* [Nepalese] lama of Nepal,' writes Chandra Das.

> Instead of asking me who I was and to what caste I belonged, our good host made a low salutation and respectfully conducted me to the place of honour and begged me to take my seat on a homely cushion made of yak hair. Other people came to look at me, but none dared ask my name and nationality. Ugyen Gyatso quickly perceived what was passing in their minds and at once addressed me as *Palbu* Lama, instead of calling me *Babu* Lama [an Indian title].[6]

Chandra Das busied himself with recording topographical features of this unexplored region, hunting for fossils and determining altitudes by the surprisingly accurate method of reading the temperature of boiling water. With the boiling point at 187° F, for instance, he knew that the Sherpa summer village of Kambachen stood at 14,600 feet, a testimonial to the hardiness of this mountain race, which sought its summer abode at a spot higher than most alpine summits.

Once across the border, on the eighth day into the journey, the Pundit realised that he was about to pay a heavy price for choosing to follow a little-travelled route into Tibet, one that he described as 'imprudent and ill-judged' and on which their safe-conduct pass would be of no help. Before them to the north soared the 19,000-foot Chathang La, much more of a Himalayan peak than a mountain pass for traders urging their yak caravans on between Nepal and Tibet. The little party advanced with apprehension across boulder fields and isolated patches of lichen and moss, heading towards the snowfields that stretched to the foot of the pass. After slogging across 3 miles of unbroken snow after a breakfast of 'ill-boiled rice', Chandra Das fell down exhausted, his lungs gasping for oxygen, which at this height is too thin to support permanent human habitation. Ugyen Gyatso was in a worse state 'on account of his corpulence'. The two travellers lay prostrate in this miserable plight, gasping for fully half an hour. Chandra Das eventually made his way off the snow that was blinding his eyes, despite his tinted glasses, and he did so in a less than dignified fashion, carried piggy-back on the shoulders of Phurchung, the new guide they had taken on in the Sherpa village. Chandra Das's plight makes clear that stamina and sheer pluck, rather than scholarly ability, were the more useful qualities where Punditry was concerned. As a rule, the best explorers were men of action rather than of the pen.

It was extremely unwise to be caught out in the Himalaya, and by this time darkness was closing in. As the Pundit relates: 'It was six in the evening, and the cliff under which we were to rest was far off. I did not want to go on, but there was no large rock to take shelter under, no water to drink, and the excessive rigour of the frost and the biting wind made it impossible for us to lie on the bare ground.'[7] The snow still lay knee-deep on the approach to the pass, which meant that every few steps the two men would sink to the ground, and then haul themselves to their feet to advance a short distance before their legs once more gave way beneath them. By the time they stumbled into their 'campsite' the temperature had dipped to below freezing. A light snow was falling as they crawled into a 4-foot-wide rock crevice, whose other inhabitant was a mountain fox called a *wamo*. The low-caste coolies had to content themselves with a spot on the open ground, sheltering under Chandra Das's waterproof cloth and two umbrellas.

They set out early the next morning, surrounded on all sides by an ocean of snow. 'The sight of stones, not to speak of vegetation,' Chandra Das recounts, 'would have been welcome to our tired eyes, but even such dreary comforts were denied us.'[8] Once again, the exhausted Pundit pleaded for a lift on his guide's back, and in this manner he was carried to within a mile of the foot of Chathang La. Here the snow, which continued to fall, was less than a foot deep, thus giving enough purchase to walk with difficulty to the foot of the ascent.

It was nothing like a technical climb by modern mountaineering standards, but no Munro-bagger would have attempted it today without ice axe, crampons and high-tech waterproofs. It turned into something of an epic for the Himalayan novices, in particular for Chandra Das, who was hauled up the scree slopes to the edge of a steep, ice-covered gradient, where the situation now turned worse. It was literally three steps forward, two steps back, as Chandra Das and Ugyen Gyatso struggled toward the elusive summit that was obliterated from view by the falling snow. The pair slithered across the ice, only to find themselves falling onto their hands and knees, sliding down the slope after every few steps. Their guide saved the day by whipping out his *kukri*, or Nepali dagger, to cut steps in the ice as he climbed. Then, digging his feet into the ice, he would drag them up to the next stance. The snow was by now swirling down with a fury, threatening to bury the climbers alive in the rising drifts. Night shadows started closing in, bringing with them the prospect of almost certain death from exposure to the elements, when, mercifully, the travellers came across a small cave into which they crawled to sit out the hours of darkness. Chandra Das cheered himself with the news that they were now past the most dangerous section of the pass, and that the vast Tibetan plateau awaited below the next morning. 'In this miserable fashion did I cross the famous Chathang La into Tibet, the very picture of desolation, horror and death, escaping the treacherous crevasses that abound in this dreadful region.'[9]

It took six hours of knee-wrenching descent before the snowfields began to give way to patches of brownish vegetation. Shortly after midday, the exhausted Pundit and his companion collapsed in exhaustion by the bank of a sluggish river that in those days marked the ill-defined boundary between Tibet, Nepal and Sikkim. Chandra Das found out to his dismay that their tribulations were not quite ended. It was now becoming apparent that in these untamed parts their much-prized safe-conduct pass represented little more than a token gesture of good intent. Their rest spot had a name, and it was not an auspicious one. *Gyamithotho* means 'Chinese border', and it was here that the Chinese general commanding the forces that had fought in the recent war with the Gurkhas had erected a stockade, vowing on his departure to prevent foreigners from ever again crossing the Chathang La into Chinese-controlled Tibet.

After a prudently brief rest they carried on, until reaching another waterway, the Zemi river, which led in a south-westerly direction to yak-grazing pasture. It was at this point that Chandra Das spotted the look of anxiety on Phurchung's face. The Pundit soon learnt to his alarm that this was Dokpa country. The Dokpas were Tibetan herders, a number of whom had been recruited by the Chinese to keep an eye on the Chathang La, with free rein to rob and administer rough justice to any foreigner found on that side of the pass. The guide hurriedly led the party into a nearby cave to sit out the remaining daylight hours until, under the shadow of darkness, they were able quietly to make their way across the mile-wide shallow river to the southern flank of Chorten Nyima La, a 17,000-foot-high pass that, in spite of its formidable altitude, afforded comparatively gentle going. Yet it was an arduous undertaking for the travellers, who had been without food for the past three days, and more so on the far side of the pass, where they were compelled to hide under boulders and at times fling themselves flat on the ground to avoid being spotted by the monks at the Chorten Nyima monastery. Hostile natives and Himalayan storms were not the only hazards lurking in these desolate hills. By now Chandra Das and Ugyen Gyatso were roaming in comparative comfort across fertile fields in the direction of the town of Tashilunpo, their destination. One afternoon in early July they strolled into Kurma, a Dokpa village of about 600 families living in brick dwellings surrounded by stone or mud walls. Here the little caravan decided on a well-earned rest, tethering their pack ponies in the nearby pasture while they stocked up on meat and other provisions. Their fortunes seemed to be picking up as they continued on their trek, until they crossed their third pass, the Kyago La, which issued

onto a vast tableland. Suddenly, across the barren plain surged
forth every Tibetan traveller's worst nightmare. Two huge
mastiffs, giant hounds that have been known to bring down a
bear, came surging wildly toward them. Their guide, Phurchung,
made a desperate attempt to drive off the mastiffs with stones, at
which they only grew more furious. Fortunately, after their last
rest stop Chandra Das and the lama had taken the precaution of
loading the pistols they were carrying. Ugyen Gyatso came to the
rescue by firing his pistol at the enraged beasts at close range, and
with luck he brought down one of the attackers, sending his
companion fleeing in panic. Tibet had by now thrown the worst it
had to offer at the travellers – enfeebling altitude, snowstorms,
bandits and murderous hounds – so the surge of joy Chandra Das
felt one fine July afternoon, on reaching the brow of a hillock
overlooking Tashilunpo, comes as no surprise. It was, and today
remains, one of Tibet's most breathtaking views. In the Pundit's
own words: 'The summit of this hill commands a beautiful view,
said to be the finest in Central Tibet. To the west was the Narthan
monastery, whose white walls and towers gleamed out from the
dark blue hills amid which it stood. Below us flowed the silvery
Penam-nyangchu [river], and far to the front rose the snow-
capped crests of the Northern Himalaya.'[10]

What a sight awaited the eyes of the travellers from the
wilderness, as they made their way along the last stretch of road
toward the Golden Monastery, home to the Panchen Lama.
Chandra Das was astonished at the sight of hundreds of yaks
carrying supplies into the great trading crossroads of Tibet. The
dusty, narrow streets throbbed with an assemblage of merchants
in their market stalls, the procession of pilgrims and monks
performing their endless circumambulations of the city's temples
and holy shrines, chanting and spinning their prayer-wheels on
their circular walks.

The Pundit built a close relationship with Phendi Khangsar, the
Minister of Temporal Affairs, during the six months he spent in
Tashilunpo, introducing the Tibetan dignitary to some of the

marvels of Western technology, such as the techniques of 'wet process' photography, while the Minister gave him a set of Tibetan texts detailing the lives of the Dalai Lamas. It was also the Minister's generosity that made possible the return journey to Darjeeling, by advancing Chandra Das enough money to cover his travelling expenses. If the Minister opened a treasure house of spiritual knowledge to the Pundit, he was equally anxious to draw on his friend's experience as a surveyor. Phendi Khangsar told him he had purchased a telescope 'at much cost' in order to see the constellations he had read of in certain stellar maps, which 'really existed in the sky'. He also asked Chandra Das to instruct him in the technique of land surveying with prismatic compass and clinometer, an instrument for measuring vertical angles at relatively poor accuracy. The Tibetan dignitary was eager to send to Calcutta for a sextant, various mathematical instruments, a chest of Western medicines and an illustrated work on astronomy, all of which were to be part of his eventual downfall.

Chandra Das and Lama Ugyen Gyatso earned the Government's rapturous praise for their exploits, which, after all, had been achieved at almost no cost to the public exchequer. The collection of manuscripts was donated to the Government Tibetan Boarding School in Darjeeling. Their fame spread far and wide, possibly beyond the frontiers of India if one is to believe some of the theories in circulation about the mysterious Russian mystic, Helena Petrovna Blavatsky, who in 1875 founded the Theosophical Society of America. Hailed as a great religious visionary by some, dismissed as an unscrupulous charlatan and even a Russian spy by others, Madame Blavatsky produced a book about her alleged spiritual masters, the Mahatmas. This gave rise to speculation that one of the disciples of her Mahatmas, whom she calls Chandra Cusho, could have been a fictional version of Sarat Chandra Das himself, and that the Mahatma Ten-Dub Ughien she speaks of is based on Ugyen Gyatso. Madame Blavatsky was obsessed with Tashilunpo and its secret archives, as well as with the figure of the Panchen Lama, which may have been derived from the Pundit and Ugyen Gyatso's connection with the Tibetan monastery. Certainly she was a contemporary of these two men, and there are even more far-fetched theories suggesting the Russian spiritualist might have accompanied Chandra Das and the lama on their journey to Tibet. Though not lacking a romantic appeal, there is not a shred of evidence to substantiate the claim made by some historians.

Chandra Das arrived back in India in December 1879 a satisfied man, the more so because he was able to inform his superiors that the Minister in residence at Tashilunpo had extended an invitation for the Pundit to return to Tibet the following year. Sadly, he was prevented from carrying this out, as Sikkim, which he would have had to cross on his journey, was in a state of political turmoil. The Buddhist kingdom was engulfed in factional rioting between Nepalese immigrants and Lepchas, the country's indigenous people, a dispute to which Britain could not afford to remain indifferent. 'The Government of India's policy with regard to Nepalese immigration into Sikkim was based on their wish to encourage economic growth in the sparsely populated kingdom, and also to counteract the pro-Tibetan leanings of the Lepchas and their rulers,' writes Amar Kaur Jaspir Singh.[11] 'Before long disputes broke out between the Nepalese settlers and the local inhabitants and representations were made to the Bengal Government. Sir Ashley Eden, Lieutenant-Governor of Bengal, invited the Maharajah [of Sikkim] to visit him at Kalimpong to settle the question.' Eden was anxious to keep the Lepchas in check, and, by doing so, effectively to block Tibet's influence in a territory that for all intents and purposes enjoyed the status of a British protectorate. But he was bound to accept that Nepalese infiltration would have to be restricted. A line was drawn across Sikkim north of the capital of Gangtok, below which Nepalese settlement would not be accepted. This only served to ignite the powder keg between both factions, a source of friction that is still exploited today by Sikkimese nationalists and pro-Nepalese elements in what is now India's twenty-first state, where less than half of the population can be considered of indigenous origin. In 1880, the upshot of these troubles was that Tibet was to remain out of bounds for Chandra Das.

The following year Chandra Das delivered an impassioned plea to his mentor, Sir Alfred Croft, seeking the Government's backing for a vast exploration project across Central Asia. Starting from the Emperor's Court in Peking, he proposed to explore thousands of miles of unknown territory, 'terra incognita to the civilised world', taking in the whole of western China, the steppes of southern Mongolia, the eastern portion of the Gobi Desert and the most easterly provinces of Tibet. In all, the journey would follow 2,000 miles in a direct line, filled with the most formidable obstacles of nature and where, as the Pundit stresses, 'man is still more hostile than devastating Nature itself'.[12] Chandra Das's letter flowed with an extraordinarily cloying high Victorian hyperbole: 'The task is, however, very great, in the performance of which I may perish, and the political and physical difficulties are so great that they can be better imagined than expressed, and the heart sinks to contemplate them. A traveller must pass, if he succeeds in surmounting those difficulties, thousands of miles in detour, through innumerable bloodthirsty, cruel and savage tribes, liable to be cut up at any moment that no traces of him will be found.'[13] One cannot help admiring the man's pluck, he having only a few months previously come very close to leaving his bones on the high passes of Tibet, and now planning to take on a huge chunk of the trackless wastes of Central Asia. It should be remembered that Chandra Das, at age 32, already held the exalted position of Deputy Inspector of Schools and enjoyed great admiration among his peers as the veteran of a courageous expedition to Tibet, an exploit that had earned him the friendship of the Minister at Tashilunpo. Small wonder that he held himself in such high esteem.

Chandra Das had enlisted his travelling companion Ugyen Gyatso to join the surveying mission, as well as another colleague, Lama Sherab, a Mongolian teacher on the staff of the Tibetan School in Darjeeling. This monk believed the project would require two years to complete and that the Government would need to advance him 20,000 rupees in travelling expenses. Croft and Horace Cockerell, Secretary to the Government of Bengal, took the Pundit's proposal into consideration. After due deliberation, they came back with a travel itinerary that left him with a less grandiose brief and with his wings somewhat clipped. Starting in September 1881, Chandra Das was to retrace his steps to Tashilunpo, and thence to Lhasa, where he was to cultivate the friendship of influential persons and 'avoid general observation as much as possible'. He was instructed to keep a diary and record in it from day to day any 'points of interest' he might note with regard to places and people. The Pundit was further expected to confine himself to Lhasa, in order to avoid the inevitable suspicions that any movements about outlying districts would have created. However, if he happened to visit a distant town or monastery, he was to take the observations necessary for a route survey, which he would have to keep in his memory. Under no circumstances was he to transfer any of these observations to a map. In other words, as far as the Survey was concerned, Chandra Das was going in as a mole behind a façade of scholarly curiosity. As for expenses, the Government once again showed its outstanding capacity for meanness by offering the travellers 5,000 rupees, a quarter of what they had requested. It speaks volumes of the Pundit's integrity that, upon his return to Darjeeling, he took the trouble to return an unexpended balance of 2,000 rupees to the Comptroller General of Indian Treasuries.

Their journey began later in the year than planned, an inauspicious start given that their route was to take them northward to the Land of Snow, with winter fast descending on the high passes leading to Lhasa. Chandra Das left his house on the evening of 7 November, the tin-roofed 'Lhasa Villa' that still stands about a mile and a half south of Darjeeling. A few minutes' walk under a full moon brought him to the door of his chief, Sir Alfred Croft, who ushered the Pundit into his drawing room to show him some plant samples that might be worthwhile hunting down in Tibet. After taking his leave 'with little confidence' that he should ever see his native land again, Chandra Das walked down to the river, where Ugyen Gyatso was waiting. Before he reached the meeting place his disguise was put to its first test. To his great relief, the Pundit succeeded in convincing a group of Bhotias warming themselves by a roadside campfire that he was a Nepali on his way into Sikkim. 'I congratulated myself on having passed unrecognised, for otherwise the story of my proceeding to Tibet would have spread all over the market of Darjeeling next day,' he writes in his travel diary.[14] The journey needed to be cloaked in secrecy, for he was anxious to avoid 'unpleasant consequences' if word of his approach were to reach the ears of Tibetan border guards. A visit to Tashilunpo on an invitation from the Minister might be allowable, but for a foreigner to gatecrash the forbidden city of Lhasa was another matter altogether. The border guards put their own lives at risk by failing to intercept trespassers and more than one had paid the supreme penalty for letting outsiders slip through the net. Led by their trusty guide of the previous expedition, Phurchung, on the second day they crossed the bridge over the Rummam, the river that marked the boundary of British territory. They were now in Sikkim proper and on their way.

Apart from being discovered by the ever-suspicious Lepchas, who are the aborigines of Sikkim, or the Bhotia merchants bent almost double under their head baskets as they toiled their way toward Darjeeling, the Pundit had other risks to confront. The coolies warned of bears lurking in their lairs in the hollows of old tree trunks, and the no-less menacing wild boar that roamed the hills. Chandra Das was also plagued by blood-sucking leeches that made for him 'with the utmost haste'. And his party was yet to tackle the mighty, snow-clad passes that loomed on the horizon. The epic crossing of one of these passes, the 20,000-foot Jongson La that straddles the Tibetan border, drew acclaim from the legendary British mountaineer Frank Smythe, leader of the 1930 Kangchenjunga expedition, who hailed it as 'one of the boldest journeys on record'.

Less than a fortnight after departing from Darjeeling, the travellers ran into trouble. As they approached the Du La (Demon Pass) near the Tibetan border, they found it cloaked deep in early winter snow. They painstakingly inched their way up in waist-high snowdrifts, driving on their reluctant ponies and yaks with the wild yells of the Tibetan hillmen. But, as Chandra Das recalls, no sooner had they struggled to the summit of one ridge, than 'the Du La rose higher up, and so we ascended peak after peak, not knowing where our troubles would end'.[15] By now they were all gasping for breath, particularly the portly Ugyen Gyatso, who was suffering badly from altitude sickness. To add to their misery, a gale-force wind blew up, throwing Chandra Das and the others to the ground several times. One of the coolies lay helpless in the snow with a bad case of frostbitten toes. The Pundit pulled off his own boots and thick Afghan socks, which he gave to the porter, putting on the Tibetan boots he had purchased for the journey. Their footwear was of little use on the higher slopes, which were coated with a treacherous film of ice. Chandra Das crawled cautiously ahead, but some of the coolies slipped under their loads and found themselves rolling precipitously down the hillside. 'I walked carefully, using my hands when my feet slipped, and when both failed I lay prostrate, trusting to my weight against the furious gale,' he relates.[16] The storm blew itself out overnight, and at daybreak the injured coolie was sent back, the rest of the party carrying on toward the border.

By the first week in December, the worst was over. The Pundit had made it past the border guard post at a safe distance, after spending an anxious moment lest the party provoked the fierce Tibetan mastiffs that slept by the watchtowers. A couple of hours before dawn on the morning of 9 December, a month and two days out of Darjeeling, they got up and dressed by candlelight in their best woollens. Chandra Das rode at the head of the procession heading toward Tashilunpo. A bitterly cold wind swept the Tibetan plateau and after a few miles the Pundit began to lose sensation in his feet, so he dismounted from his pony and alternated between riding when fatigued and walking when he felt the need to restore the blood flow to his toes. The Minister was away, travelling on matters of state, but he had left orders for the Pundit and his party to be quartered in a three-storey house that must have struck them as a royal palace after weeks of sleeping rough in the hills. To give some idea of the stateliness of their lodgings, Chandra Das recalls that the brass key to the gate was nearly half a foot in length.

Several days after his arrival, the Pundit was witness to an event that, apart from its medieval pageantry, served as the first useful piece of news-gathering for his superiors at Survey headquarters. Chandra Das awoke one morning to a great clamour and din outside his window, where some 15,000 townspeople had spilled into the streets of Shigatse to witness the portentous arrival of the envoy of the Maharajah of Kashmir at the head of an escort of more than 150 dignitaries of various nationalities, all mounted on ornately caparisoned horses. The scene was worthy of Caesar's triumphant entry into Rome, a procession of bearded, white-turbaned Muslim chieftains, Sikhs shouldering their tridents and lances, dark-skinned Ladakhis bundled in lambskin coats, Nepalese and Tibetans, and a sprinkling of Murmi and Dokpa tribesmen. Chandra Das joined the throng to learn that this was a triennial occasion, on which the Government of Kashmir dispatched an envoy to Lhasa with presents as a tribute to the Dalai Lama. The origin of this ceremony harked back to 1840, when the great Sikh general, Zorwar Singh, following his conquest of Ladakh, Baltit and Skardu (in modern Pakistan), turned his army against the famous Tibetan shawl-wool-producing provinces of Rudok and Gar. These two territories, which produced the richest quality wool used for weaving Pashmina shawls, were considered by the Dalai Lama to be his most valuable possession. The Tibetan army stood no chance against the well-trained and equipped Sikh forces, so an urgent plea was sent to the Emperor of China, Tibet's suzerain, who sent a force of more than 10,000 men to stop Zorwar Singh's advance.

The Sikh commander held the Tibetan soldiery, but he did not count on having to confront a massive force of Chinese troops. He had greatly underestimated the strength of the approaching army, and the first detachments of his own forces sent into the field were cut to pieces. An epic two-day battle raged on the Tibetan plateau until, on the third morning, Zorwar Singh was killed at the head of his army and victory was declared for the Dalai Lama. The Maharajah of Kashmir was horrified at the prospect of losing his newly conquered domain of Ladakh to the advancing Tibetan–Chinese forces, and thus sued for peace with Lhasa. Under the terms of the treaty, Kashmir agreed to pay the triennial tribute that Chandra Das now observed in awe in the streets of Shigatse.

The Government of India had for decades taken a singular interest in the highly lucrative shawl-wool trade, at that time exploited by traders along caravan routes that lay outside British territory and were in fact much more within the gravitational pull of Russia and that country's commercial interests. It was Mir Izzat Ullah, on his journey through Kashmiri territory more than half a century earlier, who had filed reports in some detail on the shawl-wool trade. The Indian agent was able to ascertain the amount of duties levied on the 800 horse loads of shawl-wool that each year plied their way from Tibet to Kashmir. He also brought word that the Maharajah of Kashmir always took pains to remain on good terms with the Dalai Lama, since any disruption in this trade would spell ruin for thousands of Kashmiri weavers and, more to the point, deprive the royal treasury of a million rupees a year in tax revenue.

This was to turn out to be an even more newsworthy day for Chandra Das. Apart from supplying Calcutta, via his superiors at the Survey, with useful particulars on commercial activities between Kashmir and Tibet concerning the shawl-wool trade, to the Pundit's surprise, only a few hours after witnessing the Kashmiri envoy's procession he was to gain a frightening insight into China's political stranglehold on Lhasa. At about one o'clock, while the shawl-wool tribute was being laid at the Panchen Lama's feet in the Tashilunpo monastery, heralds beating on drums took up position in Shigatse's main square to proclaim to the terrified onlookers that punishment was about to be inflicted on a group of wretches being paraded mercilessly through the city. This was on orders of the *Amban*, the Chinese resident who was the Emperor's all-powerful representative in Tibet. The prisoners were barely able to drag themselves around the square, being flogged whenever their legs buckled under the weight of a heavy wooden collar 3 feet in width. The men had had the misfortune of being selected as the symbolic culprits of a collective crime against the Chinese empire. One of the two Ambans stationed in Lhasa had been out on an annual inspection tour of the provinces, during which his travelling expenses were expected to be borne by the local populace to the tune of 500 rupees *per diem*. When the official came to Shigatse and demanded a rate of 750 rupees, the people openly accused him of extortion, and an angry mob surrounded the Chinese representative's house, and proceeded to bombard it with stones. In the mêlée, a few of the stones found their mark on the Amban himself, who was cut down with severe injuries. Retribution was swift and pitiless. The victims, who were minor Tibetan officials, suffered from 50 to 400 bamboo cuts on their buttocks and palms and they were forced to wear the wooden collar for six months. After observing this event, Chandra Das reported: 'Such being the state of affairs in Tibet in respect of the Amban, the Emperor's authority over the country seemed to be as great as ever, and rebellion against the authority of his representative a most unpardonable crime, which would meet with the severest punishment.'[17]

Clearly, China's presence in Tibet was an issue that would have to be dealt with if the Government of India entertained any plans of extending its imperial power north of the Himalaya, which is precisely what transpired less than twenty-five years later when Sir Francis Younghusband marched a British army into Lhasa.

Chandra Das departed the Tashilunpo monastery complex on Christmas morning to make arrangements for his journey to Lhasa with his friend the Minister, who was in temporary residence at the town of Dongtse, a day's easy journey from Shigatse. Life moved at a rather different pace in nineteenth-century Tibet, where time was not divided into units that needed to be filled with activity. Thus the Pundit spent fully four months making frequent visits to Dongtse, where the two men spent enjoyable hours together discussing sacred Buddhist texts and other scholarly matters, the Minister never suspecting the dire fate that awaited him for having befriended the Indian Pundit. On 26 April the Pundit, disguised in his 'monkish raiment', left Tashilunpo with his party.

After following the Tsangpo eastward on an uneventful 150-mile journey, they stood, a month later, gazing in wonder at the soaring walls of the Potala, the hilltop palace with its numerous towers and gilt roofs that is the historic residence of the Dalai Lama. It was late afternoon when they marched through the city gates under the watchful eyes of monks and shopkeepers who stared from their windows with a mixture of curiosity and suspicion at the passing band of newcomers. Chandra Das would certainly have been forewarned by his fellow Pundits of the executioner's axe reserved for foreigners who were suspected of spying on Tibet. The eyes that peered down at him from the Chinese-style houses – dwellings roofed with bluish glazed tiles and festooned with prayer flags – must have felt like rods of white hot steel boring into the back of his neck. What a relief, then, for Chandra Das to realise that he had been saved by a piece of perverse good luck from possible fatal interrogation. Along with Ugyen Gyatso, the party had been on foot or in the saddle that day for the better part of ten hours. The Pundit's head drooped with fatigue, and most of his face was concealed behind his snow goggles and red turban, raising alarm among the townspeople that here had arrived another victim of *lhandum*, the smallpox epidemic that was rampaging across great swathes of the country.

Consequently, as they wound their way through the city's narrow streets, people scurried to draw their shutters and bolt their doors against the killer disease. 'No one offered to molest the party as they made their way through the main street of the outer city,' recounts the Tibetologist Graham Sandberg, who was a contemporary of the Pundit. 'As Chandra Das wore coloured goggle spectacles and looked somewhat of a general wreck, the onlookers freely remarked upon his appearance. "Another sick man," exclaimed an idler at a Chinese pastry shop. "Why, the city will soon be full of such."'[18]

Chandra Das was given lodgings with the family of a Tibetan noblewoman whom he had met on his previous journey, and on 10 June a Court retainer came trotting up to his house with news that he was to be granted an audience with the Dalai Lama. Finishing his breakfast as quickly as he could, the Pundit got dressed in his Tibetan finery, all the while fairly trembling with apprehension at the prospect of having to negotiate the steep flights of steps and ladders of the Potala in his weakened physical condition after seven exhausting months on the road. He braced himself for the task as he mounted his pony, equipped with an offering of three bundles of incense sticks and a fistful of *khatas*, the white ceremonial scarves that he would present to the adolescent god-king. The audience took place in a 40-foot-long chamber, in which Chandra Das took his place along with other dignitaries seated cross-legged on a cushion about ten paces from the throne. The diary entry for this occasion reveals how deeply the Hindu Pundit had been influenced by his studies of Tibetan Buddhism. 'When we were all seated there was perfect silence in the grand hall,' he writes.

The State officials walked from left to right with serene gravity, as becoming their exalted rank in the presence of the Supreme Vice-Regent of Buddha on Earth. The great altar resembling an oriental throne and borne by lions carved in wood, on which his holiness, a child of eight, sat, was covered with silk scarves of great value. A yellow mitre hat covered his person, and he sat cross-legged with the palms of his hands joined together to bless us. In my turn I received his holiness's benediction and surveyed his divine face.[19]

The prayers were recited and the blessings given, and then the ceremony was declared ended. The Court chamberlain made the three traditional prostrations before his holiness, who departed the throne room with all the pomp that could be expected of a spiritual ruler aged 8 years. Chandra Das had achieved a master stroke as the first British agent, albeit for the moment unbeknown to the Tibetans, to be granted an audience by the Dalai Lama.

By 19 June the Pundit was back in Tashilunpo, on the first leg of his homeward journey. When Chandra Das called on the Minister he found to his horror that what for him had been a convenient subterfuge, allowing him to pass unmolested into Lhasa, was for his friend a grim reality that had brought him down to death's door. Chandra Das was ushered into the monastery meeting chamber where the Minister received him in a state of agony, his face swollen and disfigured with smallpox, eruptions covering his tongue, throat and lips. The first thing he asked his learned Indian friend, in a faltering voice, was whether there was any chance of his recovering from the disease. Chandra Das took his friend's hand and did his best to reassure him that the critical stage was probably over, little suspecting that at this point the restoration of the Minister's health was largely an academic matter.

After a five-month sojourn in Tashilunpo, Chandra Das set his face for home. Taking it at a gentle stride, a month later the Pundit rode into Darjeeling, to be greeted by a town still in the slow process of recovery from the previous week's Christmas festivities. The reports he brought back about Tibetan trade, geography and politics, and these not confined to the shawl-wool trade and Chinese political hegemony over Tibet, hold out the intriguing question of a possible secret agenda behind the Pundit's journey. It would be hard to imagine any other reason for Chandra Das, the Buddhist scholar and linguist, filling his notebooks with data on the organisation and deployment of the Tibetan army. He reports that Lhasa would be capable of putting about 6,000 regular soldiers into the field, with every family required in times of emergency to furnish at least one ready-armed *yul-mag*, or militiaman, at the call of the Government. By his calculations this would mean no less than an additional 350,000 troops at the Dalai Lama's service, out of a total population of eight and a half million. The weak spots were the provinces of Kham, famed for its warrior caste but owing only nominal allegiance to Lhasa, and Amdo, which was virtually a Chinese territory. Apart from a few cavalry units, this was very much a rag-tag infantry force armed with bows and arrows, sabres, slings, long knives and a few matchlocks. Despite China's suzerainty over Tibet, Peking played an ill-defined role in Tibetan military affairs. The *Amban* took the role of head of the country's Military Department, while the *dahpons*, or Tibetan generals, ranked immediately under the chief representative of the Chinese emperor. Yet the *Amban* had no official jurisdiction over Tibet's internal administration, and the supreme military commander, or chief *dahpon*, was not constitutionally required to take orders from the *Amban*. The viability of this ambiguous chain of command had not yet been put to the test under war conditions, but that was to come before long.

As for making a protracted defence against an invading army, it was worth noting that, Tibet being a Buddhist theocracy, the Government kept huge stores of grain for feeding the country's 30,000-strong monk population in the major monastery cities of Lhasa, Gyantse, Tsetang and Tashilunpo. The Pundit's report contains references to abundant flocks of sheep and goats throughout the country, as well as ponies, mules, donkeys and yaks. Of course, all this could be turned to a conqueror's advantage in shortening supply lines with the invader's country. Chandra Das thought that the Tibetans held an edge over their enemies by their ability to subsist largely on roasted barley, known as *tsampa*, which was moistened with tea or whey, whereas the people of neighbouring Nepal, Sikkim or Bhutan were accustomed to a diet of cooked rice with meat or vegetables. He neglected to consider another country that might have designs on Tibet's sovereignty, although his superiors took no pains to enlighten him on the issue.

Chandra Das's star swiftly took to the ascendant after his return to India. The Pundit was invited to deliver lectures on Tibetan culture and language at home and abroad, while his articles found prominence in such learned publications as the *Journal of the Asiatic Society of Bengal*. The academic world was astonished at the wealth of rare Sanskrit texts, many of them thought to have been lost, that the Pundit unearthed during a stopover at the ancient Tibetan monastery of Sakya. Chandra Das was never a man to be faulted for excessive modesty, and the honours he received would have been perceived as just reward for his life of service to the British Raj. A letter sent to the Royal Geographical Society in 1893, purportedly written by one Rowesh Chundra Dalt, CIE, bears all the hallmarks of Chandra Das's own grandiloquent style. This missive, clearly dictated by the Pundit, begs the Society to recognise Chandra Das's claims to 'some marked recognition of his services to the cause of Geography and general knowledge'. The writer states: 'I believe some of my countrymen have been awarded a Gold Medal by the Society for their services, and I venture to suggest that Mr Sarat Chandra Das's claims to a similar honour may be favourably considered by the Committee.' The letter goes on to remind the Society that the writer 'is empowered by Mr Sarat Chandra Das to mention that he attaches the highest value to a Gold Medal from the Society and that . . . it has been his ambition to obtain it'.[20] Alas, his recompense was not to be the coveted Gold Medal. The Pundit would instead have to content himself with the Royal Geographical Society's Back Award, granted for his outstanding contribution to the study of geography, having brought back some of the first detailed information on the approaches to Mount Everest, and a survey of an unknown lake on his journey to Lhasa, which he named Yamdo Croft after his chief in Darjeeling. He was given the Marquess of Dufferin and Ava's Silver Medal and was made a Companion of the Indian Empire. The Pundit was nominated a corresponding member of the Imperial Archaeological Society of St Petersburg and went on to become a prolific author, producing among other works a Tibetan grammar, a Tibetan–English dictionary, an autobiography and several treatises on religion in the Land of Snow. He was also the founder of the Buddhist Textbook Society. The Pundit known as DS worked for the Government as a Tibetan translator until his retirement in 1904 at the age of 55. In 1885 Chandra Das was sent by the Government of India to Peking, to accompany the Finance Secretary Colman Macaulay on a diplomatic mission to negotiate permits for a political and scientific mission to Tibet. He was later lionised by Macaulay in his ode 'A Lay of Lachen' (a Sikkimese village), a poem worthy of the pen of a William McGonagall:

> And Sarat Chandra, hardy son
> Of soft Bengal, whose wondrous store
> Of Buddhist and Tibetan lore
> A place in fame's bright page has won,
> Friend of the Tashu Lama's line,
> Whose eyes have seen, the gleaming shrine
> Of holy Lhasa, came to show
> The wonders of the land of snow.

Less fortunate was Chandra Das's friend the Minister of Tashilunpo, who, along with several other Tibetans, had befriended and assisted the Pundit. Shortly after Chandra Das's departure, word got out of his true identity and the nature of his mission. The supposed Buddhist scholar was in reality a British agent who had penetrated Tibet under false pretences, aided and abetted by the authorities at Tashilunpo. This is what the Lhasa authorities were led to believe, and, tragically, they were not far off the mark. The Minister, whose only crime was to have tutored Chandra Das in Tibetan Buddhist rites and holy scripture, was summarily accused of divulging state secrets to a foreigner. After all, it was he who had issued the Indian's safe-conduct pass to enter Tibet. Retribution was swift and merciless. After a rigorous imprisonment and many public floggings, he was thrown from a bridge into the Tsangpo with his hands tied behind him. This outrage gave rise to a popular legend of the day, according to which the Minister was twice dropped in the river, but failed to drown with each immersion. The bewildered executioners then hesitated to lower him in a third time, until the victim himself opened his eyes and proclaimed to a huge crowd that had gathered on the river bank that it would not be correct to mourn his death, because he was destined to go through another reincarnation. 'He said that his task was done and it was time for him to depart. He blessed the spread of Buddhism in Tibet and requested the executioners to make haste to sink him under the water.'[21] At the same time, nearly the whole of the Minister's retinue of servants was punished. Their hands and feet were cut off and their eyes gouged out, and in that condition they were left until death came to relieve their agony. *The Times* reported, twenty years after this terrible episode, that the brutality of it still shocked the city's inhabitants. 'To this day [1904] there is a sullen resentment which swells the tide of hatred and fear with which Lhasa is almost universally regarded.'[22] It was at that time that British troops of Francis Younghusband's Tibet expeditionary force were in occupation of Lhasa. One September morning Tibetan prisoners-of-war were paraded in a central courtyard and each was presented with five rupees before being released, while the Tibetans for their part set free a number of men gaoled for helping foreigners to enter Tibet. 'One of them was the now elderly steward of the Palla estate at Gyantse sentenced to life imprisonment for showing hospitality to the Bengali explorer-spy Sarat Chandra Das back in 1884,' writes Charles Allen in his history of the Younghusband mission to Lhasa. The first moment of freedom of this unnamed scapegoat of the Tibetan government's savagery was witnessed by Edmund Candler, correspondent of the *Daily Mail*, whose dispatch is quoted by

Allen: 'The old man's chains had been removed from his limbs that morning for the first time in twenty years, and he came in blinking at the unaccustomed light like a blind man miraculously restored to sight.'[23] There are no reports of any other survivors among the victims of this shameful Tibetan pogrom.

CHAPTER 7

The Holy Spy

With Chandra Das's cover effectively blown, the duty of carrying on exploration work in Tibet fell to his natural successor, Ugyen Gyatso. The jolly lama entered the Survey's secret files as agent UG and was sent to join Colonel H.C.B. Tanner's workshop to be trained in the finer points of undercover surveying. This entailed learning to use a few simple and easily concealed instruments, before the lama could be sent to Tibet 'on special duty'. Ugyen Gyatso had obviously picked up some basic skills during the months spent on the trail with his travelling companion, Chandra Das. After a week's basic training, Tanner was satisfied with the monk's ability to use a prismatic compass and determine his altitude by the hypsometer. Colonel Sir Thomas Holdich, a Survey officer who had been attached to the Russo-Afghan Border Commission, mentions in his report on Ugyen Gyatso's journey that the lama had been briefed on the methods of collecting specimens for the Calcutta Botanical Society. Whether this was a genuine spin-off from the surveying assignment or a cover-up activity is anybody's guess. Holdich adds, tantalisingly, that the monk had also been 'fully instructed by Mr Macaulay, the

Secretary to the Bengal Government, as to the information which it was desirable to collect'. For a government that was desperate to gain topographical knowledge of a country into which it would soon dispatch an invasion force, the British showed themselves astonishingly parsimonious when it came to outfitting their spies. As was the case with Chandra Das's expeditions, Ugyen Gyatso's third voyage to Tibet was to be a labour of love. 'He [the lama] made his own arrangement for the purchase of cloth, needles, tobacco, &c., to be carried as merchandise, and took care to be well provided with medicines and funds for his journey.'[1]

In the midst of one of the torrential cloudbursts that relentlessly lash Darjeeling in the monsoon season, on 9 June 1883 Ugyen Gyatso gathered his travel kitbag, along with his wife and brother-in-law, and started off on the first leg of his journey to Tibet. As he strolled up the town's cobbled streets through the Mall promenade, he stopped to inform 'certain inquisitive neighbours' that he was travelling on a visit to his home at Yangong in Sikkim, three days' march to the north. The Pundit lama and his family did indeed stop at the Yangong monastery, where he picked up a party of coolies to shoulder their loads for the demanding trek that lay ahead across the mountains. Ugyen Gyatso, or, one should say, the Survey, could not have picked a worse time to start off on a journey through this part of India. Hardly a day passes without the monsoon hitting Bengal and its northern neighbour Sikkim with an unbelievable fury, unleashing massive landslides onto the roads and sweeping away bridges across the swollen rivers. The latter almost proved to be the lama's undoing. A few hours from Yangong, he and his party were first forced to spend a morning constructing a flimsy bamboo bridge across the River Rungum, and several marches ahead they needed to employ three full days in repairing what was left of the slatted bridge over the Teesta, which roared in full flood a few inches below their terrified footsteps. So thankful was Ugyen Gyatso for his safe crossing of these torrents that, upon reaching the hamlet of Ringim, in north Sikkim, he purchased a pig, half of which he gave to his Lepcha coolies, and the other half of which he dried and carried with him as a gift for the people of Lachung, one of the last villages below the high passes into Tibet, which he reached in a few days' time.

Lachung lies along one of the main trade routes for yak caravans passing between Darjeeling and Tibet. The Lhasa government had therefore stationed an official in the village to keep a watchful eye on travellers entering the Land of Snow. It took the Pundit several days of stubborn negotiations to convince the Tibetan agent that he was but an innocent pilgrim desirous of prostrating himself before the holy shrines of Buddhism. In this he met with success, thanks, in Ugyen Gyatso's opinion, to the presence of his wife, for one could hardly conceive of a spy taking his spouse along on an espionage mission. 'The presence of his wife in his camp', writes Holdich, 'seemed to have a reassuring effect – it was a sort of guarantee that he was a *bona fide* pilgrim.'[2]

By early July preparations had been finalised for the crossing into Tibet. Yaks and ponies had been hired for transporting the party's baggage on the week-long slog through rain-soaked grassland and deep mud to the 18,100-foot Donkhya La Pass. There is a widely held belief that anyone endowed with a pair of Tibetan lungs enjoys a kind of genetic immunity to altitude sickness. The fact is that Sherpas, Bhotias and other people of Tibetan stock are as vulnerable to the effects of oxygen starvation as any European, Ugyen Gyatso being no exception to this biological reality. The lama was hit by a crippling bout of altitude sickness on the summit of the pass, suffering from the usual symptoms of shortness of breath, spasms of nausea and migraine. Nevertheless, this is where his masters at the Survey had instructed him to begin his surveying work, so, steeling himself to the task, the Pundit assembled his various pieces of equipment and set about taking the relevant bearings of the River Teesta, a dark thread snaking its way across the grey rocky landscape thousands of feet below.

Two months out of Darjeeling, Ugyen Gyatso found himself standing on the summit of Pongong La, the 16,500-foot pass, where, at the distant head of the valley, he could make out the silhouette of the bustling Tibetan commercial and administrative centre of Gyantse. The Pundit received word through the grapevine that several Sikkimese traders, personal acquaintances of his from Darjeeling, were conducting their business affairs in Gyangtse. It would have been too risky to take a chance on being recognised deep within Tibetan territory, so Ugyen Gyatso and his party set up camp in a secluded spot on the south bank of the river to wait for the all-clear signal before hustling his little caravan into the city. Three days later, the Pundit entered the gates of Gyantse, where his clandestine survey work in and around the city was to prove extremely valuable to the British forces of the Younghusband expedition, who advanced on Gyantse with the aid of reliable maps in the first stage of the 1903 Tibet invasion, a campaign that garnered official support from almost all quarters, from King Edward VII to the Government of India and *The Times* of London.

Early August found the Pundit and his companions travelling across a far more agreeable landscape of farming villages, gardens and barley fields, lying roughly along the course of the swift-flowing Nyang Chhu river. They were now in rain shadow territory and little troubled by the torrential deluge of the summer monsoon. Ugyen Gyatso's reports to Survey head-quarters on Tibetan village and religious life left few doubts in the minds of British officialdom as to the uncivilised nature of these alien tribes north of the great Himalayan divide. At Shalu monastery, a famous centre of Tantric practices, Ugyen Gyatso describes a magic rite in which an anchorite is introduced into a cave large enough for one man, where he remains for twelve years engaged in deep meditation on certain esoteric mysteries. At the end of this period, the hermit signals his readiness to return to civilisation by blowing on a trumpet made from a human thigh bone. The mystic emerges through a small hole in the ground, cross-legged in the Buddha lotus posture. He is then subjected to various tests, such as sitting on a heap of barley without displacing a single grain, to determine if he has indeed acquired esoteric powers. If the aspirant passes the test, he becomes a guru lama; if not, he is simply left to take up the routine of his previous worldly existence. Reports like this, and others depicting the oddities of Tibetan customs, were greeted with derision by Survey officers. 'Such grotesque superstitions point to a more degraded condition of the national religion of Tibet in the heart of the country than the admirers of the *Light of Asia* would care to credit.'[3]

The Pundit was now wending his way toward familiar terrain, with Shigatse and its sprawling monastery complex of Tashilunpo in his sights, 50 miles north-west of Gyantse. It must be remembered that Ugyen Gyatso, surveyor, explorer, botanist, was also a Buddhist monk ordained at Pemayangtse, one of the holiest lamaseries in the Tibetan religious hierarchy. His quest for spiritual attainment was fired by the sacred site of Shigatse, and he spent a good deal of his time visiting the city's most venerated shrines. On one of these occasions a high lama persuaded him to take a vow to repeat certain forms of prayer to the god Idam 3,000 times a day. Albeit having the best of intentions, the Pundit found this performance 'quite incompatible with his secular duties', that is, his surveying tasks, so he revisited the lama and begged to be released from his oath. To his relief, Ugyen Gyatso was let off with 1,000 incantations a day and 'as many more as he could manage'.

The blithesome, rotund lama seemed to have a knack for blundering into awkward situations – evoking an image of a Peter Ustinov character swathed in a crimson robe. Yet there was nothing frivolous about the information of commercial and military value that he contrived to gather on his journey across Tibet, at a critical time in British India's relations with its northern neighbour. From Shigatse, whose height the Pundit fixed at 12,350 feet above sea level, he set a course eastward along the southern bank of the Tsangpo, following Chandra Das's route toward the great lake complex of Yamdo Tso. Ugyen Gyatso discovered that the river is navigable by ferry service for 50 miles east of Shigatse. Below this point begin the lesser-known reaches of the Tibetan waterway, where it takes a bend southward and becomes 'rough and rapid', quite impracticable for the hide-built coracles of the country. After a difficult crossing of the Tsangpo, depicted in his report as 'a black, turbid flood', the Pundit and his wife marched ahead to the system of lakes that he spent several days exploring and surveying in great detail – in spite of the frequent rain and thick mists that enveloped the nearby mountains. The terrain in this region was more reminiscent of the drizzly Sikkim he had left behind than of the arid Tibetan plateau.

The Pundit ran into 'serious difficulty' a few days after completing his survey of the Yamdrock Tso network of lakes. Ugyen Gyatso had climbed a rocky eminence near the small village of Lha-khang to admire the rugged grandeur of the surrounding countryside. On his return to the house in which he had been offered lodgings, he found his wife and brother-in-law in a state of great distress. In their sleeping quarters stood several burly Tibetans whose scowling faces left little to the imagination of an undercover surveyor. The men had been sent by the local Jongpen, or district official, to examine the Pundit's belongings. Ugyen Gyatso's wife had concealed most of the surveying instruments, but there was enough evidence around to convince the Tibetans that they had captured a high-ranking spy. The Tibetan officials were in no mood for excuses. The Pundit, his wife and brother-in-law were arrested and kept in confinement for several days, until they were summoned before two Jongpens, one a lay official and the other a priest, who were to decide how to deal with the interloper. The Pundit could expect little mercy from his judges, who were clearly not amused by the pile of instruments, maps, botanical specimens and books before them. The decision was immediate and chilling: this was a most grievous case, warranting the involvement of the central government in Lhasa, to where all these artefacts were to be sent as evidence of a clear breach of the orders that had recently been issued, strictly forbidding anyone to draw up maps of the country.

Ugyen Gyatso knew that he had to act swiftly or risk the same fate that had been dealt to other explorers found guilty of spying, namely a public beheading. Whatever funds he had on his person were judiciously slipped to his host and a few of the junior officials, who were thus persuaded to intercede on his behalf. Some of the bribe money undoubtedly found its way into the Jongpens' pockets, for during the ensuing cross-examination their hearts suddenly softened. The Pundit was let off with a stern warning and, what is more astonishing, with the return of all his property, except for his notebook, which the Tibetans took pains to destroy, lest they were to find themselves compromised by it later falling into the hands of higher officials. Ugyen Gyatso was forced to give an undertaking not to set foot in Lhasa or mention a word to anyone about his detention in Lha-khang. The day after his release, the Pundit stole out of the village at daybreak and casually resumed his surveying work of the Tsangpo valley, while setting a course northward on the road to Lhasa.

The stone-covered expanses along this stage of the journey were infested with robbers 'with blackened faces' who preyed upon small, unarmed parties travelling to Lhasa. Ugyen Gyatso came across a lonely hut, called a *jikkyop*, standing forlorn in the middle of the plain, where he took shelter for the night. It was like stepping back several centuries in time, for the hut was kept by a 'half-savage old couple' whose bare survival seemed to depend on providing passing travellers with animal dung for fuel, in exchange for food. The Pundit, who had spent many a night shivering in caves or in open fields, was repulsed by this wretched place, which he hurriedly abandoned the following morning. The closer Ugyen Gyatso drew to the villages and vast monastery complexes on the approach to Lhasa, the more care he needed to take with his pilgrim guise in order to avoid being unmasked. At one point, the party crossed paths with a royal procession led by the Regent of Tibet – the temporal ruler as opposed to the spiritual leader, the Dalai Lama – who was on a periodic tour of his domains. This proved very inconvenient for Ugyen Gyatso, as he was unable to restrain himself from engaging in cheerful banter with the royal retainers about his adventures on the road. As the chatter rambled on, a few of the king's bodyguards began to take a keener interest in the Pundit's travels, suspecting a possible hidden motive behind his journey to Lhasa. Ugyen Gyatso only escaped being handed over to the authorities at the last minute by dispensing liberal bribes to his inquisitive companions.

On 9 October, four months to the day after his departure from Darjeeling, the Pundit surmounted a low pass, from which the lights of the holy city of Lhasa could be spotted in the distance. He took the precaution of crossing the Ki Chhu river, which he measured as 500 paces across, by moonlight, in a ferry piloted by several hopelessly drunk boatmen. The Pundit refers in passing to being almost 'torn to pieces' by savage Tibetan mastiffs when he alighted on the north bank of the river. Ugyen Gyatso had been forewarned about these ferocious beasts and took pains to supply himself with a sack stuffed with bones and scraps of meat 'with which he beguiled the dogs as they disputed his way'. By two o'clock in the morning the Pundit, not to mention his long-suffering wife, sat down under a tree to catch their breath, unsuspecting of the tribulations that lay ahead. His first task was to devise a plan to conceal his instruments and notes. Lhasa was no place to risk having these incriminating instruments exposed to the authorities, who were unlikely to be bought off so easily as a provincial Jongpen. He hit upon the idea of sealing all his surveying equipment and records in a bag, which he would leave in the care of a fellow monk at the nearby Daphung monastery, a short walk along the road to Lhasa. With this problem resolved, the Pundit settled in for a few hours' rest, only to be abruptly roused from his sleep at dawn by a group of angry villagers, who told him that the tree under which he had chosen to bed down was a place of holy veneration, and that he had only to lay a finger on a twig to be guilty of offending the guardian deities. To make matters worse, he found out that he was lucky still to be drawing breath, for this was also a meeting spot for local robbers and freebooters of every stripe, who took advantage of the neighbourhood's seclusion to plan their evil doings.

When Ugyen Gyatso reached Daphung, a short distance south of Lhasa, he explained his predicament to his friend over a cup of buttered tea. The Pundit's possessions were duly secreted behind locked doors and he went out to have a look around the great city and find a place for his party to spend the night. His first encounter was with a Chinese army sergeant who kept a tidy guesthouse near the monastery. This seemed an ideal place to spend the night. Most importantly, there was no danger of his Chinese landlord demanding to examine his baggage, as might easily have been the case in a Tibetan household. Once again, Ugyen Gyatso's proclivity for loose chatter nearly brought about his demise. Relaxing by the fire, the Pundit happened to make some indiscreet enquiries about the status of the Nepalese Resident in Lhasa, an unfortunate subject to bring up at a time when relations between Tibet and Nepal were strained to breaking point. His Chinese host's mood suddenly turned sullen. Just why, he wanted to know, was this alleged religious pilgrim taking such an avid interest in the country's political affairs? The conversation quickly turned into a cross-examination, and, fearing that he had let a spy into his midst, the Chinese officer let loose a torrent of abuse and unceremoniously turned the Pundit and his party out of his house.

Ugyen Gyatso, with his wife and brother-in-law in tow, spent the rest of the day roaming the streets of Lhasa in search of new lodgings. He eventually came across some long-lost Nepalese friends living in town, who could put him up in a spare room, in which the Pundit gratefully dropped his bags for a night's well-earned rest. However, his fame had gone before him, and it was not long before the police, who had been tipped off by the Chinese sergeant, came knocking at the door, demanding to have a look at his baggage. They left no stone unturned in their search, but fortunately failed to find any possessions of an incriminating nature, all of them having been safely stashed away at Daphung monastery. In view of the prevailing tensions between the authorities and the local Nepalese community, the Pundit's new hosts were equally indisposed to having a suspect, talkative monk from Sikkim under their roof. But they had a plan that might help him out of his predicament: Ugyen Gyatso's monastery, Pemayangtse, had a close historical kinship with the Buddhist red-hat sect of Nepal. A discreet message sent across town procured the Pundit an invitation from the Resident himself, who was only too happy to welcome a pilgrim from Pemayangtse into his house, a four-storey building that stood close to the home of his Chinese counterpart. The Nepalese Resident found the garrulous monk from Sikkim an engaging house guest, to the extent that Ugyen Gyatso's position in Lhasa was 'secured', meaning he could move freely about the city to carry out the real duties that had brought him to the Tibetan capital.

One week after arriving in Lhasa the Pundit commenced his survey of the Tibetan capital, using as his cover, quite literally, an umbrella under which he concealed the equipment that had been retrieved from its hiding place in Daphung monastery. He seemed to thrive in this environment of high intrigue, for he knew that to sit under an umbrella in full public view of Lhasa's paranoid officialdom was an open flirtation with danger. Yet he was also aware that he was engaged in trail-blazing work that, on his return, was certain to earn him the kudos of the exalted Survey of India. So for two days on end, thinking himself beyond reach of recognition, Ugyen Gyatso walked, observed and measured, painstakingly putting into practice the skills learnt in Darjeeling, so that he was able to calculate, for example, that it took exactly 9,500 paces to do a full circuit of the city.

The Pundit also found it necessary to discourage his wife from forming too close a friendship with the Resident's spouse, although, after the months of swashbuckling along the road to Lhasa, the poor woman must have been bored to distraction, spending her days confined within the four walls of the Residency. The fear was that the lama's wife might carelessly reveal the truth behind her husband's fondness for strolling about town under his umbrella. At the same time, Ugyen Gyatso took advantage of every spare moment to pump the Resident for information about the Tibetan government, its structure, its leadership and how it exercised its powers, most of which served to confirm the information that had been gathered by Chandra Das on his expedition to Lhasa.

The Pundit's luck ran out less than a week into his fieldwork. Within the pantheon of Tibetan liturgy there is a ceremony called the sky burial, in which a corpse is borne by *ragapas*, literally 'carriers of the dead', to a spot, usually a hilltop, where the body is dismembered by these men and fed to vultures that hover restlessly overhead, waiting to pounce on their gruesome meal. The *ragapas* are outcasts from society, the Tibetan equivalent of Indian untouchables, who have in most cases been branded pariahs because of past criminal offences. 'They are only permitted to live in houses or huts made of horns, no matter what their present wealth or former position may have been. These *ragapas* appear to be the pests of Lhasa. Hardened by crime, and deadened by their occupation to all sense of humanity, they band together in a turbulent and unruly crowd, and endeavour to extort blackmail from all strangers and travellers.'[4] It was Ugyen Gyatso's misfortune to have fallen foul of these wretched creatures, who prowled the streets like pariah dogs. The reason behind the *ragapas*' attack was never made clear, but the lama's eccentric appearance was undoubtedly enough to set their teeth gnashing. The upshot was that one morning a band of these snarling *ragapas* surrounded Ugyen Gyatso while at his work and proceeded to chase him into one of the city's central squares. They hurled abuse at the terrified lama, and then began chorusing the words he least wanted to hear: 'British spy! British spy!' It was something other than sheer chance that had led them to denounce what was really happening beneath that umbrella. To his alarm, one of this gang turned out to be a native of Darjeeling who claimed to recognise the Pundit. His plight was now alarming enough for Ugyen Gyatso to send in haste for his

Nepalese friends. They came rushing to the scene, along with a friendly Tibetan official. The way out of this predicament was quite straightforward: once again the Pundit was obliged to dig into his pocket to buy his tormentors' silence, at least long enough to allow him to make a safe getaway from Lhasa.

Ugyen Gyatso's main dilemma was that by now, having liberally dispensed bribes to all and sundry to buy his way out of trouble, his funds were starting to run dangerously low. This, however, did not present an insurmountable problem for the resourceful Pundit. He first needed to purchase ponies and saddles for the long journey home. Fortunately, the wife of one of the Nepalese residents in Lhasa happened to be visiting Darjeeling at that time, so by pleading his case to these acquaintances he succeeded in issuing what he called a 'promissory note' for 125 rupees, sufficient to start him on his voyage in comfort.

Ugyen Gyatso had hardly stirred from his house for days, fearful of being spotted by one of the *ragapas* or, even worse, the Chinese officials who by now had collected enough circumstantial evidence to order the lama's arrest on suspicion of spying. At dawn on 19 October he gathered his belongings and slipped out of Lhasa, not failing to take his final observations – always under cover of his umbrella – even before he was clear of town. Nearly a month later Ugyen Gyatso closed his extensive survey while crossing the Cho La Pass, moving southward over well-trodden ground toward Pemayangtse monastery. Once at his spiritual home, the Pundit entertained his brother lamas with the remainder of the funds he had obtained from Darjeeling, while leaving a small sum on deposit for one monk to turn the monastery's huge *mani* or prayer-wheel day and night. He received the blessings of the head lama of Pemayangtse, and not a moment too soon as it turned out, for when he reached Darjeeling a month later he was told that the old monk had died almost immediately after Ugyen Gyatso's departure.

Holdich, summing up the achievements of this remarkable Pundit's six-month odyssey, hailed it as 'one of the best records of Tibetan travels that has yet been achieved by any agent of the

Survey of India'.[5] In a later report, published in 1889, on the work of the Pundits, the Surveyor-General of India, Colonel H.R. Thuillier, lavished praise on the plucky monk from Pemayangtse, whom he credited for filling in a crucial gap of the Great Trigonometrical Survey's North-East Trans-Frontier map single-handed, on a mission that took him only slightly longer than six months. Thuillier waxed enthusiastic about Ugyen Gyatso's work at Yamdrok Tso lake, 'the curious double peninsula which he [the Pundit] has completely mapped'. Ugyen Gyatso was also the first to map the upper course of the River Lhobrak that flows eastward to meet the Manas in Assam. He surveyed and mapped areas of north-east Tibet 'over country till then absolutely unknown to us'. Thuillier concludes: 'The valuable geographical information which he has thus collected is interspersed with references to the social and religious customs of the Tibetans, which will doubtless prove very acceptable to the general reader.'[6]

The Pundit Ugyen Gyatso retired from active service with the Survey of India to spend his post-exploration years as Sub-Inspector of Schools in Darjeeling. On certain occasions, as one of the monks on the monastery's roll, he travelled through the valleys of his native Sikkim to attend high religious ceremonies at Pemayangtse. From time to time he would be coaxed into emerging from his retirement, when the Survey officers had need of his expertise in a liaison role to help guide their work in trans-Himalayan exploration. Ugyen Gyatso was called upon to translate the exploits of a Mongolian monk, Serap Gyatso (no relation), who turned up in Darjeeling with a tale of his travels through the lower Tsangpo valley undertaken nearly thirty years before. The monk's narrative was confined chiefly to a list of names of monasteries, sacred places and villages, with an occasional digression into history and descriptions of wild beasts, throwing little light on the geography of the Tsangpo, according to Ugyen Gyatso's account. The Mongolian lama's account was drawn from memory and, as the Survey report states, must be accepted with caution. His recollection proved surprisingly accurate, as was later confirmed in a debriefing by the explorer Kintup, although the information he brought back proved to be of minor value to the Survey's objectives of the day. 'Nevertheless, from the information, such as it is, combined with the account of K.P. [the explorer Kintup] . . . Colonel Tanner was able to compile a sketch map of the course of the Lower Tsangpo and thus furnish the first contribution to the geography of that unknown tract.'[7] Every scrap of information was of value to the Survey's data-gathering mission regarding the people and terrain that lay between British India and that uncharted land beyond the Himalaya, where lurked the Russian enemy. If nothing else, Serap Gyatso's findings helped 'in cross-checking many of the routes of which the authorities in the Survey Department had only heard'.[8]

The golden age of daredevil exploration work carried out by native agents beyond the Himalaya, an epoch spanning roughly three decades from the days of Nain Singh's monumental first journey in 1864, was entering its waning years. This is not to suggest that cloak and dagger operations north of the Himalayan divide were at an end. Far from it: Russian diplomatic and commercial influence, not to mention the build-up of a powerful Tsarist military presence close to the borders of British India, continued relentlessly throughout the 1880s. The Government of Calcutta was in receipt of daily reports of Russian agents and of troop movements fanning out in an arc across the top of India, from Afghanistan in the untamed regions of the remote North-West Frontier to the barren eastern reaches of Tibet. At about that time the Secretary of State for India, Lord Salisbury, received a letter from the British agent stationed in Tehran, informing him that the friendly Afghan warlord, Ayub Khan, a pretender to the throne, had confided 'most secretly that he had no hope or desire of being Amir' of his country. This was a most remarkable revelation, given the fanatical appetite for power that was endemic to the Afghan warlords. More exasperating was the motive for the Ayub Khan's disinterest in the job. He was convinced 'that owing to the proximity of Russia no Amir could expect to successfully oppose that power . . . and no resistance could successfully be made against the Russians unless an English army was placed permanently at Herat', near Afghanistan's western border with Iran.[9]

Dispatches were being delivered at breakneck speed from Newswriters stationed in key outposts across Central Asia. Dateline Bokhara: 'The Russians appear to be steadily consolidating their influence throughout Bokhara. During October they were improving the road between the capital and Samarkand. Sites for barracks have been purchased near Bokhara, and fortified posts established at intervals along the road to Samarkand. The administration of the country is apparently to a considerable extent under the control of Russian officers.' Meshed: 'Six guns and forty boxes of ammunition arrived from Russia. The two medium-sized guns, with ten boxes of ammunition, left for Merv. Forty-two horse-guns arrived today by train (they are probably machine guns). One hundred and fifty artillery men also arrived by the same train.' Bokhara again: 'All the Bokharan troops here are now dressed in Russian uniforms. The Correspondent accounts for about 1,200 Russian soldiers in Bokhara itself.' Askabad: 'Three hundred workmen arrived from Baku en route for Charjui. The railway has been constructed right up to the bank of the Oxus.' Dereghez: 'It is reported that the Russians are intriguing with the Arsari Turkoman tribe, whose country lies between Kerki and Charjui, on the left bank of the Oxus . . . The intention of the Russians is to cut off the Amir's control over them altogether.' Askabad reports again: 'The Russians are turning all their attention to Balkh, Mazar-Sherif and Andkhui [in Afghan territory].'[10] In they came with alarming rapidity, dispatches flooding the desks of the Intelligence Branch in Simla and the India Office in London with alarming reports of Tsarist troops massed almost on the doorstep of India. This was no time for complacency. Even now, large tracts of land situated along potential invasion routes from the north remained uncharted.

In November 1885 two travellers quietly set out on separate journeys northward under the misty autumn skies of Darjeeling. The first to depart, on 1 November, was Rinzin Namgyal (code-named RN), who, as brother-in-law to Ugyen Gyatso and a former student of Sarat Chandra Das, possessed impeccable credentials as a Pundit. His companion and protégé, PA, one of the few agents whose real name was never revealed by the Survey, started off the following morning, following in the footsteps of the man who had taught him the basic principles of surveying. Namgyal had received instructions three months earlier from the Surveyor-General, Colonel Henry Tanner, to cross into Tibet and follow an easterly course toward the untrodden reaches of Bhutan. His orders were to trace the lower reaches of the Tsangpo, in the hope of solving the riddle of whether the Tibetan river was one with the Brahmaputra that debouched into the Bay of Bengal or whether, as some explorers maintained, it converged with the Irrawaddy, the commercial lifeline of Burma. That these two great waterways of Asia lie more than 200 miles apart at their nearest juncture gives some idea of the paucity of geographical data available to the Survey in the late nineteenth century.

Namgyal had been told to head toward Bhutan by crossing the Jelap La Pass into Tibet, but the Pundit quickly became aware that he was heading for trouble. Instead, he decided to send a companion he had trained to make the crossing and carry out a survey of the area. 'As the people near the Jelap La pass were likely to recognise me and detect my motive for crossing into Tibet, I detached my companion P.A., a native of Sikkim whom I had instructed in the use of the prismatic compass, with orders to cross the Jelap La pass into Tibet,' reads the Pundit's narrative of his journey.[11] The explorers agreed to rendezvous at the junction of two rivers in Bhutan. Namgyal took with him a party of safari proportions that was certain to attract attention, consisting of 'three trustworthy companions', five Sikkimese servants and several coolies for transporting their baggage. It took a little more than a week of relatively easy trekking through lowland forest to reach the Cho La Pass, his intended route into Tibet. Here the

Pundit was warned by some friendly villagers that the pass was heavily guarded to prevent the passage of travellers, so he once more altered his plans and crossed directly into Bhutan 'through dense forest infested with tigers and bears'. All the while Namgyal proceeded to take bearings of hitherto unexplored peaks, counting the paces to each from a spot on the border between Sikkim and Bhutan, where his route survey was to begin. It took him more than five months to reconnoitre his way round Bhutan to Molakachung La, a towering pass at 17,500 feet above sea level, the summit of which, the only feature on the horizon, was 'a sea of snow'.

A few days into the forbidden Land of Snow, Namgyal and his party were discovered and taken into custody by Tibetan guards, who held them prisoners at a village called Yura in southern Tibet awaiting the arrival of the local Jongpen. Namgyal had suspected trouble might be lurking in this border region and had taken the precaution of concealing his surveying tools. This saved him from instantly facing charge as a spy. The district official was summoned, and the Pundit and his men were conducted into his presence. 'We were rudely questioned by him as to the object of our journey, but finding our story apparently truthful he remanded us back into custody with orders to await the wishes of the Lhasa authorities, who he said could alone decide our fate.'[12] Namgyal had unwittingly been caught up in Great Game drama, for Tibet was teeming with the most fantastic reports of an impending joint invasion by the Russians from the north and British forces dispatched from Darjeeling. He recounts how 'fear and consternation' had taken possession of the country at that time, to the point that taxes in the form of gunpowder and ammunition were levied from every village. Fresh guards had been forwarded with orders to strengthen all the passes into Tibet, and every crossing into the country was reinforced to avoid surprise attack by their imagined enemies.

The Pundit was allowed to proceed on his journey, but under guard by a Tibetan escort, and that precluded any possibility of survey work. 'Seeing that we were now virtually prisoners in the hands of the Tibetan, and being apprehensive of ill treatment, we concerted a plan to escape, if possible, and so leaving all impedimenta behind in the tent, we rose at midnight on the 4th May, and leaving the bank of the [River] Yura Chhu, adopted an easterly direction.'[13] The Tibetan guards, being heavy drinkers, presumably lay heaped in a stupor round the fire and the party was thus able to make good its escape unnoticed. They made a dash for the Lhobrak, the next river along the trail, a tributary of the Tsangpo, and 'with difficulty' forded their way to the right bank, where they ensconced themselves to rest in the bush. In the few hours remaining before daybreak, they tore across the land at breakneck speed, covering 12 miles from the last resting place, over the Lhobrak Pass that rises from the river. Heavy rain and a sharp biting wind forced them to spend three days holed up in a cave, following which they eventually picked up the route that had been traversed by Nain Singh in 1874, on his journey from Ladakh. Namgyal was fearful of slackening his stride, knowing full well that, if they were captured, his Tibetan pursuers could be expected to show them no mercy. After a fierce nine-month trek through Bhutan and Tibet, the Pundit and his companions reached the Assamese town of Guwahati in British India on 31 May 1886, where in most un-Pundit-like style they boarded a steamer heading south along the Brahmaputra to the Bay of Bengal delta, travelling thence by rail back to Darjeeling.

Rinzin Namgyal's journey came to far more than a tale of encounters with hostile Tibetan officials. The explorer brought back a wealth of information that he was able to compile in Bhutan before his tumultuous race for freedom. He was able to furnish the Survey with its first detailed account of Bhutan's provinces, the rivers that flowed through each of them, as well as a breakdown of the number and names of the districts within each province. The Pundit also returned with a list of more than 150 topographical names, their transliterated spelling in Tibetan and the meaning of each. Thanks to this intrepid explorer, the Survey officers in Darjeeling learnt that the Tibetans had seven names for the Tsangpo, a fact that greatly helped to clear the confusion over unexplained references to the river. For instance, the enigmatic *Gnari Chhu* ('chhu' being the Tibetan word for both water and river) was actually the Tsangpo on its passing through the Tibetan province of Gnari. The *Chang Chhu* was the 'North River', or the Tsangpo close to its source in western Tibet, and so on.

And what of PA, Rinzin Namgyal's young apprentice Pundit, who was deputed to cross and survey the Jelap La, a place to which his master dared not venture for fear of being recognised? As instructed, PA successfully traversed the pass on the boundary between Sikkim and Tibet, en route to where he was astounded to find that the Tibetans, in their ill-informed paranoia, had erected a fort fully 20 miles inside Sikkimese territory, garrisoned by a detachment of one hundred soldiers to repel the expected British invasion. Six weeks later he and his guide found themselves under interrogation in a hut in Gechukha village, where the local residents regarded with deep suspicion the Pundit's story about travelling as a pilgrim in Tibet to visit some holy Buddhist shrines. PA was shunted back and forth several times from the village to the district governor's office to plead his case. After some anxious days of deliberation, the governor finally ruled that the Pundit should return unharmed whence he came, and to this end he sent him away with an escort of soldiers to ensure they carried on over the pass into Sikkim.

When they reached Damthang village at the foot of the pass the Tibetans were 'cajoled', as the official report states, almost certainly a euphemism for 'bribed', into leaving PA and his party to their own devices, on the promise that they would, on the following day, dutifully retrace their footsteps into British territory. After three days PA considered the coast sufficiently clear to retrace his steps, only the course he took was straight back into Tibet. His travels were bold, albeit inglorious, exploits that failed to deliver any major contribution to the Survey. The Pundit directed his assistant to reconnoitre a river junction and take bearings along a range running parallel to one of them, and that was about the extent of his surveying work. Apart from confirming that he joined Rinzin Namgyal as planned some three months after leaving Darjeeling, the code name PA vanishes for ever from the Survey's records.

Intelligence gathering is a craft requiring long hours of painstaking and often tedious work that bears little resemblance to the fast-moving James Bond world of espionage. It is a calling well suited to the crossword or jigsaw puzzle addict, or, as a former British intelligence agent once remarked: 'It is really about fitting different bits of coloured paper into their proper places.' The career of Pundit Hari Ram, one of the Survey of India's last great explorers, aptly matches that job description. Code-named MH, and also 'Number 9', Hari Ram, like the Singh clan, was a native of the rugged hill region of Kumaon that straddles the southern flanks of the Himalaya. 'All but one [Sarat Chandra Das] of the pundits came from the hills, which was considered vital if the new surveyors were to pass unobtrusively into Tibet.'[14] Over a period of fifteen years, from 1871 to 1886, the longest recorded tour of duty by a Pundit attached to the Survey, Hari Ram carried out three major explorations. With the findings he brought back from each of his voyages, small but vital new pieces of geographical data were slotted into the puzzle, opening up in the process 30,000 square miles of virtually unknown territory.

Following the well-trodden path of his predecessors, in July of 1871 Hari Ram braved the monsoon deluge to begin his journey from Darjeeling, crossing the Singalila ridge (now a popular tourist trekking route) to trace the footsteps of Sir William Hooker's 1848 expedition. The timing would mean a wet and uncomfortable start to the journey, but, as he was headed north to the Tibetan plateau, it was imperative for the Pundit to carry out his surveying tasks and return to India before the winter snows blocked the passes. Montgomerie had dispatched his explorer on this mission, among other tasks, to find out local names for some of the major Himalayan peaks along the route.

As far as the father of the Pundits was concerned, the journey proper did not begin for some 60 miles north of Darjeeling, at the Wallangehoon Pass, so named by Hooker from the village south of it, but commonly known as the Tipta Pass, 'as up to that point Sir William has already given us an admirable description of the country'.[15]

The Pundit crossed the main Himalayan axis by the 16,740-foot pass to reach the village of Tashirakha, where he came up against the customary detachment of sullen Tibetan border guards, who informed him that he would not be allowed to proceed. Hari Ram had been sent out disguised as a travelling physician, but the guards were not convinced by his story. As Montgomerie tells it: 'He was rather in despair, but was fortunate enough to ingratiate himself with the chief official of a large Sikkim district whose wife happened to be very ill. I have always made my explorers take a supply of medicines with them, mostly of native kinds, with only a few ordinary European sorts to present to people on their journeys.'[16] Lacking any medical training and with very little notion of when to administer the medicines he carried, Hari Ram examined the woman and then went away purportedly to consider her case and select the appropriate medication. The Pundit had had the foresight to scour the bookstalls of Darjeeling for a Hindu translation of a treatise explaining the use of these drugs. Taking his courage in both hands, he searched through his book until he came across a reference to a disease with the same symptoms exhibited by the village chieftain's wife. He then boldly prepared the native medicines according to the prescription and gave them to the poor woman, whose ailment was never explained. Hari Ram held his breath, for he knew that on the results of his medical experiment hung the success of his trip and even possibly his freedom. Fortunately, in a few days' time the woman's condition began to improve and eventually cleared up altogether, 'very much to the astonishment of the amateur practitioner'. The Tibetans were duly impressed, for the traveller was obviously every bit the physician he claimed to be. Under the patronage of the Sikkimese headman, who sent along one of his own men to vouch for the Pundit's bona fides at sensitive crossing points, Hari Ram was granted permission to proceed into Tibet. In spite of an anxious moment at the customs house, where his baggage was checked, the guards failed to uncover the surveying instruments that had been effectively concealed in false compartments.

The Tipta Pass in the first week of September was blanketed with an early covering of snow. This is a section of the Himalayan watershed that runs nearly east and west, forming the boundary between Nepal and Tibet. The ground was elevated, broken and barren, making for rough going, so that food and fuel had to be carried on yaks for the onward journey. After three marches the Pundit and his party arrived at Tinki Dzong, the latter being the Tibetan word for 'fortress'. Here his baggage was once again subjected to a thorough search, and it was only through the good offices of his Sikkimese companion that he was given the final entry pass exempting him from any further checks in Tibetan territory. It would appear that the guards either turned up some piece of suspicious equipment or were sceptical of the Pundit's story, but the Survey's unvarnished report states that 'it was only by means of the man sent by the Sikkim official' that after many enquiries Hari Ram was allowed to proceed to Shigatse. In this case 'means' was most probably a euphemism for the first of several bribes the Pundit would be required to distribute along the way.

Hari Ram continued taking latitude and thermometer readings on his route, and in fact the Survey of India map that was drawn from the Pundit's groundwork is dotted with nearly one hundred surveying points, fixing the location and altitude of peaks, river courses and village names, almost all of which had hitherto been unknown to the Survey officers. Hari Ram was able to report back valuable political intelligence as well, and this was worth its weight in gold for the Government of India, since whatever information was obtained from the forbidden Land of Snow was of a highly sketchy nature and usually came from merchants leading their caravans down from the high passes. The Pundit reached Shigatse on 17 September, and, after making an offering of two rupees to the monastery, he was granted an audience with the high lama. That was when he learnt of the upheaval that had taken place in Lhasa only five months before, in which hundreds of people had been killed in an uprising against the Dalai Lama. The rebellion was almost certainly inspired by the Chinese, who were, 135 years ago, just as they are today, in a state of acute paranoia about the Dalai Lama's political and spiritual influence over his homeland.

By the first week in October, with the autumn wind starting to bite in earnest, Hari Ram had covered more than 120 miles in a south-westerly direction to the village of Ting Ri, astride the river of the same name and close to the Tibet–Nepal border. It was now decision time, whether to carry on surveying this unexplored Tibetan region or to head for home before he was cut off by the winter snows. There were at best only a few precious days left in which he could count on a window in the weather, so accordingly the Pundit 'pushed on as fast as he could' toward the border and on 11 October he reached the town of Nilam, the last settlement before Nepal. His baggage was once more scrutinised, this time more closely than before, because of the proximity of the border crossing. Once across, there was hardly time to draw a breath of relief before Hari Ram was confronted with the most hair-raising ordeal of his entire journey. He marched due south, following the course of the Bhotia Kosi river for a distance of 25 miles, during which he had to cross the river fifteen times. At one place the river ran in a gigantic chasm, the sides of which were so close to one another that a bridge of twenty-four paces was sufficient to span it. Montgomerie recorded the full horror of this crossing:

Near this bridge the precipices were so impracticable that the path had of necessity to be supported on iron pegs let into the face of the rock, the path being formed by bars of iron and slabs of stone stretching from peg to peg and covered with earth. This extraordinary path is in no place more than eighteen inches and often not more than nine inches in width, and is carried for more than one third of a mile along the face of the cliff at some

1,500 feet above the river, which could be seen roaring below in its narrow bed. The explorer, who has seen much difficult ground in the Himalaya, says he never in his life met with anything to equal this bit of path.[17]

Hari Ram scored some noteworthy achievements on his first trans-Himalayan expedition. He presented the Survey with the first description of the lower reaches and source of the Kosi river that flows from the Tibet highlands due south into India. The Pundit's route survey afforded a rough but acceptably accurate idea of how the mountain drainage runs between the Himalayan watershed and several points south that had been crossed previously by British explorers. He had maintained a steady pace of 2.45 feet throughout his journey, 'about what might be expected from a man of his stature', so by applying this to the number of paces recorded, the Survey was able to determine the longitude of various sections along his route, taking in key spots such as Shigatse, Sakya monastery, Nilam and Kathmandu. Most intriguing of all his feats was Hari Ram's remarkable circuit of Mount Everest, the first recorded close exploration of the terrain surrounding what had already been identified in 1852 as the world's tallest mountain. Unfortunately, the Pundit was unable to present Montgomerie with the native name for the peak. On his trek through Tibet around the north side of Everest, he was unlikely to have come into contact with anyone educated enough to be familiar with the mountain's local name of Chomolungma, which translates as 'Mother Goddess of the World'. In Nepal, all snowy mountains are called *langur*, meaning simply 'the highest point'. It was not until many years later that the Nepalese devised an indigenous name for Everest, calling it Sagarmatha, a somewhat puzzling Sanskrit term for 'Brow of the Ocean'.

Hari Ram's route survey took him 844 miles across some of the world's most inhospitable terrain, of which 550 miles were over entirely new ground, while the remainder had never been regularly surveyed before. 'The exploration . . . elucidates the geography of the basin of the Arun or Arun Kosi river, the great eastern feeder, if not the main source of the great Kosi or Kosiki river, which drains the whole of eastern Nepal,' the Survey report says, summing up the Pundit's work. 'The courses of the upper feeders of the Arun have hitherto been a puzzle to geographers. The explorer's work also defines the course of the great western tributary of the Kosi river, that is the Bhotia Kosia of which we had previously no survey.'[18]

Montgomerie was so impressed by his Pundit's initial success that, after his return to India in late 1872, Hari Ram was sent out on a second reconnaissance mission the following year. The expedition did not start off under an auspicious sign, and Hari Ram's emotional distress at the time was a key factor behind its turning into a comparatively unproductive venture. After completing a few days' refresher course in spycraft at Survey headquarters in Dehra Dun, Hari Ram returned to Pithoragarh, his village in Kumaon, to make final preparations for his journey. It was May, traditionally the hottest, steamiest month of the year in the Indian subcontinent, when the mercury frequently soars above 110° F. In these conditions, an outbreak of cholera was almost a foregone conclusion, given the lack of clean drinking water and sewage treatment. What Hari Ram could not foresee was that, in the space of a few days, the disease was to carry off his wife and three other close family members, and lay him prostrate, hovering at death's door for two months.

On 1 July, having regained his strength if not his spirits, and with the worst of the summer heat behind, Hari Ram began his trek to Nepal, whose border lay 30 miles north-east of his village as the crow flies. His orders were to explore the extreme western territory of Nepal, a tract of *terra incognita* to the Survey's map-makers. About halfway to the border crossing, in the village of Askot, the Pundit made enquiries about the best place to cross the River Kali, which demarcates the boundary with India. His cover story, as on the previous journey, was that he was a physician, this time travelling on his way to Jumla, a hill settlement lying a little more than 100 miles to the east. As the ropes used for crossing at that point were put away to keep them from rotting in the monsoon rains, the Pundit was sent further up the river to Rathi village. There, to his chagrin, he was confronted with a primitive rope pulley system, by which the traveller hangs upside down with his legs gripping the rope to drag himself hand over hand across the river. Hari Ram confesses that he had 'no nerve for it' and so had a sling fashioned for himself, to be drawn across by villagers on the Nepalese side.

The Pundit's determination to see his job through was still strong when, two and a half months after leaving his village, he arrived at the Tibetan frontier post of Loh Mantang, a fortified town ruled over by a Raja, a Tibetan Bhotia who lived in a sumptuous four-storey manor house. 'The Raja was very much averse to my proceeding further, the order of Jang Bahadur [the King of Nepal] that no one should cross the frontier being very stringent,' Hari Ram reports in his expedition account. 'However, I was determined to proceed at all hazards and at last succeeded in procuring a pass.'[19] After being held up for a week, he made his way across the 15,080-foot Photu Pass on the border to reach Tradom, a small village on the Tsangpo of twelve houses, whose owners were employed as couriers for the Lhasa government, an unpaid job for which they were compensated by being exempted from taxes. The day after his arrival Hari Ram was summoned before the chief lama of the local monastery, who gave him a chilly reception and proceeded to interrogate the Pundit about the object of his travels. Hari Ram repeated his standard tale, that he was a physician on his way to Lhasa with a pocketful of papers authorising him to carry on in that direction. His story cut no ice with the dour lama, who in fact had every good reason to refuse him passage, since letting an impostor slip through the net would put his own life in peril. The Pundit was locked up for the night. In the morning, in spite of his pleas to see the lama, he was confronted by a messenger who informed him that the lama would not be granting another interview and that he was under orders to escort Hari Ram back across the border. A year earlier the lama's obstinacy would have been treated as a challenge. Now, Hari Ram, with the memory of his wife's death and his own debilitating illness still present in his mind, lost his combative spirit. The Pundit, in keeping with the tradition of his calling always to refuse to take no for an answer, 'with great reluctance and under threats of personal violence' started off on his return journey and reached Loh Mantang on 28 September. His five-month expedition was useful inasmuch as it helped to complete the topography of remote areas of western Nepal, and also yielded information on life and customs of the region. As the Pundit himself relates, after crossing the boundary into India: 'Though disappointed at my want of success in Tibet, I felt thankful that I had been able to return to British territory with such information as I had got together.'[20]

Twelve years were to pass before Hari Ram was called from retirement into the service of the Great Trigonometrical Survey of India. The enigmatic Himalayan kingdom to the north was reported to be in an unsettled state, and the Survey had a vested interest in expanding its knowledge of that country, strategically sandwiched between British India and Tibet, where Chinese and Russian influence was growing more entrenched. Nepal had been hit by a coup in which Jang Bahadur of Nepal's ruling Rana dynasty was ousted by one of the family's younger brothers, leading to a general insurrection throughout the country. On this occasion, his instructions were to take him along the Dudh Kosi, Nepal's principal river, following its course north for roughly 140 miles to Tingri in Tibet. His proposed route could be drawn as a large anticlockwise arc commencing from this point, skirting Kathmandu to head due south back into India. It was a hazardous journey, for apart from the usual obstacles of harsh terrain and extreme climate, Nepal was in a state of turmoil that rendered every foreign traveller a potential enemy in the eyes of frightened officialdom.

Hari Ram received his instructions in April 1885 and duly proceeded to Kumaon to engage the usual complement of porters and servants for what promised to be an extended journey. He was no longer the man who had boldly struck out for the hills nearly fifteen years earlier. His family tragedy and the debilitating effects of cholera had taken their toll on his health as well as his morale. Even before setting off on his expedition, the Pundit was laid low by illness twice, each time adding a full month's delay to the start of his journey. He adopted the disguise of a physician and was equipped with the standard supply of European and native medicines, as well as gifts to be parcelled out to local officials as required. He once again set off in the insalubrious month of July, hoping to be back in warmer climes ahead of the winter snows. Luck was not with him from the start, for a fortnight after leaving Kumaon he discovered that one of his vital boiling-point thermometers used for taking altitude measurements had been smashed, as a result of an awkward fall by one of his porters, who had been carrying the instrument concealed in a hollowed walking stick. This left Hari Ram with one small thermometer that was virtually useless for high-altitude measurements. The Survey officer in charge of the expedition was later to take an unforgiving view of this incident, reporting that 'the want of hypsometrical observations deprives his route of a place in the first rank of trans-frontier explorations . . . and had he reported this [the broken thermometer] by telegram a second one could easily have been sent. He however started with only the other boiling-point thermometer and it was not long before he had cause to regret his omission.'[21]

Hari Ram had other causes for regret even before attempting to take altitude readings. A few days after the incident of the smashed thermometer, the Pundit found himself a prisoner of the Nepalese army, after having wandered into a high-security area near a copper mine manned by 400 soldiers under the command of a captain who was not taken in by his medical credentials. The explorer was subjected to a close search and interrogation, and, when it emerged that he intended to travel northward into Tibet, he was ordered to return the way he had come, no questions asked. There Hari Ram languished, stuck in a dark and foul prison for six days until he managed to persuade the officer in charge to reconsider his story. This time he was able to make effective use of the 'gifts' the Survey had supplied, with the benefit of past experience, precisely for this type of emergency.

By early August the Pundit had reached the Khumbu district on the border of Tibet, the heartland of the Sherpa people and home of Mount Everest and other Himalayan giants. Hari Ram came up against the governor of the Khumbu district, or *dzong* as it is called in Tibetan, who at first refused the party permission to carry on up toward the frontier along its proposed route, which he alleged had never been traversed by any Indian or even Nepali traveller. The Pundit had expended too much energy and time at his last detention point to tolerate a second failed mission on the whim of some obstinate petty official. He took the bold decision to use his physician ploy to ingratiate himself with the governor: goitre was endemic in the locality, Hari Ram had by now acquired a reasonable knowledge of local ailments and the drugs required to treat them, thus he proceeded to administer medication (most probably an iodine-based remedy) to those villagers afflicted with the condition. One of his patients was the governor's daughter-in-law. Treating her would be a bit chancy, but the Pundit went ahead with the treatment and luckily he succeeded in reducing the swelling in her neck. This did the trick, for after six weeks' enforced delay the governor consented to granting the Pundit a pass to travel north, moreover in the company of his son Sonam Dorje, who was taking a trading expedition in the same direction.

It took them almost six hours of unforgiving slog up a heavily crevassed icefield, made all the more treacherous by a recent covering of snow, to reach the summit of the 20,000-foot Pangula Pass leading into Tibet. By early October he was back at Tingri, for the second time, only now he could report in greater detail on the town's primitive defences, the soldiers being armed with swords, matchlocks and bows and arrows. Hari Ram gives details of their drilling practice by Chinese officers, cavalry skills and marksmanship, all of which left him singularly unimpressed. The Pundit offers other bits and pieces of information on flora and fauna, and, most interestingly for the Government of India, on trading activity between Nepal and Tibet. Goods carried northward consisted mainly of Indian tobacco leaf, cotton cloth, iron, brass and copper vessels, corals and rupee coins that were sometimes used for making jewellery. The Sherpas of Khumbu made regular trips into India, sometimes as far as Calcutta, taking with them mostly animal products like yak tails, antelope horns and pheasants. Hari Ram entered into some hard negotiations with the headman of Tingri to secure permission to continue his journey by the proposed route that would take him to Jumla, some 240 miles north-west of Kathmandu, via the unexplored regions of Jonkha fort and Nubri. The Pundit managed to put forth a convincing case that he was an inhabitant of Jumla, and, in spite of protests that this road was absolutely closed to all but government officers, the headman eventually relented to let him pass.

By late January 1886, the explorer was back at Survey headquarters to be debriefed by his superiors. He had been held up twice more on the homeward route, and on each occasion his cover stories became more elaborate. At the hamlet of Arughat, where the party was detained for three days, Hari Ram concocted a tale that he had been all the way to Nubri, a forbidden area, in search of one of his dependants, who, he alleged, had run away from his home in Jumla with a large sum of money. He was sent on his way with a warning that, because of a recent insurrection in Kathmandu, he would most likely be stopped and interrogated several times along the way. On New Year's Eve they were held for five days at a fortress called Upardangarhi, with 25-foot-high loop-holed walls, and in view of the disturbed state of the country Hari Ram's arms, consisting of an ancient double-barrelled rifle and four Gurkha kukri knives, were confiscated.

Hari Ram's name cannot be emblazoned along with those of the Singh clan or Sarat Chandra Das as one of the Survey's great explorers. But his contribution was notable, in that the Pundit traversed 420 miles of unexplored territory, and, from a cartographic point of view, he was the first to trace the Dudh Kosi, Nepal's principal river, to its source. In a way, there was in him more of the classic spy than in his illustrious colleagues. With all his human weaknesses, his persistent, painstaking efforts filled in many of those bits and pieces in the puzzle that helped make it possible to view the big picture.

CHAPTER 8

Whither Flows the Tsangpo

Trisong Detsen was the greatest of all Tibetan kings. Foremost among the many enlightened acts credited to his reign in the eighth century AD was the establishment of Buddhism as the state religion. When his son was drowned in the Tsangpo, the monarch was so distraught with rage that he ordered his servants to stand by the river bank in the exact spot of the accident, and lash the water every day as punishment for its crime. One day the spirit of the river appeared before the king in the form of Brahmaputra, whose name in Sanskrit means 'the son of Brahma'. The deity beseeched the king to see that this was an unjust punishment, and to prove his case he told him to cast a small log into the river. When Trisong Detsen saw how the piece of wood was immediately carried off downstream on the swift current, he realised that the water responsible for the prince's death had passed long since. Clearly, the water suffering punishment was not to blame for the tragedy. The legend serves to illustrate the connection, at least linguistically, between the two great waterways. The common Tibetan name for the river, *Tsang-po*, meaning 'pure one', is closely linked to *Tsang-pu*, the literal Tibetan equivalent of the Sanskrit *Brahmaputra*.

The Tibetan scholar L. Augustine Waddell unearthed an indigenous work on the geography of Tibet in the late nineteenth century. It was a treatise written about three centuries previously in which the author, a learned lama, writes that the rivers of U-Tsang (Central and Western Tibet), on uniting, discharge into the Lohita or the Sita river. 'The Lohita is, of course, a classic Indian name for the Brahmaputra river. The Sita possibly is intended for Sadiya, as the Lamas often employ notoriously corrupt forms when dealing with hearsay foreign names, for the Lamaist author is unlikely to have confused it with the Sita river, one of the four great rivers of Hindu myth.'[1] The enigma of the Tsangpo–Brahmaputra connection had for centuries occupied the minds of travellers and scholars alike, many of whom clearly perceived from the earliest days that these two rivers were one and the same. The Survey of India in particular was expending a good deal of its resources on trying to establish the link between them, since one, the Brahmaputra, flowed for several hundred miles through British territory. The question was whether it was fed by another river that came down from a land whose doors were shut to the outside world. This was a matter of utmost importance to the Government of India. If it turned out that this river was navigable upstream for 1,800 miles from the Bay of Bengal to the roof of the world, a whole new route for transporting troops and goods into Tibet would be drawn on the map. The many years of exploratory work by the intrepid Pundits had brought into focus a much more detailed picture of the Tsangpo's course across the frozen Tibetan plateau. In spite of repeated attempts to bring this debate to a scientific conclusion, one nagging question remained a thorn in the Survey's side: at precisely what spot in the unexplored regions of lower Tibet were the two rivers joined? The other great unknown was how the mighty river forced its way through the Himalaya. Did it run under these mighty, snow-capped giants through a network of caverns, or was there any truth in the legend of the existence of a great waterfall, somewhere in the yawning gorges, that brought the river down to an altitude of below 9,600 feet, which had previously been its lowest recorded height? 'The gorge's innermost reaches, the deepest ten miles of canyon, where the river surges and foams between the adjacent peaks of Namche Barwa and Gyala Peri, had repelled every intruder, from the Pundits to the British intelligence officers Frederick Bailey and Henry Morshead, who surveyed the gorge in 1913. As they all discovered, there were no trails along this portion of the river, no villages, nothing except the Tsangpo hurtling into an apparently impassable void.'[2]

By the 1870s the Great Trigonometrical Survey was growing impatient over this river mystery. Did the Tsangpo flow into the Brahmaputra or the Irrawaddy, and, if the former, why had every attempt to penetrate the secret gorges ended in failure? In 1877, Captain R.G. Woodthorpe was put in charge of the North Brahmaputra Exploration Topographical Survey. He joined Lieutenant John Harman of the Survey to explore the courses of several rivers, or more accurately tributaries of the Brahmaputra, to determine if one of these might prove to be the elusive link to the Tsangpo. A year later, after crossing and re-crossing rivers by every conceivable method, including the terrifying experience of dragging themselves across, suspended from a rope a thousand feet above the water, the explorers returned with an accurate survey of the sources and the course of the Dibong and new knowledge of some 2,200 square miles of surrounding territory near Assam. Three new rivers were entered on the map, but Woodthorpe himself was forced to conclude that 'it will only be by a much more extended exploration than we were able to make that the much-vexed question of the course of the Tsangpo will be finally set at rest'.[3]

Nem Singh, a civil servant employed in Darjeeling by the Public Works Department, had a passion for languages. In his youth he developed fluency in Tibetan and several Indian languages, as well as his native Sikkimese. In his spare time, Nem Singh acted as part-time Tibetan instructor to Lieutenant Henry John

Harman of the Survey of India, who came to recognise in his tutor certain qualities that might be of use to the Survey. Harman was attached to the Survey's Darjeeling office, where he was in charge of recruiting native explorers. One day, Harman took Nem Singh into his confidence by informing him that the Survey wished to send an explorer on a mission into the wilds of Tibet. The objective was to trace the course of the Tsangpo as far as possible, in the hope of determining the place of its juncture with the Brahmaputra. Harman himself had been out to explore the region and found that even the dog they had taken along as expedition mascot had had to be carried through the dense wall of vegetation that concealed the river's course.

Nem Singh was a seasoned traveller with a keen taste for adventure, or so it seemed. He accordingly jumped at the opportunity to exchange a routine of filing reports on road repairs for the chance to serve as an explorer for the Great Trigonometrical Survey. The fledgling Pundit was packed off to Dehra Dun, where he was given the code name GMN and a crash course in surveying techniques. In early August 1878, the same year that Ugyen Gyatso was on his journey to the north, Nem Singh departed from Darjeeling with a small party of servants, among whom was a young, illiterate tailor's apprentice named Kintup. Following Harman's instructions, the explorer headed for Lake Yamdrok Tso, but he failed to execute a survey of the far shores of this strange body of water. Instead, he carried on toward Lhasa, stopping en route to study local monastery life, which, as it later emerged to the Survey's consternation, happened to be his supreme passion. 'He spent considerable time at Lhasa and at the monasteries around. He saw the great copper cauldrons in which rice and tea were prepared for the Lamas . . . He paid a visit to the bell foundry and saw large bells two feet high.'[4] In short, in less than two months Nem Singh was back in Darjeeling with little more to show for his efforts than a travelogue, a mission that in the words of the official report 'ended in air'. Harman kept some measure of faith in his fledgling Pundit and, partly as a face-saving gesture, Nem Singh was sent to Kumaon, where he

was put through a rigorous course of instruction by the great
Nain Singh himself. In October of the same year he was off again,
and this time his expedition met with a more creditable outcome.
The Pundit was able to determine a drop in the Tsangpo of 2,000
feet between the monastery town of Tsetang, where the river runs
50 miles south-east of Lhasa, and 250 miles east to a spot called
Gyala Sindong. This is where Nem Singh, daunted by the
impenetrable terrain that lay ahead, decided to turn round and
head for home. The Pundit returned to Darjeeling with a story
passed on to him by local natives that would appear to
substantiate the prevailing theory, that the great river eventually
enters a land 'ruled by the British', or Assam.

Once back in Darjeeling, the little troupe of Himalayan travellers
went their separate ways and few took notice of the young tailor's
apprentice, who was to be found the next day, sitting cross-legged
in a market stall by the Mall mending torn garments and
stitching together the loose-fitting shalwah kameeze worn by the
hill people of Bengal. Kintup was on the verge of slipping back
into his former humdrum existence, to be distinguished from the
rest of the market traders only by the handful of travellers' tales
he had to lavish on his friends around the card table in the
afternoon tea break.

Kintup went about his daily affairs blissfully unaware that
Captain Harman was working on a scheme that would again cut
short his tailor's apprenticeship. There was in Darjeeling at that
time a Mongolian lama whose name does not figure in the Survey
records, but who was evidently a trusted Government confidant,
for this priest was the man chosen to lead the next expedition to
the lower reaches of the Tsangpo. Kintup, who had no experience
of surveying techniques but did possess extensive knowledge of
the terrain to be traversed, was offered the opportunity to
accompany the lama on this voyage. 'The two men left Darjeeling
and crossed the northern frontier of Sikkim into Tibet in August,
1880. At Tso Lamo, a beautiful lake situated among immense
snow peaks at a height of 17,000 feet, they found the traders of

northern Sikkim exchanging merchandise with the people of Gyantse. The two travellers joined the latter in the guise of pilgrims and accompanied them to their home, whence they proceeded to Lhasa.'⁵ The Survey's two agents even carried *khurshings*, a type of cradle for a pack used by pilgrims, to make themselves less conspicuous to curious travellers and officials along the route. They reached Lhasa on the first day of September and should have marched straight on, as the mission did not call for spending time in the Tibetan capital, and each passing day brought nearer the cold winter weather. Kintup noticed with growing apprehension that the lama was starting to behave in a manner unbecoming a Pundit with a mission. He bade Kintup follow him to Sera, one of the great Buddhist monasteries of the Lhasa district, where he dipped into the Survey travelling allowance to feast his old companions for six days.

When Kintup finally persuaded the lama that it was time to be moving on, they travelled by river boat and eventually reached Tsetang, where Nem Singh had begun taking measurements of the drop in the Tsangpo on its eastward course to Gyala Sindong. They were forced to halt here for twenty days while the lama recovered from an illness, most likely induced by overindulgence. It was during this halt that Kintup began to suffer the lama's mistreatment in earnest. He was steadily driven into the role of servant, being sent out to cut grass for the lama's horse and given other menial chores, a role that in due course was to take on a much graver turn. 'But he bore all his bad treatment with patience fearing lest his position might become more troublesome if he resented it.'⁶ In other words, Kintup was trapped: with or without the abuse, the lama was his only guarantee of security, for without him Kintup was deprived of any legitimate cover for travelling in Tibet.

Roughly up to this point, the two men had been following Ugyen Gyatso's route, but at a point some 250 miles beyond Lhasa the river bends sharply in a north-easterly direction. Kintup was starting to make observations on his own account, as he had witnessed on his previous travels with the Survey's explorers. He noted that at Nang Dzong, at the junction with the trail south to the great holy site of Tsari, a stream issued from the interior of the village, flowing in a northerly direction to join the Tsangpo at a distance of 'five chains' (approximately 30 feet) from Nang Dzong, the river lying to the left of the village and flowing eastward. This was a typical scrap of ostensibly trivial information that was in fact gold dust for the Survey. From these bits of geographical data the Survey officers compiled a map of Kintup's later travels that proved to be remarkably accurate.

It was at this juncture that things began to crumble into disarray. Kintup realised he was facing the prospect of a miserably failed ending to the expedition, or worse, as the case was to prove. They spent the next few weeks tracing the Tsangpo's course toward Assam, sleeping in caves or wherever they could find a night's lodging, and begging for alms along the way, as was expected of pilgrims. They moved on to the settlement of Bumkyimgog, drawing closer to where the Tsangpo begins its great bend southward to join the Brahmaputra, when the lama began to show his true colours. After collecting some provisions for their onward journey into the unknown, the lama suddenly turned the party round to return to Thun Tsung, their last rest stop along the trail. The monk had decided that he had fallen in love with their host's wife. So there they remained, the lama wooing the poor peasant woman with his worldly charms, while not neglecting the household supply of frothy *chang*, the fermented barley beer that is the staple Tibetan drink. The result was that they wasted an infuriating four months of Survey time at this house, much to the bewilderment of the landlord, while the lama lavished his favours on the woman behind her husband's back.

As the lama sank deeper into drunkenness and debauchery, his companion Kintup, with his tiresome reminders about the task at hand, was turning into something of an encumbrance. One day the priest's romantic escapade came to an abrupt end, for the landlord had discovered the shenanigans that were taking place under his roof. Far from taking to his heels, the wily lama cut a deal with the husband, a poor farmer: a sum of twenty-five rupees would be paid in compensation for the inconvenience he had caused the couple, in exchange for the lama's quiet and unhindered departure. This arrangement proved satisfactory to the farmer. However, it was Kintup who was forced to dig into his own meagre pocket money to make good the bribe, for the lama had by now squandered the expedition's funds on gambling.

The lama and Kintup made their way eastward under a dark cloud, their mood not improved by the dense jungle they had to penetrate, which slowed their progress to 5 or 6 miles per day. They eventually came to the hamlet of Gyala, the last point reached by Nem Singh before he decided he could take no more of this desperate slog. The Tsangpo runs between the settlement and a monastery next to the tiny grouping of houses. Beyond this there is no path. The Tibetan authorities require all travellers to obtain a pass at Gyala before proceeding to the next stage, Pemaköchung, about 15 miles ahead.

On their way to Pemaköchung, Kintup and the lama had to hack their way up and down steep rock faces covered with jungle foliage. The lack of any human habitation along the way forced them to spend the night in a damp cave, where the lama's thoughts turned to the much more enticing prospect of a cup of *chang* by a warm fire. Kintup busied himself reconnoitring the terrain in the three days they spent at Pemaköchung, which consisted of a small monastery with seven or eight monks in residence, with not a sign of any other human settlement in the area. There was not even a forest path to take them beyond this forlorn spot, nothing but a barricade of solid jungle, and they therefore resolved to retrace their steps to Gyala. Before leaving, Kintup took a walk to the Tsangpo, where he came across a great waterfall about 150 feet in height. He spotted a big lake at the foot of the falls with rainbows playing on the water. It was probably this feature that fixed the falls so indelibly in his mind, and he never suspected the colossal impact this discovery was to have in India as well as in England on the great Tsangpo debate.

They returned over the pass at Gyala, and the two travellers crossed the Tsangpo to trek 70 miles upstream to a bridge near Tongjuk, where it was necessary to obtain yet another permit. The lama accompanied the guardian to the village that lay about a mile from the bridge. Kintup remained behind, using this solitary moment to hide the three compasses he carried as well as the pistol he had been given by the Survey, lest he be searched when the guard returned with the lama. In the event, he need not have hurried. The lama was away four days, leaving Kintup perched at this outpost by a river crossing. When the priest finally arrived, much refreshed, he ordered Kintup to collect their belongings and make for the house of the local Jongpen, who was to furnish them with sleeping quarters. The lama could turn on the charm for those he sought to use for his own ends, but in the case of the Jongpen it appeared that he had added a sweetener. On the first morning they spent at the Jongpen's residence, one of the official's servants entered the room and demanded that Kintup hand over his personal belongings to his master. The man seemed to know exactly what he was after, for he pointed to Kintup's bag and exclaimed: 'The Jongpen orders you to bring the things which you promised to give him.' A confused but defiant Kintup replied that he had not promised the Jongpen anything, and that moreover it would be impossible to give away what he was carrying for it was Government property. The servant flew into a rage and screamed into Kintup's face: 'Your duty is not to contradict but to obey.'[7] Whereupon he snatched the pistol and one compass from Kintup's bag and stormed out of the room. This incident was the signal for the curtain to rise on the last act of this sinister farce. The lama left Kintup in his room and went to pay a social call on the Jongpen. Once again Kintup was left alone, this time for eight days, to ponder the machinations taking place between the lama and the Jongpen. When at last the priest reappeared, it was to inform Kintup that he had been called away on 'urgent business' to Poyul, a monastery in eastern Tibet. He assured Kintup that he would return in two or three days' time. In the meantime, he instructed him to wait for him at the Jongpen's quarters.

That was the last Kintup saw of the lama. Two months passed, then another, during which Kintup learnt he was to take up 'temporary employment' at the Jongpen's residence stitching clothes, the one craft in which he excelled. As the days rolled by, Kintup began to suspect foul play, fearing that the lama had fled for good. He was of course right, and his suspicions were confirmed when, one morning as he was tending horses in the stable, Kintup found out from a fellow servant that he had been sold to the Jongpen as a slave. He then understood why the lama had departed in such haste, and also why the Jongpen refused to let him wander about outside the residence.

By March 1882, Kintup had had enough. For nearly twenty months, since they had left Darjeeling, the poor tailor's assistant had suffered bullying at the hands of the treacherous lama. This he had endured solely because the man was his appointed superior, sent to lead a mission as a trusted servant of the Great Trigonometrical Survey. But the alleged Pundit had turned out to be nothing but a drunk and a womaniser, and now a deserter. This final betrayal left too bitter a taste in his mouth for Kintup to accept the role of passive victim. He was 33 years old. It would not do for a man of his age, an employee of the Great Trigonometrical Survey of India, to be humiliated and mistreated by a lowly Tibetan district official.

It was now March, and, though bitterly cold, the days allowed a traveller to cross this region of Tibet without too great a risk of frostbite. It was on one of those nights that Kintup stole out of the Jongpen's compound and made a dash for the nearby village of Namding Phukpa, to beg provisions to sustain him while he fled into the jungle, racing to stay ahead of the Jongpen's men. But this journey was not to take him back to India, where one would have expected him to go. Instead, Kintup was determined to do justice to the officers of the Survey who had entrusted the lama with the task of tracing the course of the Tsangpo. If the lama had disgraced himself by absconding, it was up to Kintup to set an example of loyalty. He would take over the mission as a Pundit and finish the job. Moving eastward as fast as his legs could carry him, he came to another village, Po Trulung, a rest stop for travellers and traders. As Kintup was neither, he naturally provoked a lot of questions about his destination and the object of his journey.

He was becoming adept at the art of deception, for his story was that he was going to the Jongpen's house on an errand. If anyone had challenged Kintup further, he could have with no effort given chapter and verse of the location. 'Crossing back and forth along the lower Tsangpo on ropes of woven bamboo and almost perishing from hunger and cold, Kintup eventually reached a small *gompa*, or monastery, in the Pemakö district, known to the Tibetans as the "promised land", where fifteen priests and thirty nuns were allowed to live together.'[8] The monastery was in a settlement called Marpung, and Kintup had raced 93 miles to this spot, only to find the Jongpen's guards hot on his heels, even as he dashed, panting, up to the monastery gates. When he was let inside, he prostrated himself three times at the feet of the abbot, hurriedly explaining all that had happened at the Jongpen's house. The lama took pity on the miserable creature cowering at his feet and went outside to speak to the Jongpen's men. It took ten agonising days for the matter to be settled, with Kintup ever in danger of being snatched from the monastery and dragged back into slavery. But at last a letter came from the Jongpen saying he would accept payment of fifty rupees for releasing Kintup from bondage. The abbot paid up and Kintup's pursuers returned home.

Kintup spent four and a half months as the abbot's servant, performing menial chores around the monastery and, of course, mending the monks' robes. Now it was time to get on with his mission, and Kintup knew what had to be done, for he had been present when Captain Harman explained the procedure in detail to the traitorous lama. The task was to cut 500 logs, each 1 foot long, with a distinguishing mark that would make them recognisable to the Survey officer in charge. The plan was ingenious in its simplicity, and it was foolproof. Once the Pundit had travelled as far south as he could along the banks of the

Tsangpo, he would cut the logs and send a letter through to Captain Harman in Darjeeling, informing him that the logs were shortly to be released, fifty each day, into the river. If they were sighted passing a predetermined spot on the Brahmaputra, the mystery of the Tsangpo was solved, for the two rivers obviously met somewhere in the deep gorges that no explorer had yet been able to penetrate.

Kintup begged the lama to grant him leave, on the pretence of going on a pilgrimage. This was the guise he had originally used when he sought sanctuary at the monastery – convincingly, it would appear, for the abbot granted Kintup his wish. Fired with enthusiasm for the chance to carry out a prestigious Survey mission, the Pundit journeyed 15 miles north-eastward through the jungle to Giling, a monastery that presides over a village of some fifty houses, where he stayed for five days on the pretext of gathering salt found on the nearby flats. Working furtively, he spent his time hacking away with his Gurkha kukri at saplings and branches until he had fashioned 500 logs of the correct size. Before leaving Darjeeling, the lama had been supplied with an instrument for boring holes in wood and a supply of small tin tubes, each containing a written paper. The plan was for a tube to be inserted into each of the logs. Kintup had either lost the drill or never had it in his possession, and as the strips of paper were of no use to the illiterate tailor's assistant, he decided to strap the tin tubes to the logs with bamboo when the time came for them to be released into the water. He then carried the logs, tied in bundles, on his back and hid them 'in a deep cave where no human foot had yet trodden'.[9] Kintup had been gone from Marpung for more than a month, so to ensure good relations with his benefactor, he returned to the monastery for a further two months before requesting permission to go on another pilgrimage, this time to visit the holy shrine of Tsari.

But Kintup did not go to Tsari. Instead he marched westward, on the arduous 250-mile trek back to Lhasa. Travelling by road and boat, he reached the Tibetan capital after the usual interrogations along the way, in which he was by now becoming something of an expert. His standard story was that he was on a pilgrimage to whichever place happened to be his destination at the time, in this case Lhasa. Kintup spent three days resting at Ramoche monastery outside the city. Luck was with him, for he did not have to search for long before he came across a Sikkimese *kazi*, or district official, whom Kintup persuaded to write a letter to the Survey on the Pundit's behalf. The letter, overflowing with pathos and innocence, was addressed to 'The Chief of the Survey of India':

> Sir: The Lama who was sent with me sold me to a Jongpen as a slave and himself fled away with the Government things that were in his charge, on account of which the journey proved a bad one. However I, Kintup, have prepared the five hundred logs according to the order of the late Captain Harman (the records fail to explain how Kintup knew that Harman was dead) and am prepared to throw fifty logs per day into the Tsangpo from Bipung in Pemakö, from the 5th to the 15th of the tenth Tibetan month of the year called *Chhuluk*, of the Tibetan calculation.[10]

The *kazi*'s wife was about to set off for Darjeeling on a family visit, so she was given the letter to deliver to one *Nimsring*, a misspelt version of Nem Singh, the Pundit who was now employed as government translator.

Kintup took his leave of the Sikkimese dignitary and prepared to retrace his steps, albeit via China, to the cave at Bipung where he had stashed his logs, there to perform the final act of what was to be Kintup's tragic debut as a Pundit. First, he felt obliged to discharge his duty to the abbot of Marpung monastery, who had shown him so much kindness. He carried on working at the monastery for nearly nine months, which was well within the timeframe he had allotted for dispatching the logs. At the end of this period, the lama told Kintup that he was so pleased with his reverence for holy places that from that day he was no longer considered a servant of the monastery and was free to go anywhere he liked. Kintup prostrated himself thrice before the abbot, as he had done when the lama rescued him from the Jongpen's soldiers. He spent the next month stitching clothes for a local farmer in order to collect enough provisions to see him back to Darjeeling. Then he was ready.

The shabby figure, clad in tattered sheepskin tunic and worn felt boots, crouched with his gaze fixed on the swiftly flowing current . . . Kintup spent the designated ten days by the river bank, taking care to avoid being observed by passing traders and pilgrims as, one by one, the specially marked logs were flung into the water. Once the job was done, the Pundit began to follow the Tsangpo downstream in a light-hearted mood, expecting to be across the border into Assam, in British India, within a few weeks. The path he took led to the territories of the tribes collectively known as Abors, a particularly fierce people with whom British explorers had experienced some nasty encounters. Kintup witnessed in the Abor country scenes he had never imagined possible, of naked people who ate snakes, tigers, leopards and bears. At one point he was taken prisoner and only managed to walk free thanks to the money he had earned working as a tailor, having to pay '306 anna coins' to his captors. Whenever he was lucky enough to find shelter for the night in a native hut, he was obliged to pay a handful of salt to every man and woman in the house. Moving among the Abors was becoming too risky for comfort, so when the Pundit got to the village of Damro, which he reckoned was only 35 miles from the Indian border, he took the painful decision to turn round and once again make for Lhasa, thence to follow a safe route back to his native Sikkim.

Kintup walked into his ancestral hilltop village of Tashiding, in West Sikkim, three months later and was greeted with the sad news that his mother had died during his travels abroad. Moreover, his family had long since assumed the Pundit had suffered the same fate on his wanderings. Finally, on 17 November 1884, after four years and three months away, the humble tailor's assistant made what he envisaged would be a triumphal entry into Darjeeling, only to be dealt the most bitter disappointment of his life. The supreme irony of all his years of tribulations, enduring the lama's brutality and the months of slavery, was that the *kazi*'s wife had reached Darjeeling much later than planned. By that time Captain Harman was dead, and the letter was delivered to Nem Singh well beyond the date on which Kintup had said he would cast the logs into the river. This being so, the letter had not been handed over to the Survey officer in charge and the logs, all 500 of them, had drifted unseen into the Bay of Bengal.

The Pundit's report was filed away and left almost forgotten for nearly thirty years, until in 1911 the British had cause to take an interest in the Abor country, where the savage tribe was causing trouble. Kintup's reports were dusted off and studied, as they were the only sources of information in existence on the tribesmen. The Pundit's story was eventually to shake the world of geography to its foundations. Had the illiterate Kintup, whose oral report was translated by Nem Singh, solved the mystery of the Tsangpo?

'On his arrival in India his story was doubted,' recalls Colonel Bailey, following his own expedition into the Tsangpo gorges. 'He was, of course, paid his bare wage, but no special rewards were given to him.' Bailey adds: 'It happened that a couple of years later the late Captain Morshead, of the Survey of India, and I were given the opportunity to follow in Kintup's footsteps. It was found that the whole story was remarkably accurate. The educated mind relies on the written word – we even make lists of our daily trivial duties. The uneducated mind retains a far surer memory.'[11]

At roughly the time of Bailey's writing, the Survey officer Sir Thomas Holdich wrote a paper for the *Journal of the Royal Geographical Society* in support of Kintup's discoveries.

Certain marked logs were put into the Tsangpo by him [Kintup] which were to float down to the Brahmaputra. I have always understood that they *did* reach the Brahmaputra and were identified. If so, it is a little difficult to see how they failed to follow a continuous stream. I think we must say that we have known now for the last twenty-five years that the Tsangpo and the Brahmaputra are one and the same river, and the credit of that discovery distinctly belongs to Kintup.[12]

Captain G.F.T. Oakes of the Survey added his authoritative endorsement of Kintup's remarkable findings. 'For many years the explorations of Kintup . . . have been received with scepticism by many owing to the romantic nature of his experiences.' Oakes points out the crucial factor that Kintup's narrative was dictated to a translator, and, curiously, he claims that it was Ugyen Gyatso and not Nem Singh who was responsible for the transcription, but that is not material to the story. 'All his names east of Tsetang, nearly one hundred and fifty in number, have now been identified, with the exception of about twenty which include many caves and camps and villages probably since abandoned.' Oakes admits that Kintup's sighting of a giant waterfall on the Tsangpo was an erroneous observation, a mistake he attributes to confusion in the dictation and translation of the story, in which the Tsangpo falls were mistaken for another, 150-foot waterfall, that in fact does exist nearby on a smaller stream that joins the Tsangpo opposite the village of Gyala. Finally, Oakes pays tribute to Kintup's heroic determination to press on against all odds. 'After the explorer [the Mongolian lama] had absconded and he [Kintup] had with difficulty escaped from slavery, that he should have continued the exploration shows the greatest pluck and perseverance and very rightly have his experiences been described as a romance of the Survey of India.'[13]

Kintup went back to earning his living as a tailor and spent years eking out a meagre existence in a Darjeeling shop. Colonel Bailey hunted him down in that town in 1913 and listened in fascination as the Pundit recounted his adventures in detail, including the fact that he never claimed to have seen the falls on the Tsangpo itself, but rather on the tributary, where they actually stand. Bailey and others prevailed upon the Government to reward Kintup for his years of service so that he could live out his remaining days in comfort. This was done the following year, when Kintup, aged 65, was granted a payment of 1,000 rupees, a considerable sum in those days. It was left to another great adventurer, the colourful British plant hunter Francis Kingdon-Ward, to confirm the linkage between the two rivers on his 1924 expedition into the hidden gorge of the Tsangpo. Kingdon-Ward, along with his travelling companion, the 24-year-old Scottish earl John Cawdor, set out from London with six cases of jam, chocolate, tea and other provisions from Fortnum & Mason. After months of hardship, the two explorers reached a point from which almost the entire gorge was visible, with the exception of a 5-mile stretch so dark and narrow that it seemed to disappear into the profoundest depths of the Earth. Nevertheless, in 1924 the riddle of the Tsangpo was pronounced solved. By that time, Kintup was ten years in his grave.

Kalian Singh's travels to gold fields in central Tibet in 1894, a mission of relatively little geographical importance, more or less brought to a close a period of some thirty years of daring trans-Himalayan survey work by native explorers. The Anglo-Russian Convention secretly signed in St Petersburg in 1907, under which the imperial powers agreed to respect one another's strategic interests in Central Asia, formally signalled the close of the Great Game. The work of the Pundits was at an end, although their legacy could serve as an example to Western intelligence agencies confronting a threat as alien and mysterious to us today, as was Tibet 150 years ago. The terrorists who in the space of less than four years killed thousands of innocent people through spectacular attacks on countries like the United States, Spain and Britain cannot be rooted out and defeated by satellites capable of reading automobile number plates or by B-52 bombers. What is required is a 'back-to-basics' strategy, along the lines of the straightforward undercover work of the Pundits. It is a tragic irony that, in the aftermath of the 11 September 2001 strikes on the World Trade Center and the Pentagon, the FBI had to put out an urgent public call for fluent speakers of Arabic, Persian and Pashtu. Prior to that date, the FBI wanted to tap the telephone conversations of several Taliban officials in New York, but lacked translators. It tried to borrow some from the Pentagon, which has its own language school – however, security clearances could not be arranged in time. The FBI then turned to the CIA, which also failed to find translators for these languages.

> Brave individuals, fluent in difficult languages and able to pass as native members of other cultures, will have to befriend and win acceptance by their own societies' enemies [suggests one military historian]. The challenge will cast the agencies back on to methods which have come to appear outdated, even primitive, in an age of satellite surveillance and computer decryption. Kipling's Kim, who has survived into modern times only as the delightful literary creation of a master novelist, may come to provide a model of the anti-fundamentalist agent, with his ability to shed his European identity and to pass convincingly as Muslim message-carrier, Hindu gallant and Buddhist holy man's hanger-on, far superior to any holder of a PhD in higher mathematics.[14]

There remains the intriguing question of why they did it. Kintup would have been easily forgiven had he made straight for home after his escape from the wicked Jongpen. Indeed, it came as a great shock to the Survey officers in Darjeeling, who had given him up for lost, to learn that, travelling alone and penniless, the Pundit had valiantly pressed on with the Tsangpo mission. Why? They were certainly not in it for the money. Chandra Das's running battle with the Survey over financing for his missions highlights the paltry material rewards these agents could expect from their spymasters, and the shoddy treatment accorded Kintup by the Survey bean-counters was truly deplorable. If not fortune, then fame? Hardly. Apart from the Royal Geographical Society gold medallist Nain Singh, the honorary Indian title of Rai Bahadur bestowed on Ugyen Gyatso and the literary acclaim earned by Chandra Das (who was in any event destined to excel in the academic world), the Pundits ranked as unsung heroes in the classic sense of the word. There is the love of adventure and risk. The Pundits undoubtedly found excitement in the prospect of journeying abroad and in disguise on a spy mission for a mighty imperial power. As Kipling's shopkeeper-cum-agent Lurgan Sahib counsels the young spy Kim: 'The pay is the least part of the work. From time to time, God causes men to be born – and thou art one of them – who have a lust to go abroad at the risk of their lives and discover news – today it may be far-off things, tomorrow of some hidden mountain, and the next day of some nearby men who have done a foolishness against the state. These souls are very few, and of these few, not more than ten are of the best.'[15] But risking one's neck on a dangerous undertaking, with no hope of coming home to some form of public recognition, is alien to the nature of the adventurer. Would anyone set out to be the first to reach the South Pole or to climb Mount Everest, if in the end the endeavour were to go unreported to the world at large? An adventurous spirit alone was not the driving force. Are we perhaps dealing with some 'special breed', set apart from ordinary men by a shared tradition of toughing it out in the face of hardship and adversity? Hardly so, when one considers the Pundits' disparate origins: a village school headmaster from the hills of Kumaon, a Bengali engineering graduate, a Sikkimese Buddhist monk, an illiterate tailor's assistant from Darjeeling. Surely there was some other motivation urging these men on against all odds, and the answer might be found in the concepts of service and duty, uncomfortable terms in today's lexicon. But the Indians of a century and a half ago were quite comfortable with the idea of devoting one's life to the service of others. Indeed, there was great merit associated with performing an act of service with full devotion and determination, and seeing it through to the end. Each of the Pundits held a special dedication to duty. It was through this selfless loyalty that they earned merit, as well as the gratitude of the Great Trigonometrical Survey of India.

Notes

Chapter 1. To Tibet with a Cross

1. Cornelius Wessels, *Early Jesuit Travellers in Central Asia* (The Hague, Martinus Nijhoff, 1924), p. 39.
2. *Ibid.*, p. 13.
3. *Ibid.*, p. 56.
4. OIOC W6971, James Walker, *The Great Trigonometrical Survey of India*, vol. 1 (Dehra Dun, Survey of India Printing Group, 1870), p. 34.
5. Clements Markham, *A Memoir on the Indian Surveys* (London, W.H. Allen & Co., 1871), p. 63.
6. *Ibid.*, p. 94.
7. *Ibid.*, p. 35.
8. *Ibid.*, p. 36.
9. George Woodcock, *Into Tibet* (London, Faber & Faber, 1971), p. 32.
10. *Ibid.*, p. 51.
11. *Ibid.*, p. 39.
12. *Ibid.*, p. 76.
13. *Ibid.*, p. 188.

Chapter 2. Mad Amirs and Englishmen

1. William Moorcroft, *Travels in the Himalayan Provinces of Hindustan and the Punjab*, ed. Horace Hayman Wilson (London, John Murray, 1841), vol. 1, p. 1.
2. William Moorcroft, *Observations on the Breeding of Horses* (Simla, Government Central Branch Press, 1886), p. 9.
3. Mountstuart Elphinstone, *An Account of the Kingdom of Caubul* (1815; repr. Karachi, Indus Publications, 1992), p. 1.
4. Moorcroft, *Travels*, vol. 1, p. 2.

5. *Ibid.*, vol. 2, p. 508.
6. Alastair Lamb, *Britain and Chinese Central Asia* (London, Routledge & Kegan Paul, 1960), p. 39.
7. Garry Alder, *Beyond Bokhara* (London, Century Publishing, 1985), p. 114.
8. *Ibid.*, p. 136.
9. OIOC Records, F/4/421, Journey of Mr Moorcroft, the Superintendent of the Stud, into Tartary, 15 June 1813.
10. *Ibid.*
11. OIOC, Moorcroft correspondence, Letter from Moorcroft to John Adam, Secretary to Government, December 1812.
12. Alder, *Beyond Bokhara*, p. 123.
13. *Ibid.*, p. 124.
14. Mir Izzat Ullah, *Travels in Central Asia* (Calcutta, Foreign Department Press, 1872), p. 65.
15. *Ibid.*, p. 16.
16. *Ibid.*, p. 11.
17. *Ibid.*, p. 13.
18. Francis Watson, 'A Pioneer in the Himalayas: William Moorcroft', *Geographical Magazine*, vol. 32 (1959), p. 214.
19. Alder, *Beyond Bokhara*, p. 334.
20. OIOC Records, F/4/1038, 3 March 1826.
21. OIOC Records, E/4/725, 1829, p. 379.
22. OIOC Records, F/4/1028, 28165, pp. 1–5.
23. Peter Hopkirk, *The Great Game* (London, John Murray, 1990), p. 104.
24. *Ibid.*, p. 129.
25. OIOC Records, F/4/1835/55181, pp. 35–54.
26. OIOC Records, F/4/1835/55182, official letters.
27. *Ibid.*
28. *Ibid.*
29. Anthony Wynn, *Persia in the Great Game* (London, John Murray, 2003), p. 137.
30. *Ibid.*, p. 12.
31. Reginald Henry Phillimore, *Historical Records of the Survey of India* (Dehra Dun, Survey of India Printing Group, 1968), vol. 5, pp. 144–7.

Chapter 3. Enter the Pundit

1. Henry Yule and A.C. Burnell, *Hobson-Jobson* (1886; Ware, Wordsworth, 1996), p. 740.

2. Thomas George Montgomerie, 'Report on the Mirza's Exploration from Kabul to Kashgar', *Journal of the Royal Geographical Society*, 41 (1871), p. 152.

3. *Records of the Survey of India*, vol. 8, part 1, pp. 158–9.

4. *Ibid.*, pp. 226–8.

5. Rudyard Kipling, *Kim* (1901; London, Penguin, 1994), p. 216.

6. Thomas George Montgomerie, *Report on the Trans-Himalayan Explorations* (Dehra Dun, Survey of India Printing Group, 1867), p. 1.

7. Kipling, *Kim*, p. 267.

8. Montgomerie, *Report*, p. 1.

9. *Ibid.*, p. 2.

10. *Ibid.*, pp. 8–12.

11. *Ibid.*, p. 15.

12. Herodotus, *The Histories*, Penguin Classics (London, Penguin, 2003), p. 215.

13. Thomas George Montgomerie, 'Report on the Trans-Himalayan Explorations Made during 1868', *Proceedings of the Royal Geographical Society* (April 1869), p. 193.

14. Markham, *Memoir*, p. 162.

15. *Ibid.*, p. 165.

16. *Ibid.*

Chapter 4. All in the Family

1. Gen. James Walker, 'Four Years' Journeying through Great Tibet', *Proceedings of the Royal Geographical Society* (February 1885), p. 65.

2. Kipling, *Kim*, p. 40.

3. Indra Singh Rawat, *Indian Explorers of the 19th Century* (New Delhi, Ministry of Information and Broadcasting, 1973), p. 85.

4. *Ibid.*, p. 74.

5. Walker, 'Four Years' Journeying', p. 76.

6. *Ibid.*, p. 77.

7. *Ibid.*, pp. 77–8.

8. *Ibid.*, p. 82.

9. *Ibid.*, p. 91.

10. *Ibid.*

Chapter 5. Spies of the Wild Frontier

1. Thomas George Montgomerie, 'On the Geographical Position of Yarkand', *Journal of the Royal Geographical Society*, 36 (1866), p. 157.
2. Algernon Durand, *The Making of a Frontier* (1899; Karachi, Oxford University Press, 2001), p. 2.
3. Kipling, *Kim*, p. 226.
4. Phillimore, *Historical Records of the Survey of India*, vol. 5, p. 447.
5. James Thomas Walker, *General Report on the Operations of the GTS of India during 1869–70* (Dehra Dun, Survey of India Printing Group, 1871), p. 56.
6. George Hayward, 'Journey from Leh to Yarkand and Kashgar, and Exploration of the Sources of the Yarkand River', *Journal of the Royal Geographical Society*, 40 (1870), p. 51.
7. Montgomerie, 'Report on the Mirza's Exploration', p. 174.
8. Kenneth Mason, 'Kishen Singh and the Indian Explorers', *Geographical Journal*, 62 (1923), p. 434.
9. John Keay, *Explorers of the Western Himalayas* (London, John Murray, 1996), p. 8.
10. Thomas George Montgomerie, 'A Havildar's Journey through Chitral to Faizabad', *Journal of the Royal Geographical Society*, 42 (1872), p. 185.
11. *Ibid.*, p. 187.
12. *Ibid.*, p. 191.
13. 'Obituary of The Havildar', *Proceedings of the Royal Geographical Society*, NS 1 (1879), pp. 600–1.
14. Mason, 'Kishen Singh', p. 434.
15. Henry Trotter, *Trans-Himalayan Explorations 1873–75* (Calcutta, Government Printing Office, 1876), p. 37.

Chapter 6. A Learned Man of Chittagong

1. Lawrence James, *Raj, the Making of British India* (1997; London, Abacus, 2003), p. 379.
2. Charles Allen, *The Buddha and the Sahibs* (London, John Murray, 2002), p. 165.
3. Sarat Chandra Das, 'Narrative of the Incidents of my Early Life', *Modern Review* (December–January 1908), p. 1.

4. *Ibid.*
5. *Ibid.*, p. 5.
6. *Ibid.*, p. 6.
7. *Ibid.*, p. 9.
8. *Ibid.*
9. *Ibid.*, p. 10.
10. *Ibid.*, p. 15.
11. Amar Kaur Jaspir Singh, *Himalayan Triangle* (London, British Library, 1988), p. 205.
12. Chandra Das, 'Narrative of the Incidents', p. 2.
13. *Ibid.*, pp. 2–3.
14. Sarat Chandra Das, *Narrative of a Journey to Lhasa, 1881–82* (Calcutta, Bengal Secretariat Press, 1885), p. 34.
15. *Ibid.*, p. 11.
16. *Ibid.*
17. *Ibid.*, p. 51.
18. Graham Sandberg, *The Exploration of Tibet* (1904; repr. Delhi, Cosmo Publications, 1987), p. 169.
19. *Ibid.*, p. 153.
20. Royal Geographical Society, *Private Correspondence*, 1893.
21. Nayan Prakash Subba, 'Spying in Lhasa', *The Statesman*, Calcutta, 2 May 2005, p. 15.
22. *The Times*, London, 31 July 1904.
23. Allen, *Buddha and the Sahibs*, p. 286.

Chapter 7. The Holy Spy

1. OIOC, *Records of the Survey of India*, Report by Thomas Holdich, vol. 8, part 2, p. 18.
2. *Ibid.*, p. 20.
3. *Ibid.*, p. 21.
4. *Ibid.*, p. 33.
5. *Ibid.*, p. 37.
6. Henry Ravenshaw Thuillier, *Report on the Explorations of [Five Pundits]* (Dehra Dun, Survey of India Printing Group, 1889), p. 3.
7. *Ibid.*, p. 3.
8. P.L. Madan, *Tibet: Saga of Indian Explorers* (New Delhi, Manohar Publishers, 2004), p. 63.

9. TNA: PRO FO65/1347, Russia Proceedings in Central Asia.
10. TNA: PRO HD2, The Great Game Meshed, pp. 1–2.
11. Thuillier, *Report on the Explorations of [Five Pundits]*, p. 37.
12. *Ibid.*, p. 50.
13. *Ibid.*, p. 51.
14. Ian Barrow, *Making History, Drawing Territory* (New Delhi, Oxford University Press, 2003), p. 138.
15. *Records of the Survey of India*, vol. 8, part 1, p. 116.
16. *Ibid.*
17. *Ibid.*, p. 118.
18. *Ibid.*, p. 120.
19. *Ibid.*, p. 145.
20. *Ibid.*, p. 147.
21. *Ibid.*, p. 384.

Chapter 8. Whither Flows the Tsangpo

1. L. Augustine Waddell, 'The Falls of the Tsangpo', *Geographical Journal*, 5 (1895), p. 260.
2. Michael McRae, *In Search of Shangri-La* (London, Penguin, 2004), p. 5.
3. OIOC V/24/3976, R.G. Woodthorpe, *Operations of the Survey of India, 1877–9*, p. 125.
4. Rawat, *Indian Explorers*, p. 177.
5. Frederick M. Bailey, 'The Story of Kintup', *Geographical Magazine*, 15 (1943), p. 427.
6. *Records of the Survey of India*, vol. 8, part 2, p. 329.
7. *Ibid.*, p. 333.
8. Ian Baker, *The Heart of the World* (New York, Penguin, 2004), p. 44.
9. *Records of the Survey of India*, vol. 8, part 1, p. 334.
10. *Ibid.*, p. 336.
11. Bailey, 'The Story of Kintup', p. 430.
12. Arthur Bentnick, 'The Abor Expedition: Geographical Results', *Geographical Journal*, 41 (1913), p. 113.
13. *Records of the Survey of India*, vol. 8, part 1, p. 173.
14. John Keegan, *Intelligence in War* (London, Pimlico, 2004), pp. 362–3.
15. Kipling, *Kim*, p. 215.

Bibliography

Primary Sources

British Library, Oriental and India Office Collection (OIOC)

OIOC, Moorcroft correspondence, Letter from Moorcroft to John Adam, Secretary to Government, December 1812

OIOC Records, E/4/725, 1829

OIOC Records, F/4/1028, 28165

OIOC Records, F/4/1038, 3 March 1826

OIOC Records, F/4/1835/55181

OIOC Records, F/4/1835/55182

OIOC Records, F/4/421, Journey of Mr Moorcroft, the Superintendent of the Stud, into Tartary, 1813

OIOC *Records of the Survey of India*, vol. 8, parts 1 and 2, 1915

OIOC V/24/3976, R.G. Woodthorpe, *Operations of the Survey of India*, 1877–8

OIOC W6971, James Walker, *The Great Trigonometrical Survey of India*, vol. 1 (Dehra Dun, Survey of India Printing Group, 1870)

The National Archives: Public Record Office (TNA: PRO)

TNA: PRO FO65/1347, Russia Proceedings in Central Asia

TNA: PRO HD2, The Great Game Meshed

Reports

Bailey, Frederick M., 'The Story of Kintup', *Geographical Magazine*, 15 (1943), 426–31

Chandra Das, Sarat, *Narrative of a Journey to Lhasa, 1881–82* (Calcutta, Bengal Secretariat Press, 1885)

Chandra Das, Sarat, 'Narrative of the Incidents of my Early Life', *Modern Review* (December—January 1908), 1–16

Hayward, George, 'Journey from Leh to Yarkand and Kashgar, and Exploration of the Sources of the Yarkand River', *Journal of the Royal Geographical Society*, 40 (1870), 51

Izzat Allah, Mir, *Travels in Central Asia* (Calcutta, Foreign Department Press, 1872)

Mason, Kenneth, 'Kishen Singh and the Indian Explorers', *Geographical Journal*, 62 (1923), 429–40

Montgomerie, Thomas George, 'On the Geographical Position of Yarkand', *Journal of the Royal Geographical Society*, 36 (1866), 157

Montgomerie, Thomas George, *Report on the Trans-Himalayan Explorations* (Dehra Dun, Survey of India Printing Group, 1867)

Montgomerie, Thomas George, 'Report on the Trans-Himalayan Explorations Made during 1868', *Proceedings of the Royal Geographical Society* (April 1869), 207–14

Montgomerie, Thomas George, 'Report on the Mirza's Exploration from Kabul to Kashgar', *Journal of the Royal Geographical Society*, 41 (1871), 152–83

Montgomerie, Thomas George, 'A Havildar's Journey through Chitral to Faizabad', *Journal of the Royal Geographical Society*, 42 (1872), 180–99

Moorcroft, William, *Observations on the Breeding of Horses* (Simla, Government Central Branch Press, 1886)

'Obituary of The Havildar', *Proceedings of the Royal Geographical Society*, NS 1 (1879), 600–1

Phillimore, Reginald Henry, *Historical Records of the Survey of India*, 5 vols (Dehra Dun, Survey of India Printing Group, 1968)

Playdell-Bouverie, Jasper, 'On a Wheel and a Prayer', *Geographical Magazine* (May 1992), 12–15

Royal Geographical Society, Private Correspondence, 1893

Subba, Nayan Prakash, 'Spying in Lhasa', *The Statesman*, Calcutta, 2 May 2005, p. 15

Thuillier, Henry Ravenshaw, *Report on the Explorations of [Five Pundits]* (Dehra Dun, Survey of India Printing Group, 1889)

The Times (London), 31 July 1904

Trotter, Henry, *Trans-Himalayan Explorations, 1873–75* (Calcutta, Government Printing Office, 1876)

Waddell, L. Augustine, 'The Falls of the Tsangpo', *Geographical Journal*, 5 (1895), 258–60

Walker, James, *General Report on the Operations of the GTS of India during 1869–70* (Dehra Dun, Survey of India Printing Group, 1871)

Walker, James, 'Four Years' Journeying through Great Tibet', *Proceedings of the Royal Geographical Society* (February 1885), 65–92

Watson, Francis, 'A Pioneer in the Himalayas: William Moorcroft', *Geographical Magazine*, vol. 32 (1959), 204–14

Secondary Sources

Alder, Garry, *Beyond Bokhara* (London, Century Publishing, 1985)

Allen, Charles, *The Buddha and the Sahibs* (London, John Murray, 2002)

Bailey, Frederick, M., *No Passport to Tibet* (London, Travel Book Club, 1957)

Baker, Ian, *The Heart of the World* (New York, Penguin, 2004)

Barrow, Ian, *Making History, Drawing Territory* (New Delhi, Oxford University Press, 2003)

Durand, Algernon, *The Making of a Frontier* (1899; Karachi, Oxford University Press, 2001)

Elphinstone, Mountstuart, *An Account of the Kingdom of Caubul* (1815; repr. Karachi, Indus Publications, 1992)

Everest, George, *An Account of the Measurement of an Arc of the Meridian* (London, Allen & Co., 1830)

Herodotus, *The Histories*, Penguin Classics (London, Penguin, 2003)

Holdich, Thomas, *Tibet the Mysterious* (London, Alston Rivers, 1906)

Hopkirk, Peter, *The Great Game* (London, John Murray, 1990)

James, Lawrence, *Raj: The Making and Unmaking of British India* (1997; London, Abacus, 2003)

Keay, John, *Explorers of the Western Himalayas* (London, John Murray, 1996)

Keegan, John, *Intelligence in War* (London, Pimlico, 2004)

Kipling, Rudyard, *Kim* (1901; London, Penguin, 1994)

Knight, E.F., *Where Three Empires Meet* (London, Longmans, Green & Co., 1895)

Lamb, Alastair, *Britain and Chinese Central Asia* (London, Routledge & Kegan Paul, 1960)

McRae, Michael, *In Search of Shangri-La* (London, Penguin, 2004)

Madan, P.L., *Tibet: Saga of Indian Explorers* (New Delhi, Manohar Publishers, 2004)

Markham, Clements, *A Memoir on the Indian Surveys* (London, W.H. Allen & Co., 1871)

Moorcroft, William, *Travels in the Himalayan Provinces of Hindustan and the Punjab*, ed. Horace Hayman Wilson (London, John Murray, 1841)

Rawat, Indra Singh, *Indian Explorers of the 19th Century* (New Delhi, Ministry of Information and Broadcasting, 1973)

Sandberg, Graham, *The Exploration of Tibet* (1904; repr. Delhi, Cosmo Publications, 1987)

Singh, Amar Kaur Jaspir, *Himalayan Triangle* (London, British Library, 1988)

Styles, Showell, *The Forbidden Frontiers* (London, Hamish Hamilton, 1970)

Waller, Derek, *The Pundits, British Exploration of Tibet & Central Asia* (Lexington, KY, University Press of Kentucky, 1990)

Wessels, Cornelius, *Early Jesuit Travellers in Central Asia* (The Hague, Martinus Nijhoff, 1924)

Woodcock, George, *Into Tibet* (London, Faber & Faber, 1971)

Wynn, Anthony, *Persia in the Great Game* (London, John Murray, 2003)

Yule, Henry, and Burnell, A.C., *Hobson-Jobson* (1886; repr. Ware, Wordsworth, 1996)

Index

Abdul (Hermann Schlagintweit's assistant) 45
Abdul Hamid (the Munshi; NA) 85–7
Abdul Wahab 95
Abode of Snow 2
Abors 182
Afghanistan
  boundaries 104
  Britain 14, 39, 88
  Hyder Shah 100
  Mirza Shuja 91–5
  Russia 151
AK see Kishen Singh
Akbar, emperor 4
Akbar Khan 39
Akhor Ahmad, Mir 106
Aling Gangri range 69
altitude sickness 32, 95, 140
Aman-i-mulk 101, 102, 103
Amar Singh 53–4
Amban 129, 133
Amdo 133
Andrade, Antonio de 7–8
Anglo-Russian rivalry 3
Arun (Arun Kosi) river 161
Askabad 152
Asmar 105–7

Asmar, Khan of 105–7
Ata Mohammed (the Mullah) 105–9
Attock 30
Awaz Ali 86, 87
Ayub Khan 151

Babu, the see Chandra Das, Sarat
Badakshan 104
Badrinath 7
Bailey, Frederick M. 17, 171, 183, 184
Bhotia Kosi river 160, 162
Bhotias 51, 53
Bhutan 18, 74, 155
Bisahiris 59, 66
Blavatsky, Helena Petrovna 121–2
Bogla 66
Bogle, George 15, 16, 17, 18, 19, 20
Bohd 3
Bokhara
  Izzat Ullah 26, 31–2
  Moorcroft 24, 25, 26, 27, 28
  Russia 99, 152
  Stoddart and Conolly 40
Bolan Pass 92
Bourguignon d'Anville, Jean Baptiste 11

Brahmaputra river
  Bogle 17
  course of 63, 71
  Tsangpo 1, 52, 80, 81, 82, 153,
    170, 171, 183
bribes 59, 144, 159
Britain 3, 9, 10
British administrators 112
Buddhism 3
Burnes, Alexander 39

Calcutta 45
Campbell, Sir George 111
Candler, Edmund 136
Caroe, Olaf 112
Cawdor, John 185
Chandra Das, Sarat (the Babu;
    SCD)
  Central Asian expedition 123,
    124–7, 130–2
  Croft 123
  duty 37
  early years 110, 111
  Kipling 21
  later career 134–5
  Sikkim 112
  Tibet 114–22
Chang Tang 76
Chathang La 116, 117–18, 119
Chief Pundit, The see Nain Singh
Chilas 52
China, Tibet 20, 33, 52
Chitral 52, 101, 104, 107
Cho La Pass 153–4
Chomolungma 161
Chomorang Pass 67
Chomorawa 80
Chorten Nyima La 119

Chumbel (Kishen Singh's travelling
    companion) 81
Chung Chu 61
Clive, Robert Clive, Lord 9, 11
Cockerell, Horace 124
colonialists 112
Conolly, Arthur 40–1
Cooch Behar 15
Croft, Sir Alfred 111, 114, 123, 124

Dalai Lama 33, 113, 131–2
Darchendo 78
David-Neel, Alexandra 2
Dawa Nangal 61
Deb Rajah 18, 20
Dehra Dun (Survey headquarters)
    54, 55
Dereghez 152
Dibong 171
Dir 100
disguise 6, 56
distance, measuring 55
Dokpas 119
Donkhya La Pass 140
Dora Pass 103, 104
Dost Mohammed 39
Du La 126
Dudh Kosi 164, 168
Durand, Algernon 88
Durand, Mortimer 88
Dzongri 115

East India Company 9, 15
Eden, Sir Ashley 122
Elphinstone, Mountstuart 25, 26,
    38
equipment, Pundits 11–12, 74, 81,
    85, 114

Everest, Sir George 13–14
Everest, Mount 134, 161
explorers, murders of western 6

Faizabad 94, 102, 104
foot-paces 55–6
Forsyth, Sir Douglas 70

Gartok 63, 69
George III: 9
Gilgit 52
GK see Kalian Singh
GM see Mani Singh
GMN see Nem Singh
Goes, Bento de 4, 5–6
gold
  deposits 65
  mines 64, 67, 68
Gopa Tajam 66
Gosain, the (Purangir Gosain) 15,
  16, 18, 19, 20, 21, 22
Great Game 3, 40, 154, 185
Great Meridional Arc of India (Great
  Arc) 12, 13, 14
Great Trigonometrical Survey of
  India (the Survey) 10, 11–14
  headquarters 54
  native agents 24, 51
  Tsangpo question 2
  Waugh, Andrew 48
Guthrie, Mr 25, 26
Gyala 176
Gyantse 141

Habibullah Khan 35
Hamilton, Alexander 15, 18, 19, 20
Hari Ram (MH; Number 9) 23,
  157–68

Harkh Dev 28
Harman, John 171, 172, 173, 183
Hastings, Lord 112
Hastings, Warren 10, 15, 19, 20,
  21
Havildar, the see Hyder Shah
Hayward, George 89, 90, 96, 101
Hearsey, Hyder 27, 29
Hedin, Sven 3
Herat 41
Herodotus 65
Himalaya 10
Hindu Kush 88, 93, 102
Hoiduthara 76
Holdich, Sir Thomas 138, 149,
  183
horses 24
  trade 27
Humboldt, Alexander von 44
Hyder, Amir Meer 31
Hyder Shah (the Havildar; the
  Sapper) 100–4, 105

Ibn Gamin 46
Inayat Ali 107
India, mapping of 10, 11
Indian Mutiny (Sepoy Mutiny) 47,
  49
Indus river 67, 69, 92, 109
Irrawaddy river 153
Izzat Ullah, Mir
  expedition 30–4
  Kabul 36
  Kunduz 37
  Metcalfe 26
  Moorcroft 25, 28, 35
  shawl-wool trade 128
  son 37–8

jade quarries 34
Jesuit missionaries 3
Johnston, Keith 48
Jongson La 125

Kabul 35, 40
Kafiristan 5
Kafirs 5
Kalian Singh (GK) 56, 60, 65
   expeditions 67, 69, 70, 185
Kambachen 116
Kamran Shah 41
Kandahar 42, 93
Kangchenjunga 112
Karakoram range 86
Kashghar 89, 95, 96, 97
Kashghar, Amir of 89
Kashmir 32, 33
Kathmandu 63, 64, 161
Kazakhstan 99
Keramal Ali, Syed 41, 42
Kham 133
Khan, Ahmad Ali 27
Khan, Ghulam Hyder 25, 35
Khardong La 45
Khelat 92
Khumbu district 166
Kim (Kipling) 17, 88–9
Kingdon-Ward, Francis 17, 184, 185
Kintup
   duty 37
   expedition 173–84
   Nem Singh 172
   Tsangpo 1, 17, 151
Kipling, Rudyard 57
   Kim 17, 88–9
Kishen Singh (AK) 56, 70, 72,
   73–82

Kohistan 109
Koonur river 104
Kosi (Kosiki) river 160, 162
Kunduz 36
Kurma 119

Lachung 140
Ladakh 35
Lahore 4
Lam-yig (Tibetan safe-conduct pass)
   114
Lambton, William 10, 11–12
Lani La Pass 76
latitude observations 63
Leh 32
Lhasa
   Chandra Das 130–1
   Izzat Ullah 33
   Kishen Singh 75
   location 3, 14, 52, 57, 64
   Manning 22
   Nain Singh 62
   Nem Singh 172
   rebellion 160
   route survey 63
   Ugyen Gyatso 146, 147
Lhobrak 150
Litang 79
Loh Mantang 163
Lowari Pass 107

Macaulay, Colman 135
Macdonald, Sir John 41, 42
Macnaghten, Sir William 39
Mala Pass 92
Mana Pass 8, 65
Manasarowar lake 28, 63
Mani Singh (GM; the Second Pundit)

expeditions 57–60, 62, 66
pseudonyms 56
Schlagintweits 45, 46
Survey, joined 51, 54
training 54
Manning, Thomas 22
maps, India 10, 11
Markham, Sir Clements 13, 70, 71,
    82, 83
Marpung 179
Meshed 43, 152
Metcalfe, Sir Charles 26, 37, 38
MH see Hari Ram
Mingmar, Yudak 67–8
Minister, the see Phendi Khangsar
Mir Jafir 9
Mir Walli 101, 103, 108
Mirza Shuja (The Mirza) 89,
    90–8
Mishmis 79
Mongolia 77
Mongolian lama (expedition to
    Tsangpo) 173–7
Montgomerie, Thomas George
    England 70
    expedition results 63, 87, 104
    expeditions 64, 98, 99
    Hari Ram 157, 158, 162
    Hyder Shah 100
    Ladakh 84–5
    native agents 51
    Schlagintweits 48
    training agents 54, 55, 56
Moorcroft, William 24–6, 27–30,
    34–7, 38–9
Morshead, Henry 171, 183
Mullah, the see Ata Mohammed
Munshi, the see Abdul Hamid

Murad Beg 36, 37
murders, of Western explorers 6

NA see Abdul Hamid
Nagchukha 78
Nain Singh (Chief Pundit; No. 1; the
    Pundit)
    Chandra Das 114
    duty 37
    expeditions 23, 57–63, 66–71
    Nem Singh 173
    pseudonyms 56
    Schlagintweits 45, 53
    Survey, joined 52, 53–4
    training 54, 55–6
Namgyal, Rinzin (RN) 153–5
Nanda Devi 51
Nang Dzong 175
Nasrullah, Amir 40–2
native agents 6, 24, 51
Nem Singh (GMN) 171–3
Nepal 28, 29, 164, 167
Nestorians 4–5
Nestorius 4
Newswriters 42, 43, 152
Nilam 161
Niti Pass 28
No. 1 see Nain Singh
No La 59
North-West Frontier 14, 52,
    88–9
Nubra valley 45
Nuksan Pass 102, 104
Number 9 see Hari Ram

Oakes, G.F.T. 184
Oudh 111
Oxus river 27, 104

PA (Pundit) 153, 156–7
Paljor (guide) 115
Pamir range 95
Pamirs 91
Panchen Lama 16, 18, 19, 113
Pandit 50
Pangong Lake 70
Pangula Pass 166
Peer Ali 95
Pemaköchung 176
Pemayangtse monastery 112–13, 142, 149
Phendi Khangsar (the Minister of Tashilunpo) 120–1, 130, 132, 135–6
Phillimore, R.H. 48
Phurchung (guide) 117, 119, 125
Plassey, battle of 9
Polo, Marco 2, 77
Pottinger, Eldred 90–1
prayer beads 55
prayer-wheels 55
Public Stud 24
pundit 50
Pundit, The *see* Nain Singh
Pundits
  equipment 11–12, 74, 81, 85, 114
  field allowance 56
  golden age of exploration 23
  motivation 186–7
  qualities 37
  training 54–6, 91, 138
  Tsangpo question 2
Punjab 14, 110
Purangir Gosain *see* Gosain, the

quicksilver 54

ragapas 148
Ramatullah Khan 100
Ranjit Singh 14
Rawlinson, Henry 40
RN *see* Namgyal, Rinzin
Roof of the World 2
Roos-Keppel, Sir George 112
route surveys 63, 69, 81–2, 103, 104, 108
Royal Geographical Society 3, 134
Russia
  Bokhara 32
  British India 41, 88, 99
  Central Asia 3, 14
  Tibet 20–1
  trade 32
  troop movements 43, 151
  Turkmenistan 111

Sachu 77
Sagarmatha 161
Sakya monastery 134, 161
Salisbury, Lord 151
Samarkand 99
Sandberg, Graham 131
Sanju Pass 73
Sapper, the *see* Hyder Shah
SCD *see* Chandra Das, Sarat
Schlagintweit, Adolf 44, 45, 46–7
Schlagintweit, Hermann 44, 45
Schlagintweit, Robert 44, 45
Schlagintweit brothers 44–8, 53
Second Pundit, The *see* Mani Singh
Sepoy Mutiny (Indian Mutiny) 47, 49, 110
Serap Gyatso 150–1
Shache 84
  see also Yarkand

Shahidulla 73
Shalu monastery 141
Shaw, Robert 48, 89
shawl-wool trade 33, 128
Sher Ali 92, 102
Sherab, Lama 123
Sherpas 167
Shigatse 127, 129, 142, 160, 161
Sikkim 45, 112, 122, 139
Singh clan, Pundits see Kalian
    Singh; Kishen Singh; Mani
    Singh; Nain Singh
Siraj-ud Daula 9
Skobelev, General 111
sky burial 148
Smyth, Edmund 53
Sonam Dorje 166
spies
    Indian traders 43
    see also Newswriters
Stein, Sir Aurel 3
Stoddart, Charles 40
Survey, the see Great
    Trigonometrical Survey of India
Survey of India 11
surveying equipment 11–12, 81,
    114
Sutlej river 69

Taklamakan Desert 34
Tandum 62, 63, 64
Tanner, Henry C.B. 138, 151, 153
Tashilunpo 120
Tashkurghan 94
Tassisudon 18
Theodosius II: 4
Third Pole 2
Thok Jalung gold fields 67, 68

Thuillier, H.R. 150
Thupten Gyatso 113
Tibet 2–3
    army 133
    Bogle 15, 19
    Britain 113
    China 20, 33, 52
    geographical enigma 52
    gold 68
    official missions 21, 22
    route surveys 64
    trade 83, 167
    Western names for 2
Tingri 166
Tipta Pass 158, 159
Tradom 163
Traill's Pass 46
training, Pundits 54–6, 91, 138
Trebeck, George 25, 26, 35
Trisong Detsen 169
Trotter, Henry 73, 105
Tsangpo Gorge 17
Tsangpo river
    Bogle 19
    Brahmaputra 1, 80, 81, 82, 153,
        170, 171, 183
    extent 2, 52
    Kingdon Ward 185
    Kintup 1, 175, 176, 180, 183
    Kishen Singh 80, 82
    Nain Singh 57
    names 156
    Nem Singh 173
    Serap Gyatso 151
    Trisong Detsen 169
    Ugyen Gyatso 142–3
Tsaparang 8
Turkestan 85

Turkmenistan 99, 111
Turner, Samuel 20, 21

UG *see* Ugyen Gyatso
Ugyen Gyatso, Lama (UG)
  Central Asian expedition 123,
    125, 126, 130
  expedition results 121
  Lam-yig 114
  Survey, joined 138
  Tibetan expeditions 116, 117,
    118, 120, 139–50
  Tibetan invitation for Chandra
    Das 112–13
undercover equipment 74
unmapped territory 52

von Humboldt, Alexander *see*
  Humboldt, Alexander von

Wakhan Corridor 95
Wali Khan, Amir 46, 48
Walker, James Thomas
  head of Survey 70
  Kishen Singh 74, 81
  Mirza Shuja 91
  Royal Geographical Society 72
  Schlagintweits 48

unmapped territory 52
Wallangehoon Pass 158
Waugh, Andrew 48
Wellesley, Arthur *see* Wellington,
  Duke of
Wellington, Arthur Wellesley, Duke
  of 11, 112
Woodthorpe, R.G. 171

Yakub Beg 95, 96, 97, 99
Yamdo Croft 134
Yamdrok Tso lake 143, 150
Yarkand
  Abdul Hamid 85, 87
  Izzat Ullah 34
  location 52
  Mirza Shuja 97, 98
  Montgomerie 84
  Schlagintweit, Adolf 47
Yassin 109
Yembi 77
Younghusband, Sir Francis 19, 129,
  136
Yunas, Muhammad 97

Zanskar range 65
Zayul 80
Zorwar Singh 127–8